Stephen Fox

Endlich Zeit für Englisch

Fortgeschrittenenkurs

Hueber Verlag

Das Werk und seine Teile sind urheberrechtlich geschützt.
Jede Verwertung in anderen als den gesetzlich zugelassenen
Fällen bedarf deshalb der vorherigen schriftlichen
Einwilligung des Verlages.

Hinweis zu § 52a UrhG: Weder das Werk noch seine Teile dürfen ohne
eine solche Einwilligung überspielt, gespeichert und in ein Netzwerk
eingespielt werden. Dies gilt auch für Intranets von Firmen und von Schulen
und sonstigen Bildungseinrichtungen.

3.	2.	1.			Die letzten Ziffern
2014	13	12	11	10	bezeichnen Zahl und Jahr des Druckes.

Alle Drucke dieser Auflage können, da unverändert,
nebeneinander benutzt werden.
1. Auflage
© 2010 Hueber Verlag, 85737 Ismaning, Deutschland
Redaktion: Jürgen Frank, Hueber Verlag, Ismaning
Zeichnungen: Wilfried Poll, München
Layout: Achim Kreuzer, Augsburg
Satz: appel media, Oberding
Druck und Bindung: Firmengruppe APPL, aprinta druck, Wemding
Printed in Germany
ISBN 978-3-19-109483-6
11.9483

Vorwort

Herzlich willkommen! Sie haben sich dazu entschlossen, mit diesem Fortgeschrittenenkurs Ihre Englischkenntnisse auszubauen.

Da Ihnen kein(e) Lehrer(in) zur Verfügung steht, müssen Sie alle Hilfsmittel nutzen, die Ihnen Buch und CDs bieten. Ein Inhaltsverzeichnis, das in Stichpunkten angibt, was in jeder Lektion behandelt wird, finden Sie auf den Seiten 4 und 5. Außerdem bietet Seite 6 eine Übersicht über die Lektionsbestandteile; machen Sie sich am besten zur Orientierung gleich zu Beginn mit dem Aufbau der Lektionen vertraut. Im Anhang finden Sie Hinweise zu den Unterschieden zwischen den zwei Hauptvarianten des heutigen Englisch, britischem und amerikanischem Englisch. Beide Varianten hören Sie übrigens auf den CDs.

Darüber hinaus enthält der Anhang eine Grammatik-Übersicht, den Lösungsschlüssel der Übungen und die Transkription sämtlicher Hörverständnistexte sowie den alphabetischen Wortschatz.

Die Randnotizen bieten zusätzliche Informationen zu dem behandelten Stoff sowie Tipps zu effektiven Lernmethoden, vor allem in Bezug auf das Vokabellernen. Nehmen Sie sich die Zeit, diese Lerntipps auszuprobieren. Suchen Sie sich diejenigen aus, die am besten zu Ihrem Lerntyp passen, oder entwickeln Sie Ihre eigene Lernstrategie. Ein Selbstlernkurs gibt Ihnen die Möglichkeit, Tempo, Rhythmus und Intensität des Lernprozesses selbst zu bestimmen. Bedenken Sie aber, dass es sinnvoller ist, öfter und in kurzen Lernperioden zu arbeiten, statt einmal im Monat eine „Mammutsitzung" einzulegen. Hören Sie sich so oft wie möglich die CDs an.

Wiederholen Sie auch die Lektionen, die Sie bereits bearbeitet haben. Dadurch wird das Gelernte verankert, sodass Sie es auch parat haben, wenn Sie es brauchen. Außerdem verbessert das Wiederholen mit den CDs Ihre Aussprache. Nehmen Sie sich auf ein separates Band auf und vergleichen Sie Ihre Aussprache kritisch mit der der Sprecher.

Ziel des Kurses ist, dass Sie so schnell wie möglich das heutige Englisch verstehen und sich in den wichtigsten Alltagssituationen adäquat ausdrücken können. Da dieser Kurs authentisches Material bietet, ist er nicht immer einfach. Aber machen Sie sich keine Sorgen, wenn Sie etwas nicht auf Anhieb verstehen: Hilfe und Unterstützung sind immer da!

Und nun wünschen wir Ihnen viel Spaß und Erfolg!

Inhalt

                                                  Seite

Unit 1 — *Why don't we share a cab?* – Teilen wir uns ein Taxi? — **7**
Szenario: **sich kennenlernen, Small Talk**
Redeabsichten: Vorschläge machen; über sich und andere erzählen
Grammatik: Verlaufsform des Präsens
Lesetext: *Correct English*

Unit 2 — *The home front* – Wer macht was im Haushalt? — **19**
Szenario: **jemanden überreden**
Redeabsichten: jemanden bitten, etwas zu tun; Vorschläge machen/annehmen/ablehnen; Pläne/Absichten äußern
Grammatik: verschiedene Möglichkeiten, die Zukunft auszudrücken
Lesetext: *Dear Ann Landers*

Unit 3 — *What do you feel like doing?* – Wozu hast du Lust? — **33**
Szenario: **Konsensfindung**
Redeabsichten: Vorschläge machen; Vorschläge annehmen/ablehnen; etwas begründen; sagen, dass man nicht einverstanden ist; Gefallen/Missfallen ausdrücken
Grammatik: *question tags*
Lesetext: *Venice, CA*

Unit 4 — *So then what happened?* – Und was ist dann passiert? — **49**
Szenario: **eine Geschichte erzählen**
Redeabsichten: über etwas berichten; etwas beschreiben; eine Meinung äußern
Grammatik: Vergangenheitsformen
Lesetext: *F—-!*

Unit 5 — *We're moving in together* – Wir ziehen zusammen — **63**
Szenario: **jemanden um einen Gefallen bitten**
Redeabsichten: jemanden um etwas bitten; eine Bitte ablehnen/einer Bitte entsprechen; sich bedanken; etwas begründen
Grammatik: indirekte Rede
Lesetext: *Cohabitation*

Unit 6 — *Shop 'til you drop* – Einkaufsmarathon — **77**
Szenario: **Dienstleistungen in Anspruch nehmen, jemanden um Informationen bitten, sich beschweren**
Redeabsichten: Wünsche äußern; etwas beschreiben; Gefallen/Missfallen ausdrücken; etwas begründen; jemanden zum Handeln auffordern
Grammatik: Verben mit *-ing* oder *to* + Infinitiv
Lesetext: *I'll be seeing you in all the new familiar places*

Inhalt

Seite

Unit 7	*So tell me about the job* – Erzähl mir doch von deiner Arbeit	**93**
Szenario:	***Informationen geben, etwas erklären***	
Redeabsichten:	Informationen einholen und geben; etwas erklären; fragen, ob der Gesprächspartner versteht/sagen, dass man (nicht) versteht; Sachverhalte umformulieren	
Grammatik:	Bedingungssätze	
Lesetext:	*Don't worry about work*	
Unit 8	*What would you recommend?* – Was würdest du empfehlen?	**107**
Szenario:	***jemanden um Rat bitten, etwas erklären***	
Redeabsichten:	Absichten ausdrücken; Zweck und Bestimmung angeben; um Rat bitten/Rat erteilen	
Grammatik:	nicht zählbare Substantive	
Lesetext:	*Just can't seem to stop*	
Unit 9	*Wake up and smell the coffee!* – Aufwachen mit Kaffeeduft	**121**
Szenario:	***diskutieren***	
Redeabsichten:	Zustimmung/Ablehnung, Wichtigkeit ausdrücken; Meinung erfragen und artikulieren	
Grammatik:	Verlaufsform des Perfekts	
Lesetext:	*Unchanging men in changing times*	
Unit 10	*The Melting Pot* – Multikulturelle Gesellschaft	**133**
Szenario:	***über etwas berichten***	
Redeabsichten:	über etwas berichten; etwas beschreiben	
Grammatik:	adverbiale Ergänzungen	
Lesetext:	*The Melting Pot*	
Anhang	***Unterschiede britisches/amerikanisches Englisch***	**146**
	Grammatik-Übersicht	**148**
	Lösungen (Übungen und *Listening*-Texte)	**162**
	Alphabetischer Wortschatz Englisch – Deutsch	**242**

Lektionsübersicht

Jede der 10 Lektionen in diesem Schnellkurs ist in **Listening** und **Reading** unterteilt, die typische Gesprächssituationen als Hörverständnistext bzw. einen thematisch passenden Lesetext enthalten. Innerhalb dieser Abschnitte gibt es folgende Rubriken:

Listening

Hier finden Sie Aufgaben zu einem Hörverständnistext (meistens einem Gespräch). In der Regel werden sowohl vor *(Pre-listening activity)* als auch nach dem Hören Fragen zum Text gestellt.

Bitte beachten Sie: Bei den Hörverständnisübungen geht es nicht darum, jedes Wort auf Anhieb zu verstehen; entscheidend ist zunächst nur, die gestellte Aufgabe zu lösen. Danach folgen Übungen zu den wichtigsten Redewendungen und dem Wortschatz sowie zur Grammatik des Textes.

1/2 Dieser Text bzw. diese Übung ist auf CD. Die erste Zahl gibt an, um welche der zwei CDs es sich handelt, die zweite den Track, den Sie ansteuern können.

Sie können die Hörverständnistexte auf verschiedene Weise anhören, je nachdem, wie schwierig Sie sie finden. Zum Beispiel können Sie
- zuhören, ohne überhaupt ins Buch zu schauen (die beste Methode, wenn Sie sich daran gewöhnen wollen, gesprochenes Englisch zu verstehen); unterbrechen Sie auch ruhig und stellen Sie fest, was Sie verstanden haben und wie das Gespräch weitergehen könnte;
- bei Dialogen, die Sie als schwierig empfinden, den Text zunächst kurz lesen und dann beiseitelegen und den Dialog noch einmal anhören;
- zuhören und dabei den englischen Text im Anhang mitlesen (weniger empfehlenswert).

Reading

Dieser Teil enthält authentische Lesetexte mit Aufgaben. Auch zum Lesetext werden sowohl vor als nach dem Lesen Fragen gestellt. Auch hier geht es darum, wie beim *Listening*, den Text zunächst in seiner Gesamtheit zu verstehen, bevor man sich mit den Einzelheiten auseinandersetzt.

Working with words

Hier werden die neuen Vokabeln des vorhergehenden Textes vorgestellt und geübt.

Language focus

Unter dieser Rubrik werden die wichtigsten Redeabsichten und -strategien des Textes unter die Lupe genommen und mit weiteren Varianten ergänzt und geübt.

Grammar focus

Hier finden Sie eine knappe Darstellung des zentralen Grammatikproblems des vorangegangenen Textes. Dabei wird zwischen Bildung und Gebrauch der vorgestellten Formen unterschieden. (Das heißt z. B.: Wie schreibe ich eine Verbform und wie wende ich sie richtig an?)

Revision

Diese Rubrik ist ein Wiederholungsteil. Hier finden Sie sowohl schriftliche als auch mündliche Übungen zum Lernstoff der *Unit*. Mit diesen Übungen können Sie die Formen und Strukturen „einschleifen", die Sie im Grammatikteil gelernt haben.

Why don't we share a cab?

Unit 1

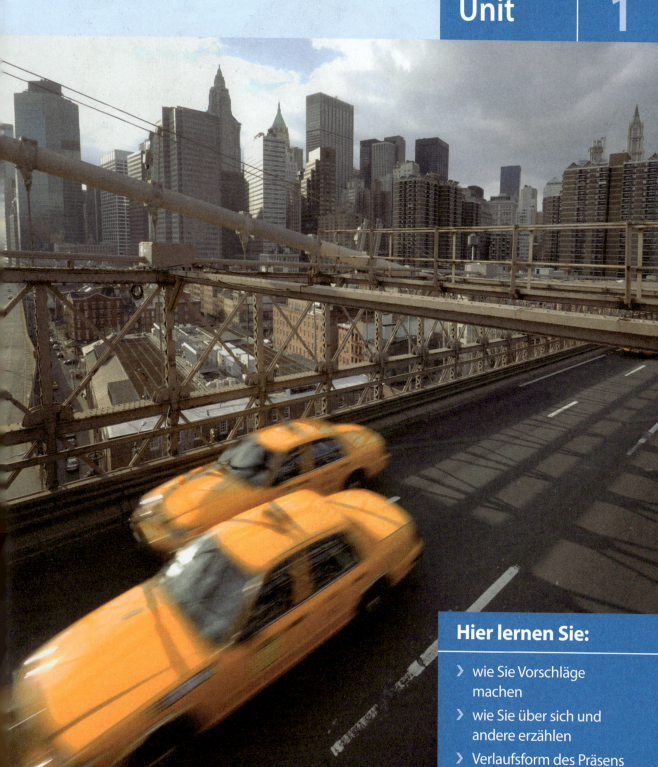

Hier lernen Sie:

› wie Sie Vorschläge machen
› wie Sie über sich und andere erzählen
› Verlaufsform des Präsens

Unit 1

Part 1

Listening

💡 Die Pre-listening-Aufgabe dient als Einstieg in das Thema des folgenden Textes.

1 Pre-listening task

Welchen der folgenden Sätze kann man verwenden, um sich einer unbekannten Person vorzustellen?

a   Hi, Sonia, how are you?
b   Hi, how are things?
c   Hello, my name's … ✗
d   Let me introduce myself. ✗
e   Hi, I'm … ✗

1/1

❗ So machen Sie diese Hörverständnisübung richtig: zuhören – Behauptungen lesen – nochmal zuhören – danach ankreuzen.

2 True or false?

Sie hören ein Gespräch zwischen Sonia und Jim. Lesen Sie zunächst die folgenden Behauptungen, hören Sie dann den Dialog und entscheiden Sie anschließend, ob die Behauptungen *true* (richtig) oder *false* (falsch) sind.

		true	false
a	Sonia and Jim know each another.		✗
b	Sonia wants to call for a taxi, but one comes before she gets the number.	✗	✗
c	Jim and Sonia could be at the airport.	✗	✗
d	They work for the same company.		✗
e	Sonia is self-employed.	✗	
f	Jim works as a communications trainer for INB.		✗
g	Someone else was originally scheduled to do the workshop.	✗	
h	Jim and Sonia split the cost of the taxi.		✗

8

Working with words

Unit 1

3 Folgende Wörter und Redewendungen kamen im Dialog vor. Zwei Übersetzungen wurden vertauscht. Welche?

to share (a cab)	zusammen (ein Taxi) nehmen
operator	(Angestellte/r bei der) Auskunft
freelance	freiberuflich
to be self-employed	geplant sein
rep = sales representative	Vertreter
to be supposed to do something	für etwas vorgesehen sein
to be signed up for	eingeschrieben sein für
to fill in/sub(substitute) for someone	für jemanden einspringen
to be expecting (a baby)	ein Kind erwarten
due	fällig
one another	einander
to be scheduled	Freiberufler sein

? Sie haben wahrscheinlich an der Aussprache gemerkt, dass der Dialog in Amerika stattfindet. Kennen Sie die britischen Äquivalente für die folgenden Wörter?
cab
convention center
operator

4 Welche Ausdrücke von Übung 3 bedeuten dasselbe wie die folgenden?

a to be registered for   b to take someone's place   c to be pregnant

5 Hören Sie den Dialog noch einmal an, achten Sie dabei besonders auf die Passagen, die im Folgenden abgedruckt sind, und kreuzen Sie die richtige Bedeutung an.

1/1

a It'd probably be a good idea to …
   1 Es war wahrscheinlich eine gute Idee, …
   2 Es wäre wahrscheinlich eine gute Idee, …

b Never mind.
   1 Vergessen Sie es.
   2 Passen Sie auf.

c You're looking at one.
   1 Sie sehen aus wie eine Eins.
   2 Da steht einer vor Ihnen.

d Any time now.
   1 Jederzeit.
   2 Gerade.

e Will do.
   1 Das will ich tun.
   2 Mach' ich.

f Let me get this.
   1 Das kriege ich schon hin.
   2 Das erledige ich.

g Same here.
   1 Das finde ich auch.
   2 Gleichfalls.

! Bitte achten Sie bei dieser Übung auf die Intonation. Sie hilft Ihnen, die Bedeutung der Ausdrücke zu erschließen.

Unit 1

Hören Sie den Dialog noch einmal und benutzen Sie dabei die Pausentaste, wenn nötig.
appropriate = passend

Language focus

6 Es gibt selten nur eine Möglichkeit, etwas auf Englisch auszudrücken. Sehen Sie sich die folgenden Ausdrücke aus dem Dialog und weitere Varianten an.

a Sonia asks Jim if he would like to share a taxi. Which one of the following expressions does she use? Would the other expressions also be appropriate?

1 Do you mind sharing a cab?
2 Is it OK if we share a cab?
3 How about sharing a cab?
4 Do you want to share a cab?
5 Why don't we share a cab?

Achtung:
Es geht hier um eine Feinheit!

b Sonia calls information to get the number of a taxi company. Which one of the following expressions does she use? Which one would not be appropriate?

1 I'd like the number of …
2 Can I have the number of …?
3 Can you give me the number of …?
4 Could you give me the number of …?
5 Would you mind giving me the number of …?

Hinweis:
In einem der Sätze handelt es sich um eine spontane Entscheidung und nicht um ein Vorhaben!

c Jim tells Sonia that he had just been thinking about calling a cab. Which one of the following expressions does he use? Which one means something different?

1 I was just about to when you walked up.
2 I think I'll call a cab, too.
3 I wanted to do just that when you walked up.
4 I was going to do that when you walked up.
5 I was thinking about doing that when you walked up.

Alle Varianten sind möglich. Prägen Sie sich diejenigen ein, die Ihnen am leichtesten fallen.

d Sonia explained why she was asked to do the workshop. Which one of the following expressions does she use? Which one would you use?

1 As the baby is due any time now, she asked me to sub for her.
2 She asked me to sub for her because the baby is due any time now.
3 (The baby is due any time now.) That's why she asked me to sub for her.
4 The baby is due any time now, so she asked me to sub for her.
5 Since the baby is due any time now, she asked me to sub for her.

weil / da

7 Ordnen Sie die Redeabsichten jeweils einer Gruppe von Ausdrücken in Übung 6 zu.

■ asking for something   b
■ expressing an intention   c
■ giving a reason   d
■ making a suggestion   a

10

Unit 1

8 Finden Sie die passenden Reaktionen.

a Why don't we share a cab?

b I'm a freelance consultant.

c Can you give me Robert's number?

d The baby is due any time now.

e It was nice to meet you.

Same here. It was nice to meet you, too. OK, fine. Oh, really, so am I.
What exactly do you do? That's very interesting. Are you sure?
That's a good idea. I didn't know that.
That's great!
I already have. Sorry, I don't have it.
No thanks, I'm not going that way. That's a good idea.
Sure, it's …
Thanks, but I'll wait for my own.
Thanks, I'd like that. Sure, why not. Let me see, here it is.

💡 Mit dem Begriff „Redeabsicht" meint man den Grund oder Anlass für eine Äußerung. Eine Redeabsicht kann man auf vielfältige Weise ausdrücken, je nach Situation. Man wird z.B. Freunden gegenüber eine Bitte anders formulieren als gegenüber Fremden. Wenn einem etwas zusteht, wird man eine andere Formulierung wählen, als wenn man keinen Anspruch auf etwas hat usw.

Unit 1

Grammar focus

Bildung

The present continuous tense

Die Verlaufsform des Präsens (*the present continuous tense*) wird gebildet mit einer Form des Verbs **to be** und der **-ing**-Form des Hauptverbs.

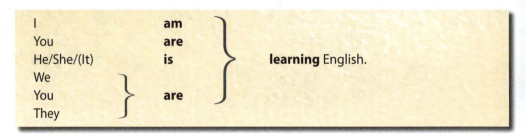

Gebrauch

Mit der Verlaufsform des Präsens werden Handlungen und Zustände beschrieben, die gerade ablaufen (a) oder für die Zukunft geplant sind (b).

a She can't come to the phone; **she's sleeping**.
b **I'm flying** to Madrid this afternoon.

9 Hören Sie noch einmal den Dialog und entscheiden Sie, ob die Verben eine zukünftige Bedeutung haben.

trade fair = Handelsmesse

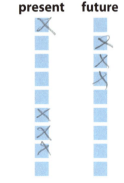

		present	future
a	Are you waiting for a taxi?	X	
b	Where are you going?		X
c	I'm going to the Marriott …		X
d	I'm going to the trade fair, too.		X
e	I'm doing a workshop …		
f	You're looking at one.	X	
g	You're kidding?!	X	
h	I'm filling in for Nancy Quinn.	X	
i	She's … expecting her second baby.		

Phrasal verbs

Phrasal verbs sind feste Verbindungen, die beispielsweise aus einem **Verb und** einer **Präposition** zusammengesetzt sind. Hier einige Beispiele aus dem Dialog:

to walk up (to someone/something)   (auf jemanden/etwas) zugehen
to sign up (for something)   sich anmelden (für etwas)
to fill in (for someone)   (für jemanden) einspringen
to sub in   vertreten

Sie werden in den folgenden Lektionen weitere *phrasal verbs* kennenlernen.

Revision

Unit 1

10 Setzen Sie das richtige Wort bzw. den richtigen Ausdruck von S. 9 ein.

a Carl quit his job at Olivetti and now works as a _____ rep.
b I can't teach my class tonight; do you think you could _sub_____ for me?
c Say hello to Judy for me, will you? – _____
d How many people are _____ for the workshop? – About 15.
e Hank and his wife _____ their first baby. – Oh really; when's it _____ ?
f When do you want me to come? _____
g Waiter, can I have the check? – _____ , Bob.

11 Setzen Sie die richtige Form des Präsens ein.

a I _____ for my parents.
b _____ they _____ to the convention, too?
c She _____ for Henry Gordon.
d We _____ a workshop during the trade fair.
e I think he _____ for a cab.
f I hope we _____ not _____ a room!
g _____ you _____ for the sightseeing trip?

wait
go
fill in
do
call
share
sign up

12 Kreuzen Sie die passende(n) Reaktion(en) an.

a Where are you going?
   1 To center city.   2 I'm calling a cab.   3 I was just about to.
b I think I'll call a cab.
   1 Same here.   2 That's a good idea.   3 Is it OK if we share one?
c Are you in computers?
   1 No, I'm not.   2 How did you know?   3 I'm going to the trade fair.
d Who do you work for?
   1 IBN.   2 You're kidding?   3 I'm a sales rep.
e Nice to meet you.
   1 Same here.   2 See you.   3 Nice to meet you too.

13 Arbeiten Sie nun die mündlichen Übungen A bis C zum Thema *present continuous* durch. Die Anweisungen erhalten Sie auf der CD.

1/2–4

13

Unit 1 Part 2

Reading

Hand aufs Herz!

14 Kreuzen Sie die Aussage an, die Ihre Ansicht über Grammatik zum Ausdruck bringt.

a I think it's boring, but I guess it's necessary.
b English doesn't have much grammar to learn.
c Words are more important than grammar.
d It's not necessary to speak correct English. The important thing is to make yourself understood.

15 Lesen Sie nun den folgenden Text.

Versuchen Sie den Text zunächst ohne Wörterbuch zu lesen.

Kennen Sie andere Floskeln auf Englisch? Gibt es im Deutschen auch solche Ausdrücke?

"Correct English"

Richard Lederer points out in his book *The Miracle of Language* that, "incredible as it may seem at first thought, practically every sentence that you speak and write during your lifetime has never been spoken or written before in human history. Except for stock phrases and conventional remarks such as "How are you?", "Thanks a lot" and "Have a nice day" almost all of your speech and writing consists of sentences that you have made up."
He goes on to tell of an experiment by a university professor who gave twenty-five students a simple cartoon and asked them to describe in a sentence what the drawing represented. What he got were twenty-five different descriptions of the cartoon. He then used his computer to determine how many grammatically correct sentences could be generated from those twenty-five sentences. The number the professor came up with was 19.8 billion! Based on this and similar studies, it is safe to say that any longer sentence that anyone may say or write has never been said or written before. This is also the case for most of what you hear on television or radio and what you read in newspapers, magazines or books.
What does this mean for those of you learning English? It means that there is rarely just one way to say something. That's good. There are, however, patterns of language that must be adhered to; that means, you must use words and put sentences together the way that a native speaker would. That's what this course is all about: helping you get a feel for the way English is used.

16 Welche der folgenden Aussagen fasst den Text am besten zusammen?

a Stock phrases are very common in English.
b Students are very creative when it comes to describing things.
c There is rarely just one way to say something in English.
d Nothing you can say has ever been said before.
e It's important to learn correct grammar.

Working with words

Unit 1

17 Ordnen Sie die synonymen Ausdrücke der rechten Spalte denen der linken zu.

to point out 10	1	fixed expression
incredible 3	2	the span of time you live
practically 4	3	unbelievable
lifetime 2	4	here: almost
stock phrase 1	10	to direct one's attention to
conventional 6	5	a comment
a remark 5	6	usual
to consist of 7	7	to be made up of
to make up 9	8	to give an account in words
to describe 8	9	to invent *verbinden*
to represent 12	11	an investigation
to determine 13	12	to portray
to generate 14	13	to obtain definite knowledge
a study 11	14	to create *beachten*
it is safe to say 17	15	seldom *selten*
rarely 15	16	to assemble
pattern 18 *Muster*	17	it can be assumed *zusammengefasst*
to adhere to 20	18	arrangement, model
to put together 16	19	to develop a sense for *entwickeln*
to get a feel for 19	20	to keep to, to respect

! Oft sind Verb und Substantiv im Englischen identisch:
Verb — Substantiv
to remark → *a remark*
to study → *a study*

! Manchmal braucht das Verb eine Präposition:
to com- → *a com-*
ment on — *ment*
to pattern → *a pat-*
after — *tern*

! Oft bekommt das Substantiv eine Endung:
to de- → *a de-*
scribe — *scription*
to inves- → *an inves-*
tigate — *tigation*

18 Tragen Sie die Wörter der linken Spalte von Übung 17 in die passende Kategorie ein.

Subjektiv (14)

noun	verb	adjective	adverb

💡 Für die deutsche Entsprechung grammatischer Begriffe siehe S. 152 im Anhang.

Welche Verben sind *phrasal verbs*?

Unit 1

Language focus

19 *Stock phrase* oder nicht?

Have a nice weekend.
See you later.
Give me a call.
Let's do lunch.
Are you serious?
I don't think so.
Can I help you?
Help yourself! *bedienen Sie sich*
Be careful!
Never mind! *i.O.*
Take care!

Enjoy your time off.
I'll see you after a while.
Hope you have good weather.
How about having lunch sometime?
I can't believe that!/You've got to be kidding! *machst du Witze*
Good luck.
May I be of assistance? *can I help you*
Please feel free to take what you want.
Please don't touch the keyboard.
Give him/her my best.
What the heck! *wen kümmert's / was soll das*

> Es lohnt sich, feststehende Ausdrücke zu erkennen, damit man sie sich merken und dann an der passenden Stelle einsetzen kann.

20 Welche der Sätze in Übung 19 bedeuten dasselbe?

_____ + _____
_____ + _____
_____ + _____
_____ + _____
_____ + _____
_____ + _____
_____ + _____

21 Formulieren Sie die folgenden Sätze mindestens zweimal um (siehe S. 12).

a Do you mind if I call you?

may I call you
is it ok if I call you

b There are patterns of language *muster* of language that must be adhered to *einhalten*; that's why you must get a feel for the way English is used.

_____
_____

c We were going to make a reservation this week.

we made a
we wanted to make

16

Revision

22 Ersetzen Sie die unterstrichenen Wörter durch ein Synonym von S. 15.

a I'd like <u>to call your attention</u> to the picture on the right.
b The sentence <u>is made up of</u> a subject and a verb.
c I've <u>seldom</u> seen that many jellyfish.
d Can you <u>tell me what</u> the man looked like?
e The new offer has <u>created</u> a lot of business.
f When abroad you must <u>respect</u> the customs of the country you are in.
g We have to go; we're <u>almost</u> out of time!

jellyfish = Qualle(n)

23 Beschreiben Sie die Tätigkeiten der abgebildeten Personen.

a

b

_____
_____

c

d

_____
_____

Unit 1

24 Kreuzen Sie die passende Reaktion an.

a How about if she subs for you tomorrow?
   1 Same here.   2 So am I.   3 That's fine with me.

b Could you give me a hand on Saturday?
   1 Are you sure?   2 That's very interesting.   3 Sure, no problem.

c I've got a new job.
   1 Good for you!   2 OK, fine.   3 Thanks, I'd like that.

d There's a lot of work to do.
   1 Let me get this.   2 Sure, why not.   3 That's why I asked you to come.

25 Wie sagt man … auf Englisch?

a Wie wäre es, wenn wir zusammen ein Taxi nehmen würden?
_____

b Ich fahre zur Messe. – Tatsächlich? Ich auch.
_____

c Wann wird das Kind erwartet? – Jederzeit.
_____

d Ich wollte mich gerade einschreiben, als Sie gekommen sind.
_____

e Er ist freiberuflicher Vertreter; deswegen ist er hier.
_____

f Ich hätte gern die Nummer von Jim McMullin.
_____

g Es war nett, Sie kennenzulernen.
_____

The home front

Unit 2

Hier lernen Sie:

> wie Sie jemanden bitten, etwas zu tun

> wie Sie Vorschläge machen/annehmen/ablehnen

> wie Sie Pläne/Absichten äußern

> verschiedene Möglichkeiten, die Zukunft auszudrücken

Unit 2

Part 1

Listening

! Siehe dazu die Grammatik-Seite dieser *Unit* (S. 24)

? Which of these phrases is the most colloquial?

colloquial = umgangssprachlich

1 Pre-listening task

Welche der folgenden Sätze würden Sie verwenden, wenn Sie jemanden fragen wollen, was er – oder sie – am Nachmittag vorhat?

a̶ What will you do this afternoon?
b   What are you doing this afternoon?
c̶   What do you do this afternoon?
d   Have you got any plans for this afternoon?
e   What's going on this afternoon?
f   What are you going to do this afternoon?

 1/5

2 True or false?

Sie hören ein Gespräch zwischen Cary und Matt. Lesen Sie zuerst die Behauptungen, hören Sie dann den Dialog und kreuzen Sie *true* für „richtig" oder *false* für „falsch" an.

		true	false
a	Matt had plans for the afternoon.	X	
b	Matt had planned to let someone else do his tax return.	X	
c	Cary wants Matt to help with the housework because she has other work to do.	X	
d	Matt says he is happy to help.		X

1/5

3 Lesen Sie die Fragen, hören Sie das Gespräch noch einmal und kreuzen Sie dann die richtigen Antworten an.

a Matt mentions several things he could do. What are they?

- [X] 1 Do his tax return.
- [ ] 2 Play tennis with Sam.
- [X] 3 Do some work at the office.
- [X] 4 Go shopping for some new shirts.

b Cary suggests several things Matt could do. What are they?

- [X] 1 Do the wash.
- [ ] 2 Clean the refrigerator.
- [X] 3 Go food shopping.
- [X] 4 Pick something up at the cleaner's.

AE *do the wash*
BE *do the washing*

20

Working with words

Unit 2

4 Alle Wörter und Redewendungen in dieser Liste kamen im Dialog vor. Zwei Übersetzungen sind vertauscht. Welche sind das?

it depends	es kommt darauf an
to get started on something	mit etwas anfangen
April first	der 1. April *(Abgabetermin für Steuererklärungen in den USA)*
(not) far off	(nicht) weit weg
a pile of stuff	ein Haufen Zeug
to catch up on something	etwas nachholen
gonna (= going to)	wollen, beabsichtigen
I better … (= I'd better)	Ich sollte (lieber) …
to be glad about something	froh sein über etwas
to give someone a call	jemand anrufen
to remind someone of something	außerdem …
to have something in mind	etwas vorhaben
to wonder	sich fragen
to give someone a hand	jemand behilflich sein
to get to something	dazu kommen (im Sinn von „nicht die Zeit haben")
to wish	(sich) wünschen
I'll bet!	Das glaub ich dir! (oft ironisch)
besides …	jemand an etwas erinnern
Now you're talking!	(etwa:) Warum nicht gleich so?!
Anything else?!	Sonst noch 'was?!
actually	eigentlich
the cleaner's	die Reinigung
What exactly …?	Was eigentlich …?

Lerntipp
Wörter, die Sie wiederholen möchten, unterstreichen Sie am besten oder Sie notieren sie hier in der Randspalte.

AE	BE
call s.o. (up)	*ring s.o. (up)*
give s.o. a call	*give s.o. a ring*

5 Welche Ausdrücke in Übung 4 bedeuten das Gegenteil der folgenden Redewendungen?

a to be sorry about something — to be glad

b to fall behind with something — to catch up

c to get a call — to give someone

d to stop doing something — to get started

Lerntipp
Immer das Antonym (Gegenteil) einer neuen Vokabel dazulernen! Oft gibt es mehrere Antonyme.

Unit 2

Language focus

Lerntipp
Prägen Sie sich ein paar Sätze ein, die Sie erfahrungsgemäß brauchen.

6 Selten gibt es in der englischen Sprache nur eine Möglichkeit, etwas auszudrücken. Vergleichen Sie die Formulierungen, die im Dialog gewählt wurden, mit weiteren Vorschlägen.

a Cary asks Matt if he's got any plans for the afternoon. Which one of the following expressions does she use? Would the other expressions also be appropriate?

(1) What are you going to do this afternoon?
2 I mean, have you got any plans?
3 What are you doing this afternoon?
4 Have you got anything planned?
5 What will you do this afternoon?

b Cary wants Matt to help with the housework. Which one of the following expressions does she use to ask him? Which one would not be appropriate?

AE BE
favor *favour*

1 Matt, would you do me a favour?
2 Can I ask you to do something for me?
3 Get busy!
(4) I was wondering if you could give me a hand.
5 Do you think you could give me a hand?

c Matt gives a reason why he can't help. How does he phrase it?

1 I can't because I've got to get caught up at the office.
2 I have to get caught up at the office.
3 Due to a lot of work at the office it's not possible.
(4) I really need to get caught up at the office.
5 Well, I've got to get caught up at the office.

Due to ... ist eher formell und wird hauptsächlich in offiziellen Bekanntmachungen verwendet.

d Matt finally gives in to Cary's request to stop at the store. Which expression does he use? Are any of the other alternatives possible?

(1) OK, *you* make up the list and *I'm* going to do the shopping.
2 OK, *you* make up the list and *I'm* going to be doing the shopping.
(3) OK, *you* make up the list and *I'll* do the shopping.
4 OK, *you* make up the list, *I'm* doing the shopping.
5 OK, *you* make up the list and *I will* do the shopping.

7 Ordnen Sie zu: Welche der folgenden Sprechabsichten passt zu welchen Beispielsätzen a–d aus Übung 6?

concede = nachgeben

conceding ♦ asking someone to do something ♦ giving a reason ♦ asking about someone's plans

22

8 Was passt zusammen? Entscheiden Sie, ob die Sätze a–e im Ton höflich oder eher familiär sind. Welche der Reaktionen im Kasten passen deshalb am besten?

Unit 2

a Do you think you could give me a hand with the ironing? (negative answer) — polite   familiar

b Have you got any plans for tonight? — polite   familiar

c Would you mind stopping at the chemist's while you're out? (positive answer) — polite   familiar

d OK, if you cook, I'll do the washing up. — polite   familiar

e Have we got enough food for the weekend? — polite   familiar

polite = höflich
familiar = familiär

No, not at all. c)
I wish I could, but …
I think so. c)
How should I know?! e)
Now you're talking! d)
I'm not sure. I'm thinking about going to … b)
Great! d)
kommt drauf an
It depends; what have you got in mind?
I'll probably go to bed early. b)
Sorry, I'm afraid I can't. I … a)
I might catch up on my work.
I hadn't really thought about it. b)
Sure, no problem. c)   Spass
You've got to be kidding!?
I'm pretty sure we do. e)
Why don't you go have a look? e)

Unit 2 — Grammar focus

Talking about the future

Das Englische kennt mehrere Möglichkeiten, zukünftige Ereignisse darzustellen, je nachdem ob es sich um Vorhersagen, Pläne oder auch um spontane Entscheidungen handelt. Dabei spielen modale und andere Hilfsverben eine wichtige Rolle.

Vorhersagen

Vorhersagen werden mit dem modalen Hilfsverb **will** gebildet:

> I guess the washing just **won't get done**. will get done (pos)

will not = won't

Die gleiche Bedeutung hat *will/won't* auch in „*if*-Sätzen":

> If I have to do everything myself, I won't get to work on my seminar.

get to = dazukommen

Wenn die Vorhersage auf aktuell vorliegenden Informationen basiert, kann man auch **going to** verwenden:

> I can see I'm **gonna get** a lot done at the office.

going to wird *gonna* gesprochen

Für Handlungen, die sich nach einem Zeit- bzw. Fahrplan oder nach einem Kalender richten, verwendet man oft die einfache Form des **Präsens**:

> April first **isn't** that far off.
> Then **I'm** outta here.

out of wird im AE *outta* gesprochen

Man nimmt diese Form vor allem, wenn es um Reisepläne geht:

> We **arrive** in Toronto on the nineteenth.

Zur Bildung der besprochenen Zeitformen siehe Grammatikübersicht, S. 157f.

Unit 2

Um eine Absicht oder einen Plan auszudrücken, hat man zwei Alternativen zur Auswahl: **Pläne**

die **Verlaufsform des Präsens**:

> What **are** you **doing** this afternoon?

oder eine Konstruktion mit **going** to:

> I thought you were **gonna give** your taxes to Sam.

Der Unterschied in der Bedeutung ist minimal. Praktisch sind diese beiden Alternativen austauschbar:

> What are you going to do this afternoon?
> I thought you were giving your taxes to Sam.

Eine eher spontane Entscheidung drückt man mit **will** aus: **Spontane Entscheidungen**

> OK, you make up the list and **I'll do** the shopping.

Bitte beachten Sie: Die einfache Form des Präsens wird *nicht* im Zusammenhang mit Vorhaben – ob geplant oder spontan – verwendet.

> ~~I give you a call later on.~~

Wie anfangs angemerkt, können auch andere Modalverben zukünftige Handlungen ausdrücken. Sie beinhalten eine gewisse Unsicherheit:

> I **should get started on** my taxes.
> I **might catch up** on my work.

Unit 2

Revision

9 Setzen Sie das passende Verb ein. *kommt drauf an*

> give ... a hand ♦ wish ♦ remind ♦ catch up ♦ depend ♦ wonder ♦ give ... a call

a Are you going to the seminar? – It **depend** ; when is it?

b I really have to **catch up** on my work.

c I **wonder** if Sheila will be able to do my taxes.

d Would you like me to **a hand** with the preparations? – Thanks, that would be great!

e I **wish** I had two pairs of hands; there's so much to do!

f Why don't you **give** Tom **a call** ? He's probably not doing anything.

g That **reminds** me: did you pick up my dress at the cleaner's?

10 Vorhersage, Plan oder spontane Entscheidung?

a I'll never understand him!
b I think I'll get started on my homework.
c I'm going to the store if you need anything.
d Where are you going this weekend?
e You won't find what you're looking for there.
f Don't worry, I'll remind you.
g I'm gonna get started on the wash.

11 Haben jeweils beide Sätze die gleiche Bedeutung?

a I won't get my taxes finished before April first.
I'm not going to get my taxes finished before April first.   *the same*

b I think they're going to give us a hand with this stuff.
I think they're giving us a hand with this stuff.   *" "*

c Here, I'll give you a hand with that.
Here, I'm giving you a hand with that.   *not " "*

d I bet you're going to need some clean shirts.
I bet you'll need some clean shirts.   *" "*

e She'll be glad to see you.
She's going to be glad to see you.   *" "*

Unit 2

12 Kreuzen Sie die passende(n) Reaktion(en) an.

a What do you mean?
   1 Yes.   2 I asked you first.   3 I mean, I'd better go.

b Can you give me a hand?
   (1) It depends.   2 I'll bet!   3 What exactly do you want me to do?

c What did you have in mind?
   1 No, thanks.   2 I guess not.   (3) I was thinking of eating out.

d I'll do the wash if you clean up.
   1 It depends.   (2) Now you're talking!   3 How should I know?

e I thought you were going to help.
   (1) I wish I could, but ...   2 I guess.   3 Glad to help.

13 Was haben die abgebildeten Personen morgen vor?

Verwenden Sie bei Ihrer Beschreibung *going to* + Hauptverb.

Stan: is going to do his tax

Jack: to do the wash

Ursula: is going to catch up on their work

Astrid: is going to do the shopping / to do the groceries

Elene: is going to do pick up the closes at the cleaner

14 Arbeiten Sie nun die mündlichen Übungen A bis C zum Thema *Zukunft* durch. Die Anweisungen erhalten Sie auf der CD.

1/6–8

Unit 2

Part 2

Reading

15 Pre-reading task

Haben Sie schon einmal einen Leserbrief geschrieben? Warum? Wollten Sie um Rat fragen oder einfach Ihre Meinung äußern?

16 Lesen Sie nun einen typischen Leserbrief.

Dear Anne Landers,
One day last weekend my parents popped in just as my husband and I finished lunch. It was one of those rare occasions when my husband had offered to do the dishes. I was shocked when my mother asked, "Why is he doing the dishes?" My mother has always been very traditional when it comes to women's roles, and her disapproving remark annoyed me. Wishing to avoid a confrontation, I simply did not respond. What I should have said was, "Maybe because this is the 21st century and I work, too." I could have added, "Maybe because I sanded and painted the bedroom walls. Maybe because I ripped up the carpet on the stairs, pulled nails and repainted the stairway. Maybe because I go to his shop and do sanding for him while he builds kitchens for a living. Maybe because I helped him put in a new floor in the upstairs bathroom. Maybe because I help him unload wood from his pickup truck. Maybe because I'm usually the one who hauls two large garbage bags filled with trash down the road to be collected. Maybe because I'm constantly picking up after him, cooking his meals and doing his laundry. Maybe because we do things for each other and I shouldn't be made to feel guilty if he does the dishes once in a while." I'd love to write more, Anne, but I've got to mop the kitchen floor and start preparing Sunday dinner. His family is coming over. If my mother reads this, I've got another shocker for her. He cooks, too. And now, if I could only get him to sew.
Doing it all in Binghamton, N.Y.

Dear Bing:
You don't owe your mother any explanation as to why your husband does the dishes. It's not her business. If the subject comes up again, you can hand her this column.
From: The Philadelphia Inquirer

maybe because ... = vielleicht, weil ...

💡 In British English the person who writes this kind of column in the newspaper is called an "agony aunt" because she (always a woman!) gives advice to people with problems. In the US there is no particular name for the person who writes this kind of column, they are usually referred to as a "Dear Abby" or "Dear Anne Landers" column.

Whom wie in **Whom do you agree with?** ist korrekt, aber heute nicht mehr gebräuchlich.

17 Beantworten Sie die Fragen.

Who does Anne Landers agree with, the mother or the wife?
Who do you agree with and why?
   I agree with ... because

Working with words

Unit 2

18 Ordnen Sie zu.

to be shocked	1	3 to go to someone's home unexpectedly
to finish lunch	2	2 to end the midday meal
to pop in	3	4 to ask if you can do something for someone
to offer to do something	4	1 to be very surprised
to be annoyed	5	5 to be a little irritated
to rip up (aufreissen)		9 to try not to let something happen
to add		8 to answer
to respond		7 to say one more thing
to avoid		10 to make smooth – glätte
to sand		6 to remove
pickup truck		12 to take off/out of
to unload		11 small truck with open loading area
to pick up after someone	13	14 to carry (something heavy)
to haul	14	15 to gather up sammeln
to collect	15	13 to gather the things someone leaves lying around
to come over	16	17 to think something is your fault
to feel guilty about something	17	18 to clean with water (usually the floor)
to mop	18	16 to visit
subject	19	20 something that is shocking (slang)
a shocker	20	21 it doesn't concern her
it's not her business	21	19 topic

Lerntipp
Versuchen Sie, mit den neuen Wörtern Sätze zu bilden.

19 Welche Verben oben bezeichnen *normale Hausarbeiten*, welche *Renovierungsarbeiten*?

Welche Verben, die zu diesen Kategorien gehören, kennen Sie noch?

20 *Do* oder *make*?

Zwei der folgenden Ausdrücke werden nicht mit dem Verb *to do*, sondern mit *to make* gebildet. Welche sind das?

your taxes	the housework	a meal	the wash(ing)/laundry
the shopping	the repairs	the cleaning	the dishes/washing up
an effort	a job	the ironing	(someone) a favour

29

Unit 2

Language & Grammar focus

Gebrauch

The present continuous tense for repeated actions

In den meisten Grammatiken liest man, dass die einfache Form des Präsens für wiederholte Handlungen und die Verlaufsform für Handlungen verwendet wird, die gerade ablaufen oder in der Zukunft geschehen werden. In der Praxis wird heute die Verlaufsform in einem bestimmten Zusammenhang auch für wiederholte Handlungen gebraucht, wie Sie im Text sehen können:

> *I'm* constantly **picking up** after him, **cooking** his meals and **doing** his laundry.

Durch den Gebrauch der Verlaufsform des Präsens verbunden mit Adverbien wie *constantly* und *always* drückt man sowohl das Momentane als auch die Wiederholung der Handlung aus.

He's always asking me to help him.

! Bitte beachten Sie diese Erklärungen!

Die einfache Form des Präsens kann umgekehrt jedoch *nicht* für Handlungen verwendet werden, die gerade ablaufen. Ein Satz wie: *I unload the pickup* bedeutet, dass man diese Tätigkeit regelmäßig ausführt, z. B. in der Arbeit, und niemals, dass man sie in diesem Moment ausführt.
Deshalb ist ein Satz wie: *I finish lunch* unwahrscheinlich, weil er nichts aussagt; erst ein Zusatz wie ... *around one o'clock* gibt dem Satz einen Sinn.

21 Bilden Sie Sätze nach dem obigen Muster.

a He / always / write letters / to the newspaper

_____

b They / constantly / pop in /at the wrong time

_____

c I / always / try to avoid / the subject

_____

d She /constantly /remind / me /about the housework

_____

e I / always /feel guilty / about something

_____

f We /constantly / offer to help

_____

g He / always / repair / something around the house

_____

Revision

22 Wie lautet das Partizip Präsens (die *-ing*-Form) der folgenden Verben?

make plans	*making plans*	persuade	_____
finish lunch	_____	mop	_____
pick up after	_____	catch up on	_____
unload	_____	rip up	_____
suggest	_____	wonder	_____
pop in	_____	avoid	_____

23 Setzen Sie das passende Verb in der angegebenen Zukunftsform ein.

> do ◆ avoid ◆ pick up after ◆ collect ◆ come over ◆ unload ◆ pop in

a Ralph and his brother _____ the pickup truck. *(going to)*

b We _____ the newspapers and bring them to the recycling centre. *(going to)*

c I _____ not _____ the dishes! *(Verlaufsform des Präsens)*

d I _____ the subject when I see them. *(going to)*

e Sarah's parents _____ later for dinner. *(Verlaufsform des Präsens)*

f I think I _____ and say hello. *(will)*

g I _____ not _____ my daughter any more. *(going to)*

24 Kreuzen Sie die passende(n) Reaktion(en) an.

a Are your parents coming tomorrow?
  1 I think so.   2 I'm afraid I can't.   3 I'm pretty sure they are.

b Would you mind taking out the garbage?
  1 Can't it wait?   2 It's not my business.   3 You've got to be kidding!?

c I wish I could help you.
  1 No, thanks.   2 I'll bet!   3 I'm out of here!

d Why don't you come, too?
  1 Because it's late.   2 Maybe I will.   3 I wish I could, but …

e Anything else?
  1 No, thanks.   2 Now you're talking!   3 Well, actually, there is something …

Unit 2

Unit 2

25 How would you …

a ask your friend to help you with the dishes?
___

b politely refuse a request from a colleague who asks you for help?
___

c tell a friend that something doesn't concern him/her?
___

d respond if someone asks what you're doing tonight?
___

e respond if someone asks if they can do something for you?
___

f tell someone that you don't mind helping them?
___

1/9

26 Hören Sie das Gespräch und tragen Sie anschließend die fehlenden Wörter ein.

● Hey, Keith, how's it going?

◆ Can't _____ , how about you?

● Good, good. Say, I wanted to ask _____ . Are you doing anything on Saturday?

◆ This coming Saturday?

● Yeah.

◆ Um, I don't think so, why?

● I was _____ if you could give me a hand at the recycling centre.

◆ I wish I _____ , old buddy, but I've got some errands to do.

● It doesn't have to be all day – just a couple of hours in the morning.

◆ I don't know …

● _____ , you'll have the whole afternoon to get your errands done.

◆ Couldn't you ask Frank?

● I already have; he _____ be away. What do you say?

◆ Oh, OK, but just until noon.

● That's the spirit!

◆ When _____ ?

● Picking you up?!

errands = Erledigungen

What do you feel like doing?

Unit 3

Hier lernen Sie:

- wie Sie Vorschläge machen
- wie Sie Vorschläge annehmen/ablehnen
- wie Sie etwas begründen
- wie Sie sagen, dass Sie nicht einverstanden sind
- wie Sie Gefallen/Missfallen ausdrücken
- *question tags*

Unit 3

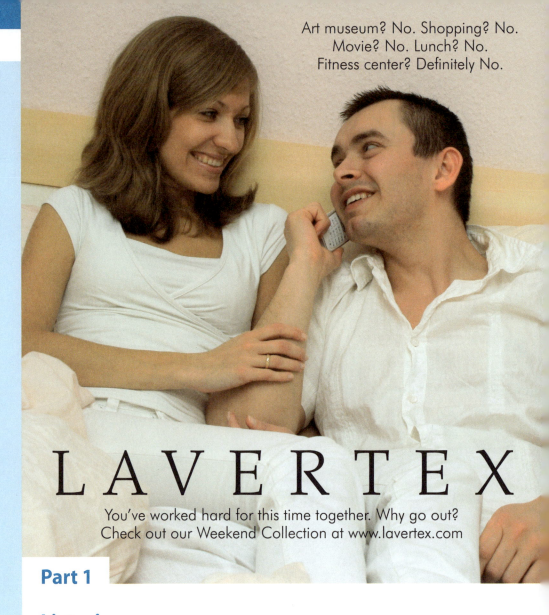

Art museum? No. Shopping? No.
Movie? No. Lunch? No.
Fitness center? Definitely No.

LAVERTEX

You've worked hard for this time together. Why go out?
Check out our Weekend Collection at www.lavertex.com

Aus Anzeigen kann man einiges lernen!

Part 1

Listening

1 Pre-listening task

Lesen Sie den Text der Anzeige und beantworten Sie folgende Fragen.

a What is the couple trying to do?
   1 plan a vacation   2 plan the day   3 plan the rest of their lives

b Do they seem to agree on what they want to do?
   1 yes   2 no

c What does the text at the bottom suggest they should do?
   1 stay home   2 go shopping   3 surf the net

d What do you think the advertisement is for?
   1 breakfast food   2 pajamas   3 bed linens

2 True or false?

Sie hören ein Gespräch zwischen Tina und Jerry. Lesen Sie zuerst die Behauptungen, hören Sie dann den Dialog und kreuzen Sie *true* für „richtig" oder *false* für „falsch" an.

		true	false
a	Jerry isn't interested in making breakfast.	☒	
b	Tina makes a couple of suggestions regarding their plans for the day.		
c	Jerry thinks one of Tina's suggestions is a good idea.		
d	Jerry and Tina agree on going out to brunch, but they don't agree right away on where to go.	☒	
e	Tina gives a specific reason for not wanting to go to the restaurant Jerry suggests.	☒	
f	Jerry and Tina can't agree on a restaurant.		☒

(handwritten next to d: übereinstimmen)

3 Lesen Sie die Fragen, hören Sie das Gespräch noch einmal und kreuzen Sie dann die richtige Antwort an.

a Jerry gives two reasons for not wanting to go to The Green Bean. What are they?
   (1) too far   2 bad food   (3) difficulty parking   4 too expensive

b Jerry and Tina finally agree on a restaurant. Which one?
   1 Point Vedra Beach   (2) The Green Bean   (3) Elliott's   4 Harry's

Unit 3

1/10

Versuchen Sie, die Aufgabe nach dem ersten Hören zu lösen!

1/10

Elliot's/Harry's = Elliot's/Harry's restaurant

(handwritten: O – j, orange juice)

Unit 3

Working with words

1/10

! Benutzen Sie das Dialogskript im Anhang nur zur Kontrolle der Rechtschreibung!

4 Setzen Sie die fehlenden Wörter in den Dialog ein.

Hören Sie anschließend den Text noch einmal und kontrollieren Sie Ihre Lösungen.

- So what do you feel like doing?
- I don't know. What do *you* want to do?
- I _____ you first.
- Well, how about breakfast in bed?
- _____ ; let me know if you need any help.
- On second _____ , …
- We could go over to my _____ .
- Any other suggestions?
- How about going to the Matisse _____ ?
- At the art museum?
- Yeah.
- What, and _____ for an hour to get in? No, thanks.
- Well, what do you _____ ?
- _____ going out for brunch?

5 Wie werden Vorschläge im Dialog formuliert? Unterstreichen Sie.

Kennen Sie noch andere Möglichkeiten, einen Vorschlag zu formulieren?

6 Setzen Sie den passenden Ausdruck in der angegebenen Zeitform ein.

AE *agree to s.th.*
BE *agree (to) s.th.*

agree with ♦ agree on ♦ agree that ♦ agree to

a Susan _agreed with_ her brother that they should make reservations. (simple past)

b I _agree that_ going to the beach at this time of day makes no sense. (simple present)

c We can't seem to _agree to_ where to go. (infinitive)

d _Do_ you _agree_ leaving now would only make things worse? (simple present)

e Can they at least _agree on_ a time? (infinitive)

f Who _did_ you _agree with_ ? (simple past)

g We never seem to be able to _agree on_ anything. (present)

7 Funktionieren die Sätze genauso mit dem Verb *to disagree*?

Language focus

Unit 3

1/11–13

8 Sie hören drei Gespräche auf Ihrer CD.

Welches Gespräch passt zu welchem Bild?

a   b   c

 Hier geht es zunächst darum festzustellen, wie viele Personen jeweils am Gespräch teilnehmen.

1/11–13

9 Welches Gespräch folgt *nicht* dem dargestellten Gesprächsmuster?

Hören Sie die Gespräche noch einmal.

Beispiele

A question is posed regarding plans. → What do you feel like doing?

Suggestions are made and discussed. → Why don't we … / How about … / Let's …

Agreement is reached. → That's a good idea. / Why not? / That's OK with me.

A plan is set out. → We could …

37

Unit 3

💡 Den richtigen Umgangston zu treffen ist nicht leicht, kann aber entscheidend sein: Prägen Sie sich daher eine oder zwei Alternativen ein, wie Sie einen Vorschlag oder ein Angebot ablehnen können, ohne dass Sie jemanden vor den Kopf stoßen.

❓ Wie fordert man im Deutschen den Gesprächspartner auf, Zustimmung zu äußern?

10 Einen Vorschlag ablehnen

Bei dem Versuch einen Konsens zu finden wird die Ablehnung eines Vorschlags, mit dem man nicht einverstanden ist, oft indirekt formuliert, da man nicht unhöflich erscheinen will. Beurteilen Sie, ob die Reaktionen aus den Dialogen direkt (d) oder indirekt (i) sind.

It doesn't look all that sunny. ▪
It's a little late to get started. ▪
I've got a better idea … ▪
What, and stand in line for an hour? ▪
I'd rather … ▪
How about …? ▪
(Yeah) Well, … ▪
Do you really think it's the right time of the year? ▪
We wanted to do something else together. ▪
Umm … ▪
Let's … instead. ▪

11 Lesen Sie den folgenden Auszug aus dem Dialog von S. 35.

Wie fordern die Sprecher einander auf, Zustimmung zu äußern? Unterstreichen Sie die zwei Beispiele im Text.

◆ Um … how about Harry's?
● We were just there a couple of weeks ago, weren't we?
◆ You're right.
● Why don't we try the Green Bean instead?
◆ That's over by eh … on the other side of town, isn't it?

Grammar focus

Unit 3

Question tags

Question tags sind kurze Fragen, die an einen Aussagesatz angehängt werden. Sie verwandeln eine Behauptung in eine (oft rhetorische) Frage.

> *We were just there a couple of weeks ago,* **weren't we***?*
>
> *We don't really know that,* **do we***?*

Bildung

Ein *question tag* besteht aus einer Form des Verbs *to be* oder einem Hilfsverb zusammen mit einem Pronomen, das sich auf das Subjekt des Satzes bezieht.
Fehlt das Verb *to be* oder ein Hilfsverb im Satz, so wird der *question tag* mithilfe des Hilfsverb *to do* gebildet:

> *You want to stay home,* **don't** *you?*

⚠ Zur Erinnerung: Hilfsverben sind z. B. die Modalverben *(can, may, must, should, will* etc.) oder *have* oder *be* in zusammengesetzten Verbformen *(I'm going, he's been* etc.).

Steht das Hilfsverb im Satz in der bejahten Form, so steht es im *question tag* in der Regel in der verneinten Form und umgekehrt.

> *We were just there a couple of weeks ago,* **weren't we***?*
> *We don't really know that,* **do we***?*

Gebrauch

Mit *question tags* versichert man sich des Verständnisses oder der Zustimmung des Gesprächspartners.

> *We were just there a couple of weeks ago,* **weren't we***?*
> *That's over by eh ... on the other side of town,* **isn't it***?*

Eine ähnliche Funktion haben im Deutschen die Anhängsel „oder" und „nicht wahr".

Unit 3 — Revision

12 Setzen Sie den passenden Ausdruck ein.

A: So what do you _____ ?

B: I don't know. What do you want to do?

A: Um, I don't know.

B: Well _____ going shopping?

A: Sure; let me know when you _____ .

B: I thought we could do something together.

A: We _____ over my parents'.

B: Any _____ ?

> get back
> could go
> other suggestions
> feel like doing
> how about

C: Why don't we call for pizza?

A: _____ , why not?

B: It doesn't _____ to me.

D: OK, I'll get one large plain and one with sausage.

C: Hey, wait a minute. Why not get one veggie?

A: That's OK with me.

B: _____

C: I meant one veggie and one with sausage.

A: OK, is everyone in _____ ?

B: Yeah, that's _____ ...

> Me too.
> fine with me
> Sure
> agreement
> matter

plain = einfach

13 Welche Reaktion(en) passen nicht zu den Vorschlägen links?

a How about going swimming?
b What about inviting Hillary?
c Let's see if we can get tickets for the late show.
d Why don't we stay home?
e Shall we go for a drink?
f Can we get together on Monday?

g Why don't we wait and see?
h Maybe we could hire a car instead?

☐ Sure, why not?
☐ I'd rather not.
☐ Sorry, ...
☐ That's OK with me.
☐ That's a good idea.
☐ Let's make it Tuesday instead.
☐ I guess not.
☐ I don't know ...

14 Welcher *question tag* passt? Ordnen Sie zu!

a That was fun,
b They can come,
c She's very nice,
d We haven't been there before,
e You're Toni's friend,
f You work with Gerry,
g You're not going,
h He'll call,
i You didn't wait,

☐ can't they?
☐ have we?
☐ isn't she?
☐ don't you?
☐ wasn't it?
☐ did you?
☐ aren't you?
☐ are you?
☐ won't he?

15 Unterstreichen Sie das Hilfsverb oder das Verb *to be* in den folgenden Sätzen und fügen Sie einen *question tag* hinzu.

a She can't come, _____ ?

b The food was good, _____ ?

c I can call and make a reservation, _____ ?

d They've been there before, _____ ?

e We hadn't really thought about it, _____ ?

f She'll drive, _____ ?

g It's been a nice party, _____ ?

16 Arbeiten Sie nun die mündlichen Übungen A bis E zum Thema *question tags* durch. Die Anweisungen erhalten Sie auf der CD.

1/14–18

Unit 3

Unit 3 Part 2

Reading

17 Welche Anzeige passt zu welcher Situation? Entscheiden Sie!

a   You don't feel like making dinner and would like to order take-away.
b   You are thinking of renting a video for the evening.
c   It's your anniversary and you would like to go out for a special dinner.
d   Friends of yours are in town and you would like to do something cultural with them in the evening.
e   You would like to go out and have dinner, preferably to an ethnic restaurant.
f   You are looking for some light entertainment on your night out.
g   You would like to do some surfing while out for a meal.

! *Preferably* (vorzugsweise) wird [prefrəbli] ausgesprochen.

! Sie müssen nicht jede Anzeige ganz genau lesen; manchmal genügt es auch, wenn Sie einen Text nur überfliegen.

1

Movie Review
Enemy of the State
★★★½ out of 4
Who's it for? It's an entertaining, paranoid thriller with wide appeal.
Credits: Starring Will Smith, Jon Voight, Gene Hackman and Regina King. Directed by Tony Scott.
Running time: 2 hours, 8 minutes.
Family guide: R. A couple of violent scenes (including one bloody shootout), mild sexual situations and some profanity. But, not as rough as many R movies, it's probably OK for young teens.

2

CASA DE TACOS

OPEN FOR LUNCH & DINNER
AUTHENTIC MEXICAN FAST FOOD

SPECIALISING IN SPICED CHICKEN, GRILLED PORK AND STEAK TACOS

ALL MEALS FROM $ 2.00–$ 5.50
810-6865 • 48 SPANISH ST.

3

SALLY O'NEALS'S
GOURMET PIZZA HOTLINE
BEST PIZZA · BEST OF THE BAY 2009
BEEF GORGONZOLA PIZZA
Lean ground beef, red onions, gorgonzola cheese atop our red pizza base.
251-0220
1319 S. Howard Ave.

4

Internet Restaurant
"Where The Past Meets The Future!"
• Electronic Postcard • E-Mail
• Printing • Scanning & More
Located at 31 Orange St. in the Authentic Old Drug Store
824-6121
Free internet access with lunch or dinner!

5

The only **in-house** roaster in Northeast Florida.

• Light Breakfast and Lunch
• Homemade Muffins & Scones
• Fresh Baked Bagels
• Fine Teas & Giftware

TWO LOCATIONS TO SERVE YOU

13245 Atlantic Blvd.
Jacksonville, FL
221-7400

930 Sawgrass Village Dr.
Ponte Vedra Beach, FL
285-9113

Green Bean Coffee House

Unit 3

6 THE COMEDY ZONE
At Gigi
Presents ...
MARK CORDES
Nov. 20 & Nov. 21
**Don't Miss the
"One Man Laugh Factory"**
For beat seats,
call today for your reservation
292-HAHA (4242)
www.comedysone.com
I-295 & San Jose Blvd.

7 *Elliott's*
ON THE SQUARE
Contemporary American Cuisine
Breakfeast · Lunch · Dinner
387 King St. · Downtown Charleston
at the Westin Francis Marion Hotel
843.724.8888

Welche englischen Wörter kennen Sie schon aus der deutschen Werbung?

8 *Ann O'Malley's Irish Pub*
904-825-4040 for takeout

Open everyday of the week 11 am till 1 am
Deli Sandwiches · Salads · Hot Soup
ON DRAFT
Newcastle Brown Ale · Murphy's Irish Stout
Guinness · Harp · Boddington Pub Ale
23 Orange Street
(Near the Old City Gate)

9 **People, Places & Quilts**
Folk Art, Fabrics, Antiques and ... quilts of course!

All handmade in the USA
871-8872
129 W. Richardson Ave,
in the ♥ of downtown Summerville

10 **CHICAGO**
THE RAZZLE-DAZZLE BROADWAY MUSICAL
PEABODY AUDITORIUM · DAYTONA BEACH
4 PERFORMANCES, NOVEMBER 5, 6, & 7
FRI. & SAT. – 7:30 PM · SAT. & SUN. 2:00 PM
FOR TICKETS CALL (407) 839-3900 OR (904) 254-4545

Unit 3

18 Lesen Sie den Artikel über Venice, Kalifornien.

Venice

Venice, CA (the closest beach community to Los Angeles, the only place around LA where you can see people outside their cars)

Living in Venice is like living in a camp for semi-demented adults. At every hour, day and night, there are people playing volleyball, running, rolling on skates, riding bikes, skateboards, surf boards, flying kites, drinking milk, eating quiche lorraine. Old people sit under umbrellas playing checkers. Bodybuilders work out in a sandy pen, and crowds line up three deep to perform on the paddle tennis courts. When do these people work? I used to wonder.

The residents of Venice fall into two groups: Those who work, and those who don't. The latter includes senior citizens, drifters, drug addicts, hopeful moviemakers and aging hippies and surfers who have made a cult of idleness and pleasure. The other group includes lawyers, dentists, real estate brokers, accountants. Many are workaholics, attached to their jobs as they are to nothing else. They work nights and weekends, eat fast food while driving to and from their work and live alone, longing, in the silence before falling asleep, for connection.

Everyone comes together on the boardwalk. The natives wear their own skates, and the tourists rent them from the places like "Cheapskates" and "United Skates of America" …

From: *Real Property*, Sara Davidson

Cheapskates und *United Skates of America* sind Firmennamen, die gleichzeitig Wortspiele sind: Das erste ist eine Anspielung auf das Wort *cheapskate*, das soviel wie „Geizhals" bedeutet, und *United Skates* bedarf eigentlich keiner weiteren Erklärung.

19 Welche der folgenden Aussagen fasst den Text am besten zusammen?

a   Venice is unlike Los Angeles in that it is a beach community.
b   Venice is unlike most other places in California – or America for that matter!
c   Venice is not a place you might want to go to – and certainly not live!
d   Venice is not as interesting as Los Angeles or – to be sure – as New York!

Unit 3

Working with words

20 Ordnen Sie Wörter aus dem Text den folgenden Kategorien zu.

Words referring to people	Words referring to leisure-time activities

💡 **Lerntipp**
Vokabeln nach verschiedenen Kriterien gruppieren = effektives und unterhaltsames Lernen

❓ Können Sie die Listen mit weiteren Wörtern, die Sie schon kennen, erweitern?

Unit 3

In den ersten zwei Übungen geht es um die Bedeutungen der Wörter, in der dritten um die Wortart.

21 Ordnen Sie zu.

demented	place to live near the sea
to work out	crazy
pen	a board game
to line up	to train
beach community	fenced in area
checkers	to wait in an orderly fashion
the latter	to give a show
boardwalk	to ask yourself
to perform	the last one mentioned
to long for	to be fond of
to wonder	to miss
to be attached to	pavement made of wood

22 Ordnen Sie die Wörter aus Übung 21 den folgenden Kategorien zu.

noun	verb	adjective	adverb

46

Revision

23 Wissen Sie, wie die abgebildeten Sportarten auf Englisch heißen?

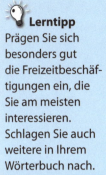

_____ _____ _____ _____

_____ _____ _____ _____

24 Setzen Sie bei den folgenden Freizeitaktivitäten das passende Verb ein.

> go (to/for) ◆ play ◆ take ◆ surf ◆ have ◆ fly ◆ see ◆ ride ◆ sail

_____	a kite	_____	a walk
_____	volleyball	_____	an exhibition
_____	swimming	_____	brunch
_____	a bike	_____	camping
_____	checkers	_____	backpacking
_____	a film	_____	out to eat
_____	a boot	_____	the net

Lerntipp
Prägen Sie sich besonders gut die Freizeitbeschäftigungen ein, die Sie am meisten interessieren. Schlagen Sie auch weitere in Ihrem Wörterbuch nach.

Lerntipp
Welches Gefühl verbinden Sie mit bestimmten Aktivitäten? Was hört man dabei? Mit allen Sinnen zu lernen steigert den Lernerfolg.

Unit 3

25 **Kreuzen Sie die passende(n) Reaktion(en) an.**

a What do you feel like doing?
   1 Sure, why not.   2 I don't know.   3 We could go to brunch.

b How about staying home and watching TV?
   1 Fine.   2 That's OK with me.   3 You've got to be kidding!?

c Why don't we get started?
   1 No, thanks.   2 Me, too!   3 Good idea!

d What are you thinking about?
   1 Greece.   2 I've got it!   3 Sounds like a plan to me!

e I'd rather go somewhere else, wouldn't you?
   1 Ah, come on!   2 On second thought …   3 Well, actually, no.

26 **Unterstreichen Sie das Hilfsverb oder das Verb *to be* in den folgenden Sätzen und fügen Sie einen *question tag* hinzu.**

a He's looking forward to coming, _____

b We've already seen that film, _____

c It's going to rain, _____

d The service was excellent, _____

e They can't afford it, _____

f Seeing them again will be fun, _____

g You want her to succeed, _____

1/19

27 **Schreiben Sie einen Dialog nach dem vorgegebenen Muster.**

Hören Sie anschließend auf der CD, wie das Gespräch verlaufen könnte.

A fragt eine(n) Freund(in), was er/sie heute Abend unternehmen möchte.

B ist unsicher und fragt, was A machen möchte. A schlägt vor, zusammen essen zu gehen oder so ähnlich.

B erwidert, dass er/sie lieber zu Hause essen möchte, und schlägt vor, dass man später ins Kino gehen könne.

A findet, dass das Wetter zu schön sei, um ins Kino zu gehen, und schlägt vor, draußen etwas zu unternehmen.

B akzeptiert den Vorschlag an und fragt, ob A schon eine konkrete Idee habe.

A schlägt vor, einen Blick in die Zeitung zu werfen, und sagt, er/sie werde später anrufen.

B ist damit einverstanden und verabschiedet sich.

A verabschiedet sich auch.

So then what happened?

Unit 4

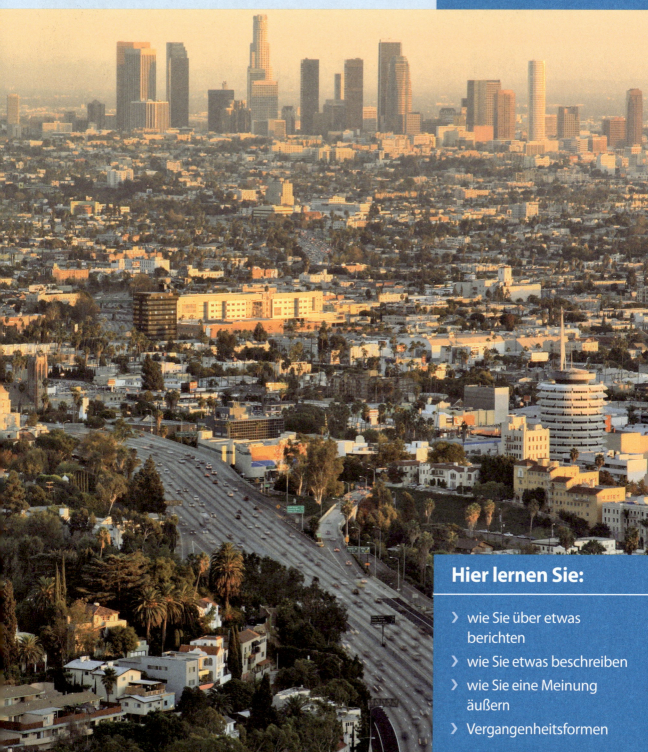

Hier lernen Sie:

> wie Sie über etwas berichten
> wie Sie etwas beschreiben
> wie Sie eine Meinung äußern
> Vergangenheitsformen

Unit 4

Part 1

Listening

1 Pre-listening task

Mit den Worten *"Once upon a time ..."* beginnen alle englischen Märchen. Und wie leitet man heute eine Erzählung im Alltagsgespräch ein? Ordnen Sie die folgenden Anfänge nach der Brisanz der zu erwartenden Geschichte.

a   You'll never guess what happened!
b   Have you heard about ...?
c   I'll never forget what happened that day.
d   By the way, I ran into ... recently.
e   A funny thing happened on the way to ...

! Natürlich gibt es noch viel mehr Formulierungen!

 1/20

2 True or false?

Sie hören ein Gespräch zwischen zwei Freundinnen, Karen und Nancy. Lesen Sie zuerst die folgenden Behauptungen, hören Sie dann den Dialog und kreuzen Sie anschließend *true* für „richtig" oder *false* für „falsch" an.

		true	false
a	Nancy and Karen have both been to California.	☐	☐
b	Nancy liked San Francisco better than Los Angeles.	☐	☐
c	Nancy and Karen agree that Venice is crazy.	☐	☐
d	Nancy lived in Venice.	☐	☐
e	Nancy tells Karen a funny story about her visit to Sea World.	☐	☐
f	Nancy's boyfriend David got arrested for indecent exposure.	☐	☐
g	Nancy is still seeing David.	☐	☐

💡 Weil man nicht *alles* verstanden hat, denkt man oft, man habe *nichts* verstanden. Aber in Wahrheit hat man eine ganze Menge verstanden!

Working with words

Unit 4

3 Zwei Übersetzungen in der folgenden Liste sind vertauscht. Welche sind das?

hotel chain	Hotelkette
discount	Rabatt
to take advantage of something	etwas ausnutzen
It's a trip!	(etwa:) Das ist ein Erlebnis!
weird	sonderbar
to be spread out	verteilt sein
Tell me about it!	Wem sagst du das!
to room with someone	eine Wohnung mit jemandem teilen
to get along with someone	mit jemandem gut auskommen
to call it quits	sich trennen, (eine Beziehung) beenden
to keep in touch	in Kontakt bleiben
loony	Verrückte(r)
brilliant	(hier:) toll
to be a good sport about something	vorfahren
row	Reihe
to splash	mit Wasser bespritzen
to get soaked	klatschnass werden
secluded	abgelegen
to dry off	trocken werden
indecent exposure	(Erregung öffentlichen Ärgernisses durch) unsittliches Entblößen
to pull up	etwas locker nehmen
to get out (of a car)	aussteigen
to get arrested	verhaftet werden
soggy	feucht
to dry out	trocknen
poky	Knast
highlight	Höhepunkt

4 Welche Verben aus der Liste bedeuten dasselbe wie die folgenden Verben?

a   to get wet/drenched _____

b   to drive up _____

c   (the opposite of *to get wet*) (2x) _____

d   to end (a relationship) _____

e   to be apprehended by the police _____

Lerntipp

Sprechen Sie neue Vokabeln auch laut aus. Wie beurteilen Sie selbst Ihre Aussprache? Wenn Sie nicht mehr sicher sind, wie eine Vokabel ausgesprochen wird, achten Sie im Dialog darauf.

Unit 4 — Language focus

5 Eine Geschichte erzählen

Setzen Sie die folgenden Sätze in die richtige Reihenfolge, sodass sie eine Geschichte ergeben.

Introduction		a Seems she's met someone else and she's thinking of leaving Mike.
Background information		b So anyway, we got talking and before you know it she starts telling me she's having marital problems.
The plot		c I was flabbergasted!
Highpoint		d You'll never guess what happened to me yesterday!
Comment		e On my way to work I ran into an old friend, Marlies. You remember her: we were neighbours in Clivden. She and her husband Mike and Del and I used to be inseparable.

flabbergasted = verblüfft

 Als zusätzliche Übung: Versuchen Sie, eine kurze Geschichte nach diesem Muster zu schreiben.

Unit 4

6 Echt?

Mit bestimmten Ausdrücken gibt man dem Gesprächspartner zu erkennen, dass man seiner Geschichte interessiert folgt. Welche Wörter gehören nicht dazu?

really?	no!	are you?
you're kidding?	I see	anyway
yeah	so then what happened?	mm...
uhuh	actually	that's odd
I can imagine!	wow!	what?
oh, right	does he?	have they?

Lerntipp
Stock phrases sollten Sie auswendig lernen. Dann haben Sie sie immer parat.

7 Schreiben Sie eine passende Reaktion aus Aufgabe 6 unter jede Äußerung in der Geschichte unter 5.

8 Elipse

In alltäglichen Gesprächen lässt man gern unwichtige Wörter weg. Dies gilt besonders, wenn man eine Geschichte erzählt, weil die Zusammenhänge dann sowieso klar sind. Lesen Sie folgende Sätze aus dem Hörtext. Können Sie feststellen, was fehlt? (Hinweis: Es fehlen Wörter an fünf Stellen!)

a Bet you were out rollerblading with the rest of the loonies. – Actually, I was – and loved every minute of it!

b How crazy is that place? – About as crazy as they get!

c It was hilarious! – Wish I could have seen that!

d We found this park nearby – just what the doctor ordered.

like
Viele halten den überflüssigen Gebrauch des Wortes *like* für eine Unart, aber es ist aus dem Sprachgebrauch mancher Sprecher einfach nicht wegzudenken.
He got (like) a discount at other hotels.
David is (like) standing there wringing out his shorts ...

Eine andere solche Floskel, die bei manchen Sprechern viel zu häufig vorkommt, ist *"ya know?"*, eine Art *question tag*.

Unit 4

Gebrauch der Zeitformen

Grammar focus

Talking about the past

Das **Präteritum** *(the simple past tense)* wird für Handlungen und Situationen verwendet, die zu einem bestimmten Zeitpunkt in der Vergangenheit stattgefunden haben:

> Where **did** you **go** (when you were living in California)?

Will man die Dauer einer solchen Handlung oder Situation betonen, so verwendet man die Verlaufsform *(the past continuous tense)*:

> Before I found my own apartment I **was rooming** with a friend in Venice.

Das **Perfekt** *(the present perfect tense)* wird verwendet, wenn es in erster Linie um die Auswirkung einer vergangenen Handlung oder Situation auf die Gegenwart geht:

> **Have** you ever **been** to California?

Will man betonen, dass eine Handlung oder Situation bis in die Gegenwart andauert, so verwendet man die Verlaufsform *(the present perfect continuous tense,* siehe Lektion 1). Diese Zeitform kommt logischerweise selten vor, wenn man von Vergangenem erzählt.

Mit dem **Plusquamperfekt** *(the past perfect tense)* beschreibt man Handlungen und Situationen, die vor einer anderen Handlung oder Situation in der Vergangenheit stattgefunden haben. Zeitadverbien weisen oft auf die Abfolge der Ereignisse hin:

> And he **had** just **got finished** saying: „I think we should move."

Will man die Dauer einer solchen Handlung oder Situation betonen, so verwendet man die Verlaufsform *(the past perfect continuous tense)*:

> We just **hadn't been getting along**, so we decided to call it quits.

1/20

9 Hören Sie den Dialog noch einmal. Welche Vergangenheitsform kommt am häufigsten vor? Welche am seltensten?

Talking about the past

Haben Sie beim Zuhören gemerkt, dass die Sprecher auch Präsensformen verwendet haben, um das Geschehen zu vergegenwärtigen? Auch im Deutschen setzt man dieses Stilmittel ein, um eine Erzählung lebendiger zu machen. Voraussetzung für solche Einlagen im Präsens ist, dass der Zusammenhang eindeutig ist, d. h. dass klar ist, dass das Geschehen in der Vergangenheit spielt.

Man gebraucht dabei sowohl die einfache als auch die Verlaufsform des Präsens:

> David **is** (like) **standing** there **wringing out** his shorts with the rest of his clothes **hanging** in the tree and these two cops **get out**.

Die Verlaufsform beschreibt die andauernde Handlung (*is standing* (and) *wringing out his clothes*) bzw. Situation (*his clothes* **are hanging** *in the tree*) und die einfache Form die momentane Handlung (*two cops* **get out**). Mit der einen Form malt man sozusagen den Hintergrund, vor dem die andere Handlung stattfindet.

Unit 4

Gebrauch der Zeitformen (Fortsetzung)

10 **Hören Sie den Dialog noch einmal. Wie viele solcher „Präsens-Einlagen" gibt es im Verlauf des Gesprächs?**

a eine   b zwei   c drei

Unit 4

Revision

11 *Simple past* oder *past continuous*? Setzen Sie die Verben in der richtigen Vergangenheitszeit ein.

a I _____ with a friend when we _____ . room, meet

b We _____ in touch for a while but keep

I haven't heard from them in years.

c We _____ a discount at the hotel. get

d She _____ a real good sport about it. be

e Our clothes _____ when the police _____ . dry out, pull up

f _____ you _____ ? get arrested

g We _____ very well while were on the trip. get along

12 *Simple past* oder *present perfect*? Streichen Sie die falsche Form durch.

a Where did you go? – We *went/have gone* to L.A.
b Did you go to Venice? – Yes, I *did/have*.
c Have you been to See World? – Yes, I *did/have*.
d So then what happened? – Well, we *explained/have explained* the situation.
e I wish I could have seen that. – Yes, it *was/has been* pretty funny.
f Have you seen David since then? – No, I *didn't/haven't*.
g Have you ever been arrested? – Once, when we *were/have been* in New York.

13 Was machte Paul in dem angegebenen Zeitraum?

a 7.00 – 7.30 _____
b 7.45 – 8.15 _____
c 8.30 – 9.10 _____
d 9.15 – 9.30 _____
e 9.30 – 10.15 _____

56

Unit 4

14 **Ordnen Sie der Frage die passende Antwort zu.**

a Do you know Liz?
b How long have you lived there?
c When did you see the film?
d Where is your jacket?
e When are you leaving?
f What happened?
g Are you new here?

☐ Since 1999.
☐ As soon as we've finished packing.
☐ I haven't seen it yet!
☐ No, I've never met her before.
☐ Yes, we've just moved from London.
☐ I think I left it at the cinema.
☐ I think I've broken my thumb.

15 **Setzen Sie den passenden Ausdruck ein.**

a Larry doesn't really know what he's doing, _____
b First you have to arrange for transportation. _____
c And then she put it on her head! _____
d _____, I don't really care!
e Do you know what I mean? _____
f I'd like you to come to the picnic. _____
g They've got this thing about fitness. _____

Actually
Really?
does he?
Yes, go on.
I see.
You're kidding?!
Tell me about it!

16 **Arbeiten Sie nun die mündlichen Übungen A bis F zum Thema Vergangenheitsformen durch. Die Anweisungen erhalten Sie auf der CD.**

1/21–26

Lerntipp
Was tun, wenn Sie Schwierigkeiten mit einer mündlichen Übung haben? Hören Sie einige Aufgaben und die Lösungen an, beginnen Sie wieder von vorne und wiederholen Sie die ersten Sätze. Fahren Sie mit der Übung fort.

Unit 4

Part 2

Reading

17 Pre-reading task

Kennen Sie im Deutschen Wörter, die Sie in gemischter Gesellschaft nicht benutzen würden? Gibt es Wörter, die Sie sagen, aber nicht schreiben?

18 Lesen Sie nun den folgenden Text.

> Dieses und manch anderes Tabu-Wort aus dem Englischen erfreut sich seit Kurzem im Deutschen großer Beliebtheit.

F---!

Here comes the most commonly used and shocking taboo word in the English language. Fifty years ago it could not have been placed in a printed book without strong objections from editors and publishers, let alone readers. Indeed, it was not until the 1980's that it was listed – along with a scholarly note on its likely origins – in most dictionaries. Even today, when newspapers feel obliged to allude to the word, in verbatim news accounts, the convention is to print f---. The word, of course, is *fuck*. The very sight of the whole word, there on a page, is still a shock. Not at all because of the sexual meaning, which by this time, in an age of open frankness about all sexual matters, has almost been lost. The word shocks because of the explosive violence contained in it, the malevolence, the expression of contempt. Its first meaning remains, of course, sexual intercourse, but the several other, meaner meanings are:

"to mishandle; bungle, usually used with up, to meddle or interfere." If you are strolling past a construction site in mid-Manhattan, you will surely hear this word used more frequently than any other in the English language and you are just as likely to hear it repeatedly around the computers in pleasant Wall Street offices on a bad business day. ...

The word was usually left out of dictionaries, I suppose, as a matter of taste, and in a way this was a kind of encouragement. There seems to have been something like an enduring consensus, reflected in our dictionaries, that there are some words so abusive when seen in print, so cursed and cursing, as not to be acceptable on a page. It is somehow a different matter to shout the word, or to hear it spoken; we can put up with that as we must. But we are not obliged to look at it.

Based on: *Et cetera, et cetera, Notes of a word-watcher*, Lewis Thomas

19 Welche der folgenden Behauptungen fasst den Text am besten zusammen?

a Although the word in question is rare in spoken English, it is often found in written English.
b Although the word in question has become commonplace in spoken English, it is seldom written.
c Although the word in question is offensive to many people, it is often used.
d Although the word in question is commonplace in other languages, it is not in English.

Working with words

Unit 4

20 Ordnen Sie zu.

to feel obliged	gebräuchlich, alltäglich
objection	Einwand, Bedenken
commonly used	geschweige (denn)
let alone	sich verpflichtet fühlen
verbatim	eine Andeutung machen
to allude to something	Wort für Wort

intercourse	Bericht
contempt	Brauch
account	Offenheit
frankness	Bosheit
malevolence	Abscheu
convention	Geschlechtsverkehr

to interfere	gemein
to meddle	schlecht behandeln
to bungle	verpfuschen
to mishandle	sich einmischen
mean	sich einmischen

encouragement	spazieren
to stroll	annehmen
to curse	bleibend, fortdauernd
suppose	Ermutigung
enduring	beleidigend
abusive	verdammen

Können Sie die Vergangenheitsformen der Verben in dieser Liste nennen?

21 Setzen Sie die fehlenden Wörter ein.

	noun	verb	adjective	adverb
a		to be frank		
b			abusive	
c	encouragement			
d			shocking	

Unit 4

Talk, talk, talk!

22 Verbinden Sie die Synonyme.

a divulge
b tell
c break the news
d have your say
e rant and rave
f improvise
g gossip
h chat

☐ spread rumours
☐ rattle on
☐ report
☐ disclose
☐ narrate
☐ converse
☐ speak your mind
☐ speak off the cuff

23 Was passt zusammen?

a narrate
b leak
c broadcast
d whisper
e gossip
f speak your mind
g rattle on
h improvise

☐ unsubstantiated
☐ wide audience
☐ spontaneous
☐ descriptive
☐ softly
☐ open
☐ unending
☐ indiscreet

24 Wo liegt die Hauptbetonung bei den folgenden Wörtern?

al·lude
ver·ba·tim
ma·lev·o·lence
mis·han·dle

in·ter·fere
a·bu·sive
con·ven·tion
en·cour·age·ment

in·de·cent
dis·count
ob·jec·tion
con·tempt

1/27

Lerntipp
Die richtige Betonung eines Wortes hilft, es korrekt auszusprechen. Übertreiben Sie ruhig am Anfang; so prägen Sie sich die richtige Betonung besser ein.

60

Revision

25 Setzen Sie das passende Wort ein.

bungle ◆ think better ◆ verbatim ◆ mean ◆ stroll ◆ interfere ◆ feel obliged

a At first he was going to go, but then he _____ of it.
b You don't have to come along; please don't _____ .
c I've got it; let's take a _____ down to the high street.
d She can't keep her nose out of our business; she _____ always _____ .
e He _____ the job again; we'll have to do it over!
f I can't quote her _____ , but she said something to the effect that she was thinking of quitting.
g That's an awfully _____ thing to say!

26 *Simple past* oder *present perfect*?

a I _____ in Boston in 1999 but I _____ there since then.   live, not be
b I _____ to get her a couple of times.
  – I think she _____ to Finola's for the weekend.   try, go
c _____ you _____ the new Woody Allen film?
  – Yes, I _____ it Sunday night.   see
d When _____ you _____ to Spain?
  – Spain? I _____ to Spain.   go, never be
e Laura, _____ you ever _____ Steven?
  – Yes, I think so. _____ we _____ at Tony's last year?   meet, not meet
f When we _____ it quits he _____ a good sport about it.   call, be

27 *Simple past* oder *past perfect*?

a Yes, it _____ a good film, but I _____ it before.   be, see
b She _____ just _____ when I _____ .   leave, arrive
c I _____ never _____ to the West Coast, so
  I _____ them play tour guide.   be, let
d I _____ just _____ my laptop when the new
  models _____ .   buy, come out
e I _____ it, although I _____ never _____
  Indonesian food before.   like, have
f We _____ just _____ from the first downpour when
  it _____ to rain again.   dry out, begin
g We _____ to keep in touch, but of course we
  never _____ .   promise, do

Unit 4

61

Unit 4

1/28

28 Hören Sie die folgenden Sätze und kreuzen Sie die passende(n) Reaktion(en) an.

a 1 You don't say!   2 Wow!   3 About as crazy as they get.
b 1 Do they?   2 Really!   3 Right!
c 1 Actually, ...   2 OK.   3 To tell you the truth, ...
d 1 You don't say!?   2 Does she?   3 You're kidding?!
e 1 Are you sure?   2 I see.   3 What?

29 Wie sagt man's auf Englisch?

a Habt ihr noch Kontakt?
– Nein, seit wir uns getrennt haben, nicht mehr.
b Venice ist eine sonderbare Stadt.
– Wem sagst du das!?
c Kommst du gut mit ihr aus?
– Ja, wir teilen uns seit fünf Jahren eine Wohnung.
d Ich habe früher für eine Hotelkette gearbeitet.
– Tatsächlich?
e Wurde er verhaftet?
– Ja, er hat die Nacht im Knast verbracht.

past continuous

simple past

a   b   c   d

1/29

Hören Sie nun die Geschichte zu den Bildern auf der CD und kontrollieren Sie Ihre Lösungen.

We're moving in together

Unit 5

Hier lernen Sie:

› wie Sie jemanden um etwas bitten
› wie Sie eine Bitte ablehnen/einer Bitte entsprechen
› wie Sie sich bedanken
› wie Sie etwas begründen
› indirekte Rede

Unit 5

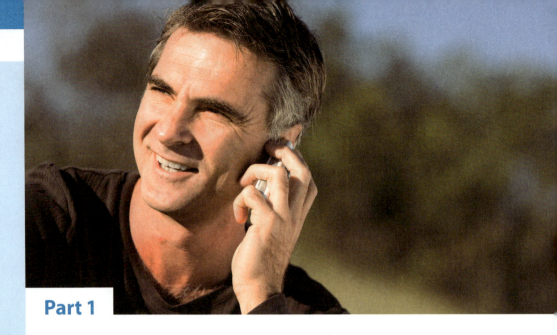

Part 1

Listening

Bitte beachten Sie: Manche Sätze sind in beiden Situationen denkbar!

1 Pre-listening task

Welche der folgenden Sätze würden Sie hören, wenn jemand Freunde um Hilfe beim Umzug bittet (G für *Gefallen*) und welche, wenn diese Person die Freunde einlädt (E für *Einladung*)?

a What are you doing on Saturday?
b Did I mention that Tina is making her famous chili?
c When did you say it was?
d I told the others about 10 o'clock.
e You're not getting started at the crack of dawn, are you?
f Thanks old buddy, I appreciate it.
g Don't mention it.

1/30

2 True or false?

Sie werden ein Gespräch zwischen zwei Freunden, Tommy und Phil, hören. Lesen Sie die folgenden Behauptungen, hören Sie den Dialog und entscheiden Sie danach, ob die Behauptungen richtig oder falsch sind.
Handelt es sich um eine Einladung oder eine Bitte um Hilfe?

		true	false
a	Tommy and Phil haven't spoken with each other in a while.		
b	Tina is Tommy's girlfriend.		
c	Phil knows Tina.		
d	It's not the first time Tommy has asked Phil to give him a hand moving.		
e	Tommy needs help because he's doing the moving himself.		
f	Phil is eager to help.		
g	Phil is not an early riser.		

Working with words

Unit 5

3 Zwei Erklärungen in der folgenden Liste sind vertauscht worden. Welche?

to complain	sich beklagen/beschweren
he's history	(etwa:) der ist weg
to hang in there	(etwa:) hartnäckig bleiben, sich behaupten
to see someone	(hier:) befreundet sein mit jemandem
seriously	(hier:) im Ernst
to stand up straight	sich gerade hinstellen
expertise	Expertise, Fachkenntnisse
light fixture	Beleuchtungskörper
to hook something up	etwas anschließen/installieren
stuff	Zeug
redo	renovieren
in your dreams!	(etwa:) ich bin dabei!
good move!	(etwa:) gute/kluge Entscheidung!
count me in!	das hättest du wohl gern!
to convince	überzeugen
at the crack of dawn	bei Tagesanbruch
to handle something	(hier:) mit etwas umgehen können

4 Welche der Ausdrücke von Übung 3 bedeuten dasselbe wie die folgenden?

a to gripe/grumble _____

b to date someone _____

c to install _____

d to deal with something _____

5 Das Verb *move*

Das Verb *move* hat mehrere Bedeutungen. In dieser Lektion kommt es in der Bedeutung „umziehen" vor. Was bedeuten die folgenden Verbindungen mit *move*? Ordnen Sie dem Verb die passende Ergänzung zu.

a move away
b move in
c move out
d move in together

of your house
from the old neighbourhood
with someone
to a new apartment

Lerntipp

Wollen Sie sich die englischen Begriffe für die Gegenstände in Ihrer Umgebung merken? Schreiben Sie die Wörter auf selbstklebende gelbe Zettel und heften Sie sie eine Zeit lang an die Gegenstände.

Oft als *stock phrases* zu hören:
Hang in there!
In your dreams!
Good move!

Lerntipp

Nehmen Sie weitere Verben und fügen Sie Präpositionen hinzu. Wie verändern sie die Bedeutung des Wortes? Schlagen Sie bei Bedarf im Wörterbuch nach; Sie finden dort die Varianten unter dem Hauptstichwort.

Unit 5

Language focus

1/31–33

! Achten Sie beim ersten Hören auf den Inhalt der Gespräche. Die Lösung der Aufgabe ergibt sich dann von selbst.

6 Hören Sie die Gespräche an.

Sie werden drei Gespräche hören, in denen jeweils eine Person eine andere um einen Gefallen bittet. Welches der Gespräche folgt nicht dem dargestellten Gesprächsmuster?

■ Gespräch 1
■ Gespräch 2
■ Gespräch 3

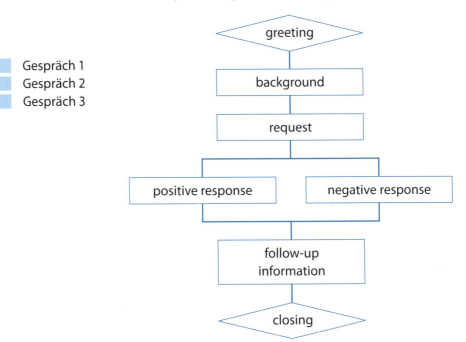

? Je weniger direkt eine Bitte formuliert ist, umso höflicher ist sie. Haben Sie gemerkt, dass Tommy im Dialog auf S. 64 eigentlich gar keine Bitte ausspricht? Wie ist das in den Dialogen auf dieser Seite?

7 Ordnen Sie die Bitten in die Kategorien „neutral", „höflich" und „sehr höflich" ein.

a I was wondering if you could …
b Can you …?
c I was wondering if you could possibly …
d Would you mind …?
e Do you think you could …?
f I wanted to ask if you could …
g Could you …?
h How about …?
i I would really appreciate it if you would …
j Would you …?

neutral	polite	very polite

8 Nein sagen – aber höflich!

Lehnt man eine Bitte ab, gehören ein Ausdruck des Bedauerns und eine Begründung dazu, wie Sie sie in einem der obigen Gespräche gehört haben.

a Unterstreichen Sie diese Formulierung im folgenden Textausschnitt.

Carl: I wanted to know if you could do me a favour and come in for a couple of hours tomorrow.
Lynn: Tomorrow?
Carl: Yeah, any time is OK with me.
Lynn: Jeez, Carl, I'd really like to help, but I'm leaving for Toronto tomorrow.
Carl: Darn it! You were my last hope.
Lynn: I'm really sorry.

b Mit welchen der folgenden Ablehnungen könnte man den Textteil ersetzen, den Sie unterstrichen haben?

1 Sorry, but I make it a point not to work on the weekend.
2 You've got a lot of nerve asking me!
3 No, I'm busy.
4 I wish I could, but I'm already doing something.
5 I'm really sorry, but I really need the day off.
6 I don't like to work for friends.
7 Sorry, but you're outta luck.

Unit 5

! Fast so wichtig wie sich zu verständigen: den Gesprächspartner nicht vor den Kopf zu stoßen!

Jeez! = Oje!
Darn it! = Verdammt!

! Prägen Sie sich eine oder zwei Floskeln ein, damit Sie sie für den Ernstfall parat haben.

Unit 5

Gebrauch

Grammar focus

Reported speech

Mit der indirekten Rede (*reported speech*) gibt man bereits gemachte Aussagen wieder. Hier ein paar Beispiele aus dem ersten Dialog:

> ... you said you were having a problem with your boss.
> ... Fitz said he'd try to make it.

Das Gegenstück zur indirekten Rede ist die direkte Rede, d.h. es wird wörtlich zitiert:

> "I'm having a problem with my boss."
> "I'll try to make it."

Bildung

Die indirekte Rede wird durch ein Verb des Sagens eingeleitet. Dieses Verb steht im Präsens, wenn man wiedergibt, was jemand gerade oder generell sagt bzw. denkt:

> He **says** they're moving in together.
> He **thinks** her chili is out of this world.

! Bitte beachten Sie die Aussprache:
say [sei]
says [sez]
said [sed]

Meistens aber steht das einleitende Verb im *simple past*. Aussagen können mit dem Bindewort *that*, Fragen mit *if* oder einem Fragewort eingeleitet werden:

> Phil **asked if** Tommy was still seeing Tina.
> Tommy **said** (**that**) he was moving in with her.

Die Zeitform in der wiedergegebenen Aussage hängt von der Zeitform des Verbs im ersten Satzteil und von der ursprünglichen Aussage ab. Die allgemeine Regel lautet: „eine Zeitform zurück". *Will* wird *would*. Sehen Sie sich einige Beispiele an:

ursprüngliche Aussage	wiedergegebene Aussage
"I'**m** free on Saturday."	He said he **was** free on Saturday.
"I'**m having** a problem."	You said you **were having** a problem.
"Tina **is making** her famous chili."	He told me Tina **was making** her famous chili.
"I'**ll try** to make it."	He said he'**d try** to make it.

Pronomina ändern sich entsprechend von der direkten zur indirekten Rede:

> "I need **your** technical expertise."   **He** said he needed **my** technical expertise.

Ratschläge und **Bitten** bzw. **Befehle** werden mit *to* + Infinitiv wiedergegeben. Die angesprochene Person wird dabei erwähnt:

"Take care!"	He told/encouraged **me to take** care.
"Give me a hand, will you?"	He asked **me to give him** a hand.
"Tell her I said hello."	He told/asked **me to say hello to Tina**.

Typische Verben, auf die der Infinitiv mit *to* folgt:

Ratschläge	**Bitten**	**Befehle**
advise	ask	tell
encourage	beg	order

Weitere Verben, nach denen der Infinitiv mit *to* stehen kann:

agree, offer, promise, refuse
He agreed/offered/promised/refused to help.

Vorschläge werden mit der *-ing*-Form des Hauptverbs wiedergegeben:

"Why don't you give Pete a call?"	He suggested giving Pete a call.

Typische Verben, auf die die *-ing*-Form folgen kann:

suggest, propose, recommend
He suggested/proposed/recommended giving Pete a call.

Es geht bei der indirekten Rede nicht immer darum, eine bereits gemachte Aussage oder Frage wörtlich wiederzugeben, sondern oft nur um eine sinngemäße Entsprechung oder Zusammenfassung. Zum Beispiel könnte man den Satz *"I don't need your back this time"* folgendermaßen wiedergeben: *He promised I wouldn't have to do any lifting.*

Bitte beachten Sie!

Unit 5

Revision

9 Setzen Sie das passende Verb ein.

> handle ◆ need ◆ want to ◆ appreciate ◆ mention ◆ complain ◆ convince

a How are you? – Oh, I can't _____ .

b I don't have to install the kitchen? – Not unless you _____ .

c I don't _____ your back this time, just your technical expertise.

d Did I _____ that Tina is making her famous chili?

  I thought that would _____ you.

f I think I can _____ that.

g Thanks a lot; I _____ it.

10 Setzen Sie die folgenden Aussagen in die indirekte Rede.

a I can't complain.
He said he _____

b What are you doing on Saturday?
He asked what I _____

c What time do you want me?
She asked what time I _____

d I've got a moving company.
He said he _____

e I'll order pizza.
She said she _____

f I think I can handle that.
He said he thought he _____

g I'm having a "senior moment".
She said she _____

= Ich bin aber heute vergesslich.

Unit 5

11 Tommy erzählt, was Phil ihm gesagt hat. Wie lauteten die ursprünglichen Aussagen?

a He said if I was having a housewarming, he was free.
___

b He asked if I remembered the last time he had helped me move.
___

c He said he couldn't stand up straight for a month.
___

d He asked if he had to install the kitchen.
___

e I told him not unless he wanted to.
___

f He said I could count him in.
___

g Then he asked who else was going to help.
___

12 *to* + Infinitiv oder *-ing*-Form? Streichen Sie die falsche Form.

a He encouraged me *to call/calling* someone else.
b She suggested *to make/making* chili.
c He asked me *to come/coming* at 10.
d He asked me *to say/saying* hello to Tina.
e She recommended *to relax/relaxing*.
f She proposed *to send/sending* him an article on stress management.
g She promised *to call/calling* when she got back.

13 Kreuzen Sie die passende(n) Reaktion(en) an.

a Do you think you could come tomorrow, too?
   1 Sure.   2 I'll have to call you.   3 Sorry, I'm doing something already.

b I'd really appreciate it if you'd take these with you.
   1 Same here.   2 I'd be happy to.   3 You're outta luck!

c Would you mind giving us a hand?
   1 No, not at all.   2 When?   3 Sure, no problem!

d How about lending her your car?
   1 Forget it!   2 You're kidding, right?   3 I'm using it myself.

e I was wondering if you could possibly let me use your apartment?
   1 Um, I'll have to think about that.   2 See you.   3 I'm really sorry, but …

14 Arbeiten Sie nun die mündlichen Übungen A bis E zum Thema indirekte Rede durch. Die Anweisungen erhalten Sie auf der CD.

Lerntipp
Wenn Ihnen gerade die Konzentration fehlt, um die mündlichen Übungen zu machen, können Sie sich schon bekannte Übungen einfach nochmal anhören und sich berieseln lassen.

1/34–38

Unit 5

Part 2

Reading

15 Pre-reading task

Wie bezeichnet man im Deutschen eine Person, mit der man fest liiert ist bzw. mit der man zusammenlebt, aber nicht verheiratet ist?
Und im Englischen?

16 Lesen Sie nun den folgenden Text.

? Mit welchem Begriff behilft man sich also? Mit Ausnahme von *mistress* und *paramour* werden sie je nach Situation alle benutzt, wenn auch mit leicht ironischem Ton.

Cohabitation

For years it has been evident that we lack a good word to describe, much less introduce, the person of the opposite sex with whom one is living but to whom one is not married. "What's really needed," David Behrans of *Newsday* explains, "is one new word that will capture all the elements of blissful, unmarried cohabitation. The word must at least blend a reference to residency, a suggestion of sexuality, a shading of emotional care, a hint of permanence, and a dash, perhaps, of economic sharing." Our dictionaries cry out so loudly for such a precise word that tens of lexical candidates have rushed in to try to fill the gap. Few, if any, of these pretenders have earned a thumbs up.
Friend, boyfriend, girlfriend, and *companion* are too coy and too euphemistic to describe the relationship at issue and fail to identify the live-in arrangement. *Lover* (can't married folks be lovers, too?), *mistress*, and *paramour*, though fine, old words, do not convey that anybody is living with anybody else; on the contrary, they all have intimations of romantic secrecy. ... *Partner* sounds too commercial or clinical, while *cohabitor* is a mouthful that is cold and passionless. *Roommate* identifies the joint living arrangement but not the emotional arrangements, *significant other* suggests a close, sharing relationship but not necessarily the cohabitation, and *mate* calls to mind tossing seas or the jungle: "Me Tarzan, you Jane."

From: *The Miracle of Language,* Richard Lederer

17 Welche der folgenden Aussagen fasst den Text am besten zusammen?

a Most words for people in relationships in English have negative connotations.
b English can't seem to find the right word to describe people in relationships.
c English doesn't have enough words to describe people in relationships.
d English has plenty of words to describe people in relationships.

Working with words

Unit 5

18 Ordnen Sie zu.

to lack	Verweis
much less	Zusammenwohnen
to capture	(hier:) einfangen
blissful	fehlen
cohabitation	schon gar nicht
to blend	wohnhaft sein
reference	mischen
residency	(glück)selig
shading	Hinweis
care	(hier:) schreien nach
hint	sich darauf stürzen
dash	Schattierung
to cry out for	Sorge
precise	eine Lücke füllen
to rush in	präzise
to fill a gap	Prise
pretender	Andeutung
to earn a thumbs up	zur Debatte stehen
coy	Bewerber/in
to be at issue	angenommen, akzeptiert werden
to fail	(hier:) Lebensgefährte/in
to convey	unterlassen
intimation	kokett
mate	vermitteln

Lerntipp
Unterstreichen Sie oder notieren Sie Wörter in der Randspalte, die Sie wiederholen möchten.

19 Ordnen Sie die Wörter in der linken Spalte der passenden Kategorie zu.

noun	verb	adjective	adverb

Oft haben Verb und Substantiv dieselbe Form, z. B.:
Verb   Substantiv
to lack → *a lack*
to blend → *a blend*
to care → *a care*
to hint → *a hint*

Unit 5

1/39

Längere Wörter haben logischerweise immer eine zweite Hauptbetonung.

Lerntipp
Solche Übungen dienen dazu, Ihnen ein Gefühl für die Verwendungsmöglichkeiten eines Verbs zu vermitteln.

20 Wo liegt die Hauptbetonung bei den folgenden Wörtern?

de·scribe   can·di·date
op·po·site   eu·phe·mis·tic
co·ha·bi·ta·tion   pre·cise
ref·er·ence   in·ti·ma·tion
e·mo·tion·al   con·tra·ry
per·ma·nence   ev·i·dent

Kontrollieren Sie nun Ihre Lösungen anhand der CD.

21 Wortverbindungen

Welches Wort passt nicht zum Verb?

a	to lack	1	permanence	2	a word	3	cohabitation
b	to call	1	to order	2	a gap	3	to mind
c	to convey	1	interest	2	a meaning	3	a candidate
d	to sound	1	exciting	2	sexuality	3	clinical
e	to fill	1	space	2	a gap	3	a hint
f	to identify	1	a problem	2	a person	3	a reference
g	to capture	1	residency	2	a moment	3	someone's interest

Revision

22 Lesen Sie die Nachricht.

> Sal,
> When you read this I'll be at Tony's. He called and asked if I could give him a hand - he's putting down new carpeting.
> I told him I could only stay for an hour or so, so don't worry, I'll be back in plenty of time.
> Marge called and said she wouldn't be able to make it tonight.
> See you around 4.   K

a Welche drei Aussagen stehen in der indirekten Rede?

___

b Wie lauteten die ursprünglichen Aussagen?

___

23 Was passt zusammen?

a "Sure, count me in."
b "Good move."
c "How's it going?"
d "Things are crazy at the moment!"
e "I don't need your back."
f "No, really, work is going OK."
g "I'll leave it on the porch."

He **explained** where I could find it.
He **promised** me I wouldn't have to carry anything.
He **thought** it was a good idea.
He **complained** about his workload.
He **assured** me he would come.
He **inquired** how I was doing.
He **insisted** that things were going well at work.

porch = Veranda

24 True or false?

Lesen Sie die folgenden Behauptungen, hören Sie den Text auf der CD und kreuzen Sie die richtige Lösung an. Es geht um das gleiche Thema wie im Text auf S. 72.

The speaker ...   true   false
a uses first person, so the tone is somewhat personal.   ☐   ☐
b feels that the situation is more complicated now due to
   changing lifestyles.   ☐   ☐
c associates the terms boyfriend and girlfriend with young
   people.   ☐   ☐
d seems to be anti-gay.   ☐   ☐
e finds English wanting when it comes to describing
   non-traditional relationships.   ☐   ☐

wanting = lückenhaft

Unit 5

Unit 5

25 Wie sagt man's auf Englisch?

a Wie geht's? – Ich kann nicht klagen.

b Könntest du mir morgen helfen? – Tut mir leid. Ich wollte morgen arbeiten.

c Ich wünschte, ich könnte, aber ich habe ihr gesagt, dass ich hier bleiben würde.

d Du hast gesagt, dass du Probleme in der Arbeit hättest. – Ja, ich erinnere mich.

e Es tut mir sehr leid, aber ich brauche einen freien Tag.

f Sie sagte, sie würde ihr berühmtes Chili machen.

26 Was hat sie gesagt?

a "I'm leaving for Toronto tomorrow."   „What did she say?"

b "I just read an article on stress management."   „What did she say?"

c "I'll try to make it."   „What did she say?"

d "Talk to you when you get back."   „What did she say?"

e "I'm leaving."   „What did she say?"

Shop 'til you drop

Unit 6

Hier lernen Sie:

- wie Sie Wünsche äußern
- wie Sie etwas beschreiben
- wie Sie Gefallen/Missfallen ausdrücken
- wie Sie etwas begründen
- wie Sie jemanden zum Handeln auffordern
- Verben mit *-ing* oder *to* + Infinitiv

Unit 6

Part 1

Listening

1 Pre-listening task

Sie möchten aus irgendeinem Grund ein paar Schuhe umtauschen. Mit welcher der folgenden Formulierungen haben Sie die besten Erfolgsaussichten, mit welcher die schlechtesten? Welche sind zu höflich? Welche Formulierung passt überhaupt nicht?

Können Sie die Bedeutung des Wortes *exchange* aus dem Kontext erschließen oder kennen Sie das Verb schon?

a Would you be so kind as to exchange these shoes?
b I'd like to exchange these shoes.
c I like exchanging these shoes.
d Exchange these shoes, will you?
e Would it be possible for you to exchange these shoes?

2 True or false?

2/1

customer – salesperson: Welche Handlungen sind typisch?

Sie werden ein Gespräch zwischen einer Verkäuferin und einer Kundin hören. Lesen Sie die folgenden Behauptungen, hören Sie den Dialog und entscheiden Sie danach, ob die Behauptungen richtig oder falsch sind.

		true	false
a	The customer wants to return the shoes because they don't fit.	☐	☐
b	The salesperson doesn't want to take the shoes back because the customer can't prove that she bought them at the store.	☐	☐
c	Because they don't have the shoes in her size, the customer has to go and try to get a refund for the shoes.	☐	☐
d	Before the store employee can give the customer a refund she has to get some information on the shoes.	☐	☐
e	Because the customer doesn't have her receipt for the shoes, she has to accept a sale price, even though she didn't buy them on sale.	☐	☐

Working with words

Unit 6

3 Zwei Erklärungen in der folgenden Liste sind vertauscht worden. Welche?

to exchange	tauschen, umtauschen
heel	Absatz
to come off	beweisen
receipt	Kassenzettel
to throw away	wegwerfen
to be out of something	etwas nicht vorrätig haben
refund	Rückerstattung
to get your money back	sein Geld zurückerstattet bekommen
counter	Theke
to pay cash	bar bezahlen
to charge something	etwas mit Kreditkarte bezahlen
store credit	Gutschein
article	Artikel
do you mind …?	macht es Ihnen etwas aus …?
to be reduced	herabgesetzt/reduziert sein
to prove	sich lösen
to sign	unterschreiben
(the) same to you	ebenfalls

 Lerntipp
Wenn Sie Ihr Englisch ernsthaft verbessern wollen, versuchen Sie, regelmäßig zu lernen. Lieber häufige kurze Lerneinheiten als gelegentliches stundenlanges Pauken.

4 Welche der Ausdrücke von Übung 3 bedeuten dasselbe wie die folgenden?

a to toss out _____

b to run out of something _____

c to put something on your credit card _____

d to be on sale _____

OUR GUARANTEE TO YOU
Your shoes have been handcrafted using the finest materials available. We guarantee our product to be free of defects in workmanship and materials under normal wear. Should a problem arise, simply return the shoes to us for repair or replacement. Model no.: 5590 B
Fancy Free Shoes, Inc.
Chicago, IL 60028

Unit 6

Lerntipp
Wortschatz wiederholen – immer im Kontext lernen!

AAA = triple A = Automobile Association of America

5 Ordnen Sie die folgenden Dienstleistungen der passenden Kategorie zu.

live music venue ◆ real estate agency ◆ chiropractor ◆ massage ◆ attorney ◆ movie theater ◆ acupuncture ◆ dentist ◆ comedy club ◆ car rentals ◆ airline reservations ◆ guided tours ◆ tanning studio ◆ dining out ◆ accommodations ◆ doctor ◆ bike + skate rentals ◆ playhouse ◆ financial planner ◆ beauty salon ◆ AAA

Professional Services	General Services	Entertainment	Travel Services

6 Wie hätten Sie es gern?

Ordnen Sie folgende Adjektive der passenden Kategorie zu. Achtung: Mehrere Adjektive passen zu mehr als einer Kategorie.

fast ♦ reasonable ♦ well-lit ♦ helpful ♦ polite ♦ well laid out ♦ knowledgeable ♦ strong ♦ accessible ♦ conveniently located ♦ patient ♦ good quality ♦ cheerful ♦ courteous ♦ environmentally friendly ♦ spacious ♦ friendly ♦ well-informed ♦ discreet ♦ well-built ♦ flexible ♦ articulate ♦ long-lasting

Staff	Product	Location

Ergänzen Sie die Listen mit weiteren Adjektiven, die Sie kennen.

Language focus

7 Sie Hören drei Dialoge.

2/2–4

a **Kreuzen Sie die Behauptungen an, die zutreffen.**

1 All three situations involve a customer complaint.
2 All three complaints take place in a store.
3 All three complaints involve defective merchandise.
4 All three customers are satisfied with the outcome of their conversations.
5 The language used in all three complaints is non-confrontational, that is, both customer and service employee want to resolve the problem in a way that is acceptable to both parties.
6 The tone of the dialogues is unfriendly/polite/overly polite.

b **Hören Sie die Dialoge noch einmal und notieren Sie Wörter und Ausdrücke, die bestätigen, dass Ihre Antworten richtig sind.**

Auch in diesen Gesprächen geht es darum, den richtigen Ton zu treffen. Das ist wichtig, denn letztendlich sind Sie manchmal auf die Kulanz der Angestellten auch angewiesen.

Unit 6

Grammar focus

Verb + ing or infinitive?

8 Lesen Sie die E-Mail und unterstreichen Sie die richtige Verbform.

to straighten out = klären

hassle = Ärger

Dear Madam or Sir,

My wife and I stayed at your hotel from 29 June to 1 July and we (a) wanted to tell/telling you that although we (b) enjoyed to stay/staying at the Wellington Inn once we did get a room, we think there is room for improvement at the reception.
When I called and made our reservations, the person I spoke to (c) promised to hold/holding our room until 9 o'clock as we knew we would be arriving late. Well, although we (d) managed to arrive/arriving on time, we were first told our room had been given to someone else. Apparently the person I had spoken to had (e) forgotten to make/making a note of my request to hold the room. The gentleman who was at the desk (f) invited us to have/having a drink in the lounge while he (g) tried to straighten/straightening things out. We would have preferred to go/going to our room as we had had a long drive, but (h) agreed to give/giving him some time. We had hardly (i) finished to order/ordering when he came and told us he had (j) managed to find/finding us a double. The only problem was that it was on the street side and was quite loud. I categorically (k) refused to be put/being put in a room no one else wanted! We (l) continued to sip/sipping our drinks while Mr. Singh (m) tried again to work/working something out. (I give him a lot of credit for keeping his cool under the circumstances – I was not an easy guest!) After another ten minutes he returned and asked us if we (n) minded to stay/staying in two single rooms – just for the one night. We agreed and were moved into a lovely double the next day. Certainly this was not a major catastrophe, but I think you (o) need to look/looking at the way reservations are handled at your hotel so that this type of thing doesn't happen again. After a tiring trip the last thing you need is this kind of hassle. The incident was especially unfortunate since we were otherwise pleased with the accommodations and staff, who (p) made us to feel/feel at home whenever possible.
I (q) hope to have/having been of service to you and (r) look forward to stay/staying at your hotel in the future.
Sincerely,
Jason and Amy Crenshaw

9 Ordnen Sie zu.

Für den Fall, dass zwei Verben aufeinander folgen, kennt das Englische verschiedene Muster, wie Sie auf Seite 82 gesehen haben. Tragen Sie die Verben aus dem Brief in eine der unten stehenden Spalten ein.

verb + *-ing*	verb + *to* + infinitive
enjoy doing something	want to do something

Unit 6

Auch Personen, die fließend Englisch sprechen, machen bei diesen Konstruktionen gern Fehler!

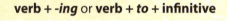

verb + *-ing* or verb + *to* + infinitive

verb + pronoun + *to* + infinitive	verb + pronoun + infinitive

10 Sie Hören sechs Sätze auf der CD. Ordnen Sie die darin enthaltenen Verbkonstruktionen einer der obigen Spalten zu.

2/5

11 Welche Verbkonstruktion kommt am häufigsten vor, welche am seltensten?

Unit 6 Revision

12 **Setzen Sie das passende Verb in der richtigen Form ein.**

> come off ♦ be out of ♦ pay cash ♦ throw away ♦ sign ♦ prove ♦ reduce ♦ exchange

a Were you able to _____ the sweater?
b The handle _____ the cup and I'd like it replaced.
c _____ you _____ or did you charge the gift?
d I don't see any in your size; I think we _____ them in blue.
e Can you _____ that you bought the article here?
f I think these shirts _____
g Would you please _____ here?

13 ***to* + Infinitiv oder *-ing*-Form? Streichen Sie jeweils das Verb, das *nicht* passt.**

a Vince *promised/told/agreed* to let us know if he couldn't come.
b The salesperson *asked/wanted/made* us to follow her.
c We *need/tried/don't mind* to talk about our plans.
d I don't think he *minds/wants/enjoys* shopping.
e I *forgot/can't stand/hate* to tell you this, but I've already paid for it.
f We *wanted/didn't mind/decided* to leave, but Kim wouldn't let us go.
g She *refused/agreed/made* to refund my money.

14 Schreiben Sie die Sätze unter das passende Bild.

I stopped to see what was on sale.
I stopped looking for sales.

15 *to* + Infinitiv oder *-ing*-Form? Streichen Sie die falsche Form.

a He encouraged me *to ask/asking* someone else.
b She suggested *to ask for/asking for* a cash refund.
c He asked me *to come/coming* at 10.
d She recommended *to relax/relaxing*.
e She proposed *to send/sending* him an article on stress management.
f He asked me *to say/saying* hello to Tina.
g She promised *to call/calling* when she got back.

16 Kreuzen Sie die passende(n) Reaktion(en) an.

a How can I help you?
 1 I'm just looking, thank you.   2 No, thank you.   3 I'd like to return this.

b I'd like to exchange these glasses.
 1 Yes.   2 I'll have to give you a store credit.   3 Have you got your receipt?

c I'll see if I can get a cash refund approved.
 1 Thanks.   2 Thanks, I appreciate it.   3 You're welcome.

d I'll have to give you a store credit.
 1 Forget it!   2 I guess.   3 I'd prefer a cash refund.

e Thanks for your help.
 1 I don't mind.   2 Same here.   3 You're welcome.

Unit 6

Unit 6

Part 2

Reading

17 **Pre-reading task**

Was fällt Ihnen auf, wenn Sie durch die Fußgängerzone einer fremden Stadt irgendwo in Deutschland schlendern? Benetton, Douglas, McDonald's – nichts Unbekanntes zu entdecken, alles vertraut. In den USA ist das nicht viel anders – das zeigt der Lesetext dieser Lektion.
Welche der folgenden Adjektive aus dem Text haben eine ähnliche Bedeutung und was könnten sie mit diesem Thema zu tun haben?

idiosyncratic one-of-a-kind
mind-numbing quirky
distinct eccentric
shabby well-worn

18 Lesen Sie nun den folgenden Text.

I'll be seeing you in all the new familiar places

A few months ago my supermarket decided to rearrange all its merchandise. The cereals were moved to where the detergents used to be, the pet food now replaces the bottled water, and I'm still trying to find the raisins. One of the stock boys told me they're on aisle 5, but I'll be damned if I can find them. I had shopped there long enough to understand the idiosyncratic way that things were displayed: I felt at home. Now I'm in a strange land, in need of a road map.
When I asked my favorite checkout clerk why this cruel little game was being played on me, he said the company bigwigs decided they wanted to make all their stores exactly

---

Lerntipp
Prägen Sie sich eine „schwierige" Vokabel zusammen mit einem Bild ein. Je subjektiver, persönlicher das Bild, desto besser die Chancen, dass Sie sich die Vokabel merken.

Einige weit verbreitete Ketten in den USA:
Starbucks (Café)
The Gap (Jeans-Shop)
Restoration Hardware (Baumarkt)

the same. Right down to the green beans.

"You mean, so when I go grocery shopping the next time I'm out in Santa Monica, I'll know where the black olives are?" I asked.

"Exactly," he replied.

Alas. Are there no surprises left in America anymore? Does everything have to be exactly the same everywhere we go? Will this mind-numbing homogenization of America never cease?

I'm convinced I'll wake up one morning to discover that Starbucks has opened a takeout kiosk in the corner of my kitchen.

The Gap, Restoration Hardware, Abercrombie & Fitch. Barnes & Noble, CVS. In every town. On every corner. Enough already!

Years ago I lived in Saratoga Springs, a beautiful little tourist town nestled in the foothills of the Adirondack Mountains of upstate New York. When I moved there in 1973 it had a distinct personality. There was no place quite like it on earth. There was a certain shabby elegance to the place. A patina. It was a town filled with interesting nooks and crannies, one-of-a-kind stores, quirky eateries and eccentric people. Liz Hood ran Montana Book on Broadway. There were well-worn chairs in the front window where you could spend a winter's afternoon perusing the latest Cheever.

Bernie Serotta ran Farmer's Hardware, an institution more than a store. It offered up kitchen utensils, handmade children's toys and Bernie himself, who always had a story to tell and was more than happy to share it. It was not a place to go if you were in a hurry.

And the men over at Glickman's sold oxford cloth shirts straight out of the boxes they were shipped in. The wood floors creaked under your feet and the fluorescent light hummed overhead.

All are gone now, of course. I returned to Saratoga last summer after a few years' absence to find a Sheraton, a Starbucks and an Eddie Bauer lining the main boulevard. A Borders bookstore is on the way. Can Banana Republic be far behind?

Tourists who come searching for something unique now just find more of the same. But I fear that may be what they want. The safety of familiarity.

Yes, of course I liked the familiarity of my grocery store before it was so rudely rearranged. But it was my grocery store, one of a kind. I know I'm 50, but I don't want to know what's around every corner. I can still handle a surprise every now and then.

Really, I can.

Craig Wilson, USA Today

Unit 6

Abercrombie & Fitch (Bekleidungsgeschäft)
Barnes & Noble (Buchhandlung)
CVS (Drogerie/Apotheke)
Eddie Bauer (Sportgeschäft)
Borders (Buchhandlung)
Banana Republic (Kleidungsgeschäft)

19 Welche der folgenden Aussagen fasst den Text am besten zusammen?

a Uniformity brings convenience, but it also leads to monotony.
b Uniformity brings convenience, and it also leads to familiarity.
c Uniformity brings convenience, but it also leads to rudeness.
d Uniformity brings convenience, but it also leads to homogenization.

Wie sehen Sie das?
Nostalgie statt Effizienz?
Romantik oder Pragmatismus?

Unit 6

Lerntipp
„Wortspinnen" sind eine gute Möglichkeit, Wortschatz zu wiederholen.

Working with words

20 **Vervollständigen Sie die Wortspinne mit Vokabeln aus dem Text.**

Ergänzen Sie sie dann mit anderen Wörtern, die zu den Kategorien gehören.

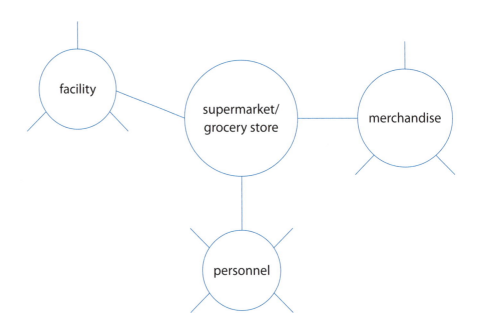

Lerntipp
Entscheiden Sie selbst, welche Wörter für Sie nützlich sein könnten.
Die anderen müssen Sie nur passiv kennen.

21 **Ordnen Sie zu.**

to decide
to rearrange
to replace
I'll be damned!
way
to display

　　　 to show
　　　 to substitute
　　　 to put in a new place
　　　 method
　　　 (exclamation)
　　　 to make up one's mind

homogenization
to be convinced
hardware store
to discover
nestled
foothills

　　　 beginning of the mountains
　　　 to find out
　　　 sheltered
　　　 to be sure of something
　　　 shop where tools are sold
　　　 uniformity

patina
nooks and crannies
eatery
to peruse
to be in a hurry
oxford cloth

　　　 hidden areas
　　　 restaurant
　　　 type of material
　　　 to have little time
　　　 to look slowly
　　　 coating

22 Wo liegt die Hauptbetonung bei den folgenden Wörtern?

cour·te·ous
re·ar·range
re·place
damned
sur·prise
con·vinced
en·vi·ron·men·tal·ly friend·ly
hard·ware store
nes·tled

u·ni·for·mi·ty
ho·mo·ge·ni·za·tion
pe·ruse
nooks and cran·nies
pat·i·na
flex·i·ble
real es·tate a·gen·cy
ac·com·mo·da·tions
knowl·edge·a·ble

a·cu·punc·ture
chi·ro·prac·tor
con·ve·nient·ly lo·cat·ed
ac·ces·si·ble
spa·cious
rea·so·na·ble
dis·creet
po·lite
ar·tic·u·late

Kontrollieren Sie nun Ihre Lösungen anhand der CD.

23 Ordnen Sie zu.

a quirky
b idiosyncratic
c cruel
d creaking
e mind-numbing
f unique
g well-worn
h handmade

☐ sofa
☐ surprise
☐ toys
☐ personality
☐ opportunity
☐ uniformity
☐ floors
☐ way of doing things

Unit 6

Lerntipp

Noch einmal zur Erinnerung: Übertreiben Sie am Anfang die Betonung neuer Vokabeln. Dadurch prägt sich die richtige Aussprache besser ein.

2/6

Können Sie die rechte Spalte mit weiteren Möglichkeiten ergänzen?

Unit 6

Grammar focus

Gebrauch

Das Passiv

Will man über die Person sprechen, die eine Handlung ausführt, verwendet man die Aktivform:

> A few months ago my supermarket decided to rearrange all its merchandise.

Will man dagegen die Aufmerksamkeit auf das Ziel der Handlung lenken, verwendet man das Passiv:

> The cereals **were moved** to where the detergents used to be.
> I asked a checkout clerk why this cruel little game **was being played** on me.

In diesem Fall ist die handelnde Person entweder zweitrangig oder unbekannt. Wird die handelnde Person doch erwähnt, dann mithilfe von *by*:

> The cereals **were moved by** the stock boys.

Bildung

Das Passiv wird mit einer Form des Hilfsverbs *to be* und dem Partizip Perfekt des Hauptverbs gebildet:

> The cereals **are moved** frequently.
> The cereals **were moved** to where the detergents used to be.
> The cereals **have been moved** to where the detergents used to be.
> The cereals **had been moved** to where the detergents used to be.
> The cereals **will be moved** to where the detergents are now.

Die Verlaufsform wird mit einer Form des Hilfsverbs *to be* gefolgt von *being* plus dem Partizip Perfekt des Hauptverbs gebildet:

> The cereals **are being moved** to where the detergents used to be.

Nach Modalverben verwendet man den Infinitiv des Hilfsverbs *to be*. Die Vergangenheit wird gebildet mit *have been* und dem Partizip Perfekt des Hauptverbs:

> Why **must** all supermarkets **be made** the same?
> The cereals **may have been moved** to where the detergents used to be.

Revision

Unit 6

24 Setzen Sie das passende Verb in der passenden Zeitform ein.

> rearrange ◆ peruse ◆ convince ◆ decide ◆ replace ◆ display ◆ be in a hurry ◆ surprise

a Have you _____ where you want to eat?
b One of the cups in my china is broken; I want to _____ it.
c I hope to _____ her to come with us.
d I started to _____ the want ads, but stopped when she rang me.
e I can't stand _____ when I'm shopping.
f I'll have to _____ my appointments if we're going to meet for lunch.
g The staff usually _____ a cheerful attitude.

want ads = Suchanzeigen

25 Unterstreichen Sie die Passivform.

a The regulations concerning returns are contained in this pamphlet.
b Clothing is taxed at the same rate as furniture.
c The shop closes in half an hour.
d Our products are sold at better department stores.
e The sportswear has been reduced 20%.
f We will arrange shipment if you wish.
g I'm looking for the shoes that were displayed in your ad.

26 Tragen Sie das Verb im Passiv ein.

a Coupons can _____ at any store. — redeem
b Coupons cannot _____ for catalogue purchases. — use
c Coupons cannot _____ if lost. — replace
d Purchases must _____ with a credit card. — make
e Coupons cannot _____ in conjunction with other special offers. — use
f Original coupons must _____ at the time of purchase. — present
g Coupons cannot _____ for cash. — redeem

$25 OFF
any regular price purchase of $100 or more (excludes some merchandise)
Coupon valid for merchandise only.
Not valid with any other coupons, promotions, or for purchases of gift certificates.
Not redeemable for store credit or cash. Expires 09/04/12.
CASUAL CORNER

Unit 6

27 **Setzen Sie das angegebenen Verb ins Passiv.**

a Proof of purchase _____ .

b The return must _____ by the manager.

c These restaurant ratings _____ on a scale of 1 to 10.

d The chef _____ by his competitors.

e The salads _____ at your table.

f Gifts can _____ around the world.

g The package will _____ within 24 hours.

require
approve
base
inspire
prepare
send
deliver

28 **Setzen Sie die folgenden Sätze ins Passiv.**

Erwähnen Sie die Person, die die Handlung ausführt, sofern Sie es für wichtig halten.

a The boss told the manager that his contract would not be renewed.

b Urban Magazine named the Green Onion one of the ten best restaurants in the city.

c They closed the shop six months ago for renovations.

d Someone sold the last one yesterday.

e Donna Karan designed it.

f I had to postpone the appointment.

g They bake the bread on the premises.

29 **Wie sagt man's auf Englisch?**

a Ich möchte diese Hose zurückbringen.

b Würde es Ihnen etwas ausmachen, drüben zu warten?

c Ich hoffe Sie bald wiederzusehen.

d Sie luden uns ein, sie nach dem Einkaufen zu treffen.

e Ich kann es nicht ausstehen, warten zu müssen.

f Ich trage die Hose erst seit Kurzem.

g Sie sagte zu mir, ich müsste in den dritten Stock.

2/7–10

30 **Arbeiten Sie nun die mündlichen Übungen A bis D zum Thema *Passiv* durch. Die Anweisungen erhalten Sie auf der CD.**

So tell me about the job

Unit 7

Hier lernen Sie:

- wie Sie Informationen einholen und geben
- wie Sie etwas erklären
- wie Sie fragen, ob der Gesprächspartner Sie versteht
- wie Sie sagen, dass Sie (nicht) verstehen
- wie Sie Sachverhalte umformulieren
- Bedingungssätze

Unit 7

Part 1

Listening

1 Pre-listening task

Lesen Sie die folgende Stellenanzeige und notieren Sie sich die Tätigkeiten, die zu diesem Beruf gehören.

> **Norfolk – The Furniture Place**
> is the leader in custom home furnishings. Do your friends come to you for decorating tips? Do they say you should be an interior decorator? Come check out one of the fastest growing furniture stores in the nation. You need exceptional people skills, a great eye for design and a winning attitude. Call Linda Hines for an appointment 877 4536.

2/11

2 True or false?

Sie hören ein Gespräch zwischen den Geschwistern Barbara und Jake über einen neuen Job. Kreuzen Sie die Aufgaben an, die Barbara in der neuen Stelle erwarten würden. Vergleichen Sie sie mit Ihren Antworten zu Aufgabe 1.

a call prospective customers
b make appointments
c visit clients at their home
d give advice
e arrange financing
f do paperwork
g commission the actual work
h go to trade fairs

Lerntipp
Prägen Sie sich besonders gut die Tätigkeiten ein, die zu Ihrem Beruf gehören. Schlagen Sie auch weitere in Ihrem Wörterbuch nach.

Working with words

Unit 7

3 Zwei Übersetzungen in der folgenden Liste sind vertauscht. Welche sind das?

impression	Eindruck
to enjoy	genießen
certainly	bestimmt
basically	grundsätzlich
sales	Verkauf
to spend time	eine Bestellung bearbeiten
customer	Kunde
home furnishings	Einrichtung
window treatment	Fenstergestaltung
curtains	Vorhänge
sheers	Stores
valance	Querbehang
transparent	durchsichtig
rod	Stange
material	Stoff
prospective	voraussichtlich
tele-marketing	Telefonmarketing
appointment	Termin
to decorate	(hier:) einrichten
custom-made	nach Maß angefertigt
in your dreams!	das hättest du wohl gern!
to be able to afford something	sich etwas leisten können
health benefits	Leistungen zur Gesundheitsfürsorge
pricey	teuer, exklusiv
to process an order	Zeit verbringen
financing	Finanzierung
company car	Firmenwagen
vote of confidence	Vertrauensbeweis

💡 **Lerntipp**
Können Sie diese Vokabeln richtig anwenden? Versuchen Sie, mit neuen Wörtern Sätze zu bilden.

4 Welche Verben passen zu welchem Substantiv? Zu jedem Substantiv passen mehrere Verben.

> make ◆ place ◆ wait on ◆ cancel ◆ keep ◆ postpone ◆ advise ◆ help ◆ process ◆ confirm ◆ expedite ◆ reschedule

... a customer	... an appointment	... an order

💡 **Lerntipp**
Prägen Sie sich Verben am besten zusammen mit einer oder zwei passenden Ergänzungen ein.

Unit 7

Work, work, work!

5 Bringen Sie die Aktivitäten in eine logische Reihenfolge.

- get recommendations
- hear from the prospective employer
- get the job / get a rejection
- apply for a job / send in your resume
- quit / get sacked/fired
- get a promotion / get demoted
- put together a resume
- check the want ads
- get transferred
- go for an interview
- fill out an application
- look for a new job

2/12–14

6 Listening

Sie hören drei Personen, die über ihre Arbeit erzählen. Welche Berufe üben sie aus? Markieren Sie sie.

real estate agent	driving instructor	sales assistant
travel agent	mechanic	photographer
undertaker	building contractor	university lecturer
electrician	police officer	public health inspector
maintenance engineer	headhunter	advertising executive
social worker	buyer	circus performer
interior decorator	medical technician	computer programmer
secretary	food-service employee	financial consultant

Lerntipp
Prägen Sie sich besonders gut die Berufe ein, mit denen Sie am meisten zu tun haben.

2/15

7 Hören Sie nun die oben genannten Berufe und sprechen Sie nach.

Markieren Sie anschließend den Hauptakzent.

96

Language focus

8 Giving information / Explaining

Ordnen Sie die folgenden Sätze der passenden Sprechabsicht zu.

> Am I making myself clear?
> Are you following me?
> What's the word for ... in English?
> What I'm trying to say is ...
> Excuse me? / Pardon me?
> How do you say ... in English?
> Sorry, I didn't get that.
> I don't know the word in English.
> What I mean is ...
> It's used for ...
> It's a kind of / sort of ...
> Sorry, I don't understand.
> Do you know what I mean?
> Could you repeat that, please?
> I don't know what you call it in English.
> What was that?
> Do you understand what I'm saying?

- checking to see if the other person understands
- signalling that you don't follow
- rephrasing something
- expressing that you don't know how to say something

Unit 7

! Prägen Sie sich jeweils eine Variante gut ein, denn solche Sätze braucht man öfters, wenn man eine Fremdsprache lernt!

Unit 7

Bildung

Grammar focus

If-clauses

Sogenannte *if-clauses* oder Bedingungssätze verwendet man, um die Möglichkeit des Eintretens einer Handlung oder Situation auszudrücken. Sie bestehen aus einem Hauptsatz und dem mit *if* (wenn) eingeleiteten Nebensatz, der die Bedingung bzw. Voraussetzung enthält. Die Reihenfolge dieser Satzteile ist beliebig. Die vier Hauptvarianten sind:

1	*If they **offer** you a job, you **take** it.* Wenn einem ein Job angeboten wird, nimmt man ihn.	generell
2	*If they **offer** me the job, I'**ll take** it.* Wenn man mir den Job anbietet, nehme ich ihn.	mögliche Zukunft
3	*If they **offered** me the job, I'**d take** it.* Wenn man mir den Job anbieten würde, würde ich ihn nehmen.	Hypothese
4	*If they **had offered** me the job, I **would have taken** it.* Wenn man mir den Job angeboten hätte, hätte ich ihn genommen.	nicht mehr möglich

Die Verbformen im Überblick:

main clause = Hauptsatz

	if-clause	main clause
1	simple present tense	simple present tense
2	simple present tense	future tense (will / going to / present continuous)
3	simple past tense	would + infinitive (= conditional)
4	past perfect tense	would + present perfect simple tense (= conditional past)

Achten Sie auf die abweichenden Verbformen. In den irrealen Bedingungssätzen (Typ 3 und 4) kommt – anders als im Deutschen – das *conditional* nur im *main clause*-Satzteil vor.

Statt *was* wird oft *were* in der ersten Person Singular *(I)* in Typ 3 verwendet:

*If I **were** you, I'**d take** the job.*

Im Hauptsatz bei Typ-2-Sätzen kann man die verschiedenen Zukunftsformen verwenden:

*If they **offer** me the job, I'**ll take** it.*
*If they **offer** me the job, I'**m going to take** it.*
*If they **offer** me the job, I'**m taking** it.*

Unit 7

Wie bereits erwähnt, beschreiben *if*-Sätze mögliche Handlungen und Situationen. Dabei nimmt die Wahrscheinlichkeit, dass das Geschehen eintritt, ab:

1. Das erste Beispiel beschreibt einen Zusammenhang.
2. Das zweite Beispiel beschreibt ein Ereignis, das wahrscheinlich eintreten wird.
3. Das dritte Beispiel beschreibt ein Ereignis, das eintreten könnte.
4. Das vierte Beispiel beschreibt ein Ereignis, das so hätte eintreten können, in Wirklichkeit aber nicht eingetreten ist.

In *if*-Sätzen kommen oft **Modalverben** vor:

Gebrauch

1. If they **can't get the financing**, they don't buy.
2. If you **must** know, I'**ll explain** it.
3. If I **could** help you, I **would**.
4. If we **could** have come, we **would have**.

Wie im Deutschen können die *if-clauses* auch mit dem Hauptsatz beginnen:

I'd help you if I could.

Im Hauptsatz steht oft der **Imperativ**, wenn im *if*-Satz Präsens steht:

Call us tomorrow if you need an answer right away.
Don't make an appointment if you're not sure you have time.

Bitte beachten Sie: Manchmal wird der *if*-Satz weggelassen. Sehen Sie folgende Beispiele aus dem Dialog:

I'll know in a couple of days (if I've got the job).
I'd be working out of the office (if I got the job).

Unit 7

Revision

9 Verbinden Sie die Satzteile.

a If you apply
b If the stuff wasn't so pricey
c If I get the job
d If the interview had gone better
e If I knew what happened
f If I got a discount
g If you had dressed appropriately

    you would have made a better impression.
    I would reconsider.
    you could get the job.
    I would be in a better position to help you.
    I might have had a chance.
    I might buy something.
    I'll have to move.

10 Tragen Sie die richtige Form des Verbs ein.

a If we _____ the company, we'd need a consultant.

b If you _____ the interview, you'll never get the job.

c If you _____ me, I wouldn't have forgotten the appointment.

d If we _____ so caught up in our work, we would have noticed you come in.

e If she _____ mad, I'd be surprised.

f I won't get in the way if you _____ in mine.

g If I _____ I was spinning my wheels here, I would quit.

expand
sweat
remind
be
get
not get
think

11 Tragen Sie die richtige Präposition ein.

at ◆ in ◆ on ◆ to ◆ of ◆ to ◆ from ◆ for

I wasn't happy _____ (a) the company I was working for, so when I decided to look for a new job, the first thing I did was dig out my old resume. Of course it needed to be updated. I sat down _____ (b) the computer and typed in any pertinent new information. The next thing I did was read the want ads _____ (c) the paper and _____ (d) the web. Once I had found what I was looking for, I sent off a couple of applications _____ (e) the personnel departments _____ (f) the companies looking for people _____ (g) my field. It didn't take long before I got replies _____ (h) them – most of them were rejections, but there was one invitation _____ (i) an interview. And that's how I ended up working _____ (j) IBC.

Unit 7

12 Setzen Sie die passende Zeitform des angegebenen Verbs ein.

a If you _____ more time with her, you'd certainly like her. — spend

b If the material is good, the product _____ longer. — last

c If the job _____ of tele-marketing, I wouldn't have taken it. — consist

d If you _____ the prospective customers, you'd make more sales. — visit

e If the furniture _____ so pricey, I'd be able to afford it. — not be

f If you _____ the order now, the customer would get it tomorrow. — process

g If you _____ the office, it would make a big difference. — decorate

13 Setzen Sie den passenden Ausdruck ein.

responsibilities ♦ calls ♦ holidays ♦ appointments ♦ correspondence ♦ travel agency ♦ colleagues ♦ conference ♦ department

"It was my first day on the job, so one of my _____ (a) showed me the ropes. First she took me around and introduced me to the others in the _____ (b). After that she showed me duties: First of all, I have to take incoming _____ (c) and put them through to the right people. Then I'm responsible for keeping track of the boss' _____ (d). Of course I have to do the _____ (e) and filing and generally organise the office. One thing I don't have to do is make coffee; there's a cafeteria open most of the day that takes care of that. One of my other main _____ (f) is travel planning: making hotel and plane reservations, making sure that members of the department have their travel documents on time and that we get the best rates from our _____ (g). I'm also in charge of planning the odd _____ (h) during the year. Beyond that, I have to keep an eye on people's _____ (i), you know, co-ordinate them so that everyone's not away at the same time. And, well, I think that's about it, but then I think that's quite enough, don't you?"

to show someone the ropes = jemanden in alles einweihen

14 Arbeiten Sie nun die mündlichen Übungen A bis E zum Thema *if-clauses* durch. Die Anweisungen erhalten Sie auf der CD.

2/16–20

101

Unit 7

Part 2

Reading

15 Pre-reading task

Im folgenden Text geht es um Stress in der Arbeit. Sind Sie gestresst? Wenn ja, was verursacht diesen Stress, was können Sie dagegen tun? Notieren Sie einige Stichworte.

16 Lesen Sie nun den folgenden Text.

Self-help books, also Ratgeber, haben einen großen Anteil am englischen und amerikanischen Buchmarkt.

Don't worry about work

Is work making you crazy? Do you come home from your job every day in a snit? Richard Carlson, best-selling author of the *Don't Sweat the Small Stuff* books, has some advice for you: Chill out! Carlson, a 37-year-old stress-management consultant and motivational speaker who's sold more than ten million books, has just come out with *Don't Sweat the Small Stuff at Work*. Writer John Rubino caught up with Carlson in Miami, where he was counseling corporate executives on the art of lightening up.

Question: Why did you expand your "small stuff" focus to the office? Have you been getting a lot of questions about work problems lately?

Unit 7

Answer: Yes – practically every day. People say, "God, if only my co-workers weren't so annoying" or "If I just had more time …" You can't always have more time, of course, but you can feel like you do, by spending less energy reminding yourself how busy you are.

Question: What do you mean when you say: "Lose respect for worry"?

Answer: Some people think that worry helps you pay attention and take more care. But in fact, any success you have is despite your worry. Worry just gets in your way. When you give worry less respect, it starts to let up. Say you're anxious about public speaking. If you say, "This worry is ludicrous," and you overcome it, you begin to see big strides in your career.

Question: How can you keep a demanding boss from driving you nuts?

Answer: I've had bosses like that; almost everyone has. You can do what roughly 90 percent of people do – complain, talk behind your boss's back – or you can say, "Maybe there's something I could do differently. Maybe I can try to learn from him or her." If you're caught up in how difficult this person is, you can't see any of the gifts your boss may have to offer.

Question: How should you deal with someone who gets mad at you on the job?

Answer: If you're working for a living, there's always going to be someone who's mad at you. Always. Just accept this fact. If you see a waitress who doesn't sweat the small stuff, you see a waitress who gets good tips.

Question: Asking for a raise is a big source of anxiety. Is there a low-stress way to make sure you're paid what you're worth?

Answer: So much is in the timing. If someone's in a bad mood and you ask him or her for something that's really important to you, it makes no difference how rational your request is. You're going to fail. Demanding rather than asking is rarely effective either.

Question: How do you respect a deadline without sweating it?

Answer: People focus on the stress of deadlines without understanding how useful they are. Having a deadline helps you get the job done instead of spinning your wheels. So try to see each one as a source of motivation: "I've got until Thursday to finish this, and I will".

From: **Good Housekeeping**

Lerntipp
Entspannt lässt sich auch besser lernen. Machen Sie zwischendurch eine kurze Pause und wiederholen Sie danach das, was Sie gerade gemacht haben.

17 Welche der folgenden Behauptungen fasst den Text am besten zusammen?

a Your work isn't that important.
b There will always be some reason to get upset.
c Worrying gets in the way of success.
d Deadlines are made to be missed.

Unit 7 — Working with words

Lerntipp
Die Bedeutung einzelner Wörter kann je nach Kontext unterschiedlich sein – das ist im Deutschen nicht anders.

18 Ordnen Sie zu.

to sweat	to give advice
in a snit	advisor
Chill out!	angry
consultant	head of a company
to catch up with someone	(hier:) to speak to
to counsel	(hier:) to worry about
corporate executive	Take it easy!
lighten up	colleague
to expand	relax
small stuff	to cause to remember
co-worker	disturbing
annoying	to grow
to remind	things that aren't important
despite	ridiculous
to get in the way	step
ludicrous	in spite of
stride	to hinder
demanding	to get on someone's nerves
to drive someone nuts	asking a lot
to be caught up in something	to waste your time
roughly	to get angry
to get mad	approximately
anxiety	date something must be finished
worth	fear
deadline	to be occupied with something
to spin your wheels	origin
source	value

Lerntipp
Wortpaare merkt man sich besser als einzelne Wörter.

19 Welche Substantive passen zu welchem Adjektiv? Zu jedem Adjektiv passen mehrere Substantive.

motives ◆ buyer ◆ seat covers ◆ job ◆ piece of clothing ◆ hotel ◆ employer ◆ furniture ◆ order ◆ restaurant ◆ material ◆ partner

pricey	transparent	prospective	custom-made

Revision

20 Setzen Sie die passende Form des Verbs ein.

> get in the way ◆ drive someone nuts ◆ expand ◆ remind ◆ sweat ◆ get mad ◆ spin your wheels ◆ be caught up in

a Don't _____ it; I'm sure you'll get the job.
b May I _____ you that we're beginning in roughly an hour?
c Why _____ she _____ at me; was it something I said?
d If I were you, I'd look for a new job; you're just _____ there.
e Will you stop that; you're _____ !
f He has no time at the moment; he _____ his work.
g Go ahead and do it; I certainly don't want to _____

21 Was passt zusammen?

a to catch up with
b to remind someone
c to sweat
d to expand
e to be caught up in
f to drive someone nuts
g to spin your wheels

your business
an interview
to do something
a friend
at a job
with an annoying habit
your work

habit = Gewohnheit

22 Verbinden Sie die Satzteile.

a If she asks me,
b If I needed money,
c If I can't get anyone,
d If you need help,
e If you want me to,
f If you can't come,
g If you have to go,

we'll clean up.
we'll understand.
I'd ask you for it.
I'll pick you up.
I'll give you a hand.
I'll give you a ring.
I'll go.

Unit 7

Unit 7

23 Kreuzen Sie die passende(n) Reaktion(en) an.

a Could you repeat that, please.
   1 Sure.   2 Come again?   3 What I said was …

b Do you know what I mean?
   1 No problem.   2 I think so.   3 I'm not sure.

c I don't know what you call it in English.
   1 I think it's … 2 Neither do I.   3 Really?

d Excuse me?
   1 You're welcome. 2 I don't mind.   3 What I meant was …

e What I'm trying to say is …
   1 It's a kind of … 2 I see.   3 I know what you mean.

24 Lesen Sie die folgenden *if*-Sätze aus dem Lesetext: Entsprechen sie Typ 1, 2, 3 oder 4?

a "God, if only my co-workers weren't so annoying" … ☐
b "If I just had more time …" ☐
c If you say, "This worry is ludicrous," and you overcome it, you begin to see big strides in your career. ☐
d If you're caught up in how difficult this person is, you can't see any of the gifts your boss may have to offer. ☐
e If you're working for a living, there's always going to be someone who's mad at you. ☐
f If you see a waitress who doesn't sweat the small stuff, you see a waitress who gets good tips. ☐
g If someone's in a bad mood and you ask him or her for something that's really important to you, it makes no difference how rational your request is. ☐

25 Wie sagt man's auf Englisch?

a Wenn ich du wäre, würde ich neue Vorhänge bestellen.

___

b Weißt du, was ich meine? – Ich glaube ja.

___

c Wenn sie mir einen Firmenwagen geben, nehme ich den Job.

___

d Wenn ich einen Termin ausgemacht hätte, hätte ich ihn jetzt verschieben müssen.

___

e Hör auf, du machst mich wahnsinnig.

___

f Darf ich dich daran erinnern, dass sie eine ziemlich anspruchsvolle Mitarbeiterin ist.

___

What would you recommend?

Unit 8

Hier lernen Sie:

- wie Sie Absichten ausdrücken
- wie Sie Zweck und Bestimmung angeben
- wie Sie um Rat bitten/Rat erteilen
- nicht zählbare Substantive

Unit 8

Part 1

Listening

1 Pre-listening task

Wann haben Sie zum letzten Mal jemanden um Rat gefragt? Worum ging es, um eine private oder um eine berufliche Angelegenheit?
Wann haben Sie zum letzten Mal jemanden beraten? Worum ging es?

2 True or false?

Sie werden ein Gespräch zwischen zwei Personen, Andrew und Diana, hören. Lesen Sie die folgenden Behauptungen, hören Sie den Dialog und entscheiden Sie danach, ob die Behauptungen richtig oder falsch sind.
Handelt es sich um eine private oder um eine nicht private Angelegenheit?

		true	false
a	Andrew and Diana are probably colleagues.	☐	☐
b	Andrew asks Diana for advice because she knows more about computers than he does.	☐	☐
c	Mobility is an important criterion regarding Andrew's choice of computer.	☐	☐
d	Diana is able to recommend a computer to Andrew immediately.	☐	☐
e	Diana gives her supplier a call to see if she can get Andrew a deal on a computer.	☐	☐
f	Andrew has doubts about the supplier because of the name of the company.	☐	☐
g	Diana doesn't think it's necessary to price-shop because she knows the company's prices are competitive.	☐	☐

Working with words

Unit 8

3 Zwei Übersetzungen in der folgenden Liste sind vertauscht. Welche sind das?

around these parts	(scherzhaft:) in dieser Gegend
advice	Rat
inconvenient	lästig, ungünstig
obsolete	veraltet, überholt
to recommend	Preise vergleichen
account	(hier:) Kundenakten
spreadsheet	(hier:) Kostenvoranschlag
access	Zugang
request	Bitte
supplier	Lieferant
deal	ein (gutes) Geschäft
to quote	(hier:) einen Preis nennen
quote	Tabelle(n)
outfit	(hier:) Firma
competitive	konkurrenzfähig, marktgerecht (Preise)
price-wise	preislich
to shop around	empfehlen
to be/make sure	aufpassen, sich vergewissern

Lerntipp
Nutzen Sie Reise- oder Wartezeiten, indem Sie mit Vokabeln „spielen": sie gruppieren, neu ordnen usw.

4 Ordnen Sie jedem Verb die passende Ergänzung zu.

a to put in
b to quote
c to know
d to develop
e to get
f to do
g to mention
h to have

   a deal
   your homework
   access
   a price
   a request
   someone's name
   your stuff
   a strategy

Lerntipp
Prägen Sie sich Verben am besten zusammen mit einer passenden Ergänzung dazu ein.

5 Welches Wort passt nicht in die Kategorie?

phrasal verb	Adjektiv	Verb = Substantiv
shop around	competitive	request
make sure	lately	shop
quote	obsolete	recommend
put in	serious	deal

Wissen Sie noch die Bedeutung des Begriffs *phrasal verb*? Wenn nicht, schlagen Sie in *Unit* 1 nach.

Unit 8

Working with words

6 Ordnen Sie zu.

computer / pc ◆ screen ◆ keyboard ◆ key ◆ mouse ◆ cable ◆ disk drive ◆ switch ◆ USB port ◆ loudspeaker

💡 Ergänzen Sie die Liste mit Begriffen, die Sie eventuell brauchen. Wo Sie diese Begriffe auf Englisch finden können: im Wörterbuch, wenn es einigermaßen *up-to-date* ist, in einem Fachwörterbuch oder im Internet – auf der Website einer Hard- oder Software-Firma oder vielleicht in einer Computerzeitschrift.

110

Language focus

7 Um Rat fragen oder einen Rat erteilen?

Ordnen Sie die folgenden Sätze aus dem Dialog richtig zu.

I find that …
I thought maybe you could give me some advice.
That way you can …
What would you recommend?
If I were you I'd …
That's what I wanted to talk to you about; you're the expert.
Do you think it would be a good idea to …?
Well, you're probably going to need …
What kind of notebook did you have in mind?
Why don't you …?
My guess is you're going to need …
It can't hurt to …

Lerntipp
Stock phrases sollten Sie auswendig lernen. Dann haben Sie sie immer zur passenden Gelegenheit parat.

asking for advice	giving advice

Kennen Sie noch andere typische Wendungen, um um Rat zu fragen oder darauf zu reagieren?

8 Welche der folgenden Ausdrücke sind <u>keine</u> stock phrases?

Glad to help.
Will do.
No problem.
Talk to you later.
It depends.
It's just a matter of cost.
Good idea.

Let me see.
Thanks a lot.
Not at all.
Is that possible?
I know what you mean.
Definitely.
Is this a serious outfit?

Kennen Sie die Bedeutung aller Redewendungen?

Unit 8 — Language focus

9 Welcher Satz aus dem Dialog spielt auf dasselbe Problem wie der Cartoon an?

"Before you go, could I interest you in an upgrade?"

2/22–24

10 Hören Sie die folgenden drei Gespräche.

Eine Person fragt jeweils eine andere um Rat. Welches der Gespräche verläuft *nicht* nach dem dargestellten Gesprächsmuster?

- Gespräch 1
- Gespräch 2
- Gespräch 3

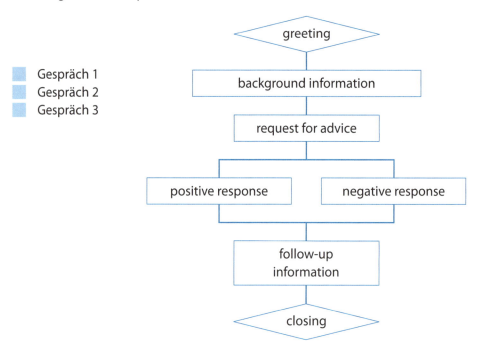

Zusätzliche Übung: Schreiben Sie einen kurzen Dialog nach dem Muster.

11 Gesprächsstrategien

Wenn man um Rat gefragt wird, will man oft nicht zu direkt antworten. Unterstreichen Sie Wörter und Ausdrücke in den folgenden Sätzen aus den Dialogen, die diese Zurückhaltung erkennen lassen.

a Well, you're probably going to need almost as much RAM as you've got on your desktop computer here.
b Well, my guess is you're going to need between two and three thousand.
c You know what: why don't you give them a call yourself?
d I find they're the best around price-wise, but, sure, it can't hurt to shop around.

Grammar focus

Non-countable nouns

Es gibt im Englischen eine Reihe von Substantiven, die weder Ein- noch Mehrzahlform kennen, weil sie grundsätzlich als nicht zählbar gelten. Zwei Beispiele aus dem Dialog auf Seite 108:

> *I thought maybe you could give me some **advice**.*
> Ich dachte, Sie könnten mir vielleicht einen Rat(schlag) geben.
>
> *OK, I'll give them a call and see if they can fax me some **info**.*
> Gut, ich rufe sie an und frage, ob sie mir Informationen zufaxen können.

Will man doch bei solchen Substantiven so etwas wie Ein- und Mehrzahl andeuten, so verwendet man jeweils eine Umschreibung mit *a piece of* oder dem unbestimmten Zahlwort *some*:

advice		**Rat**	
a piece of advice	*some advice*	einen Rat(schlag)	Ratschläge
information		**Information**	
a piece of information	*some information*	eine Information	Informationen

Eine Umschreibung mit *a lot of* bzw. *much* (in Fragen und in negativen Sätzen) deutet eine große bzw. kleine Menge an:

I've got a lot of information bzw. *I don't have much information.*

Einige wichtige nicht zählbare Substantive im Englischen:

nicht zählbar		**zählbar**
baggage/luggage	Gepäck	*a piece of baggage/luggage*
equipment	Ausrüstung	*a piece of equipment*
furniture	Möbel	*a piece of furniture*
homework	Hausaufgaben	*a part of the homework*
information	Information	*a piece of information*
knowledge	Wissen	*a bit/piece of knowledge*
money	Geld	*a coin/note/bill*
news	Nachrichten	*a piece of news*
traffic	Verkehr	(*a bit of traffic*)

Das dazugehörige Verb steht immer im Singular.

*The information you gave me **was** false.*
*My homework **is** done.*

12 Welche der oben genannten Wörter kommen im Dialog auf S.108 vor?

Unit 8 — Revision

13 Setzen Sie das passende Verb in der entsprechenden Form ein.

> do ♦ get ♦ know ♦ put ♦ have ♦ check ♦ mention

a Beate works with computers. She really _____ her stuff!

b Did I _____ that they're coming?

c Could you _____ the price at the other supermarket, please?

d Did you _____ your homework before going shopping?

e Could you _____ that in writing, please?

f If you ask Nola maybe she can _____ you a deal on a printer.

g I'm sorry, but I don't _____ access to that information.

14 Kreuzen Sie die passende(n) Reaktion(en) an.

a How far along are you?
  1 Sure.   2 We're just about finished.   3 Not very far.

b It's kind of inconvenient not having a notebook.
  1 Same here.   2 I know what you mean.   3 You'll get one!

c What would you recommend?
  1 It depends.   2 For you?   3 Sure, no problem!

d There's always something new on the horizon.
  1 That's true.   2 I guess you're right.   3 It can't hurt to shop around.

e Thanks a lot.
  1 No problem.   2 Glad to help.   3 Not at all.

15 Wie sagt man's auf Englisch?

a Sie kennt sich gut aus; ich bitte sie um Auskunft.
_____

b Ich dachte, sie könnte mir einen Rat geben.
_____

c Haben sie schon ihre Hausaufgaben gemacht?
_____

d Die Nachrichten sind nicht gut.
_____

e Habe ich schon erwähnt, dass die Ausrüstung neu ist?
_____

2/25–27

16 Arbeiten Sie nun die mündlichen Übungen A bis C zum Thema *non-countable nouns* durch. Die Anweisungen erhalten Sie auf der CD.

Part 2

Reading

17 **Pre-reading task**

Welche Errungenschaft(en) der modernen Technik haben Ihr Leben am stärksten beeinflusst? Haben Sie aufgrund dieser Errungenschaft(en) mehr oder weniger Freizeit?

18 Lesen Sie nun den folgenden Text über die Situation in Amerika.

Just can't seem to stop

Computers have increased the pace of our lives and we have got into the habit of multitasking

It was the golden promise of the computer age – computers would make life so much easier, said the hi-tech apostles, whose visions of robot-maids, networked homes and computerised care are still endlessly hyped by an unquestioning pro-technology media. But 40 years after the invention of the personal computer, those promises and assumptions are beginning to look a little suspect. A new generation of critics are starting to question some of the most basic tenets behind the hi-tech revolution.
Things may be getting faster and faster, but are they getting better and better? they ask. Have we become so enslaved to our machines that the very concept of time is dictated by the millisecond processing abilities of computers? In short, are we adopting the relentless pace of the computers that were built to serve us? ...
Multitasking was a concept developed by engineers to allow then feeble computers to process two calculations at a time. ... Now, not only is multitasking a widely used word in the English language, for many people it has become an essential tactic for getting through the day.
Interestingly enough, a local newspaper in Silicon Valley – the capital of technological innovation – recently ran a story lamenting the demise of the two-day weekend. "The weekend has been slashed from two days to one," the paper noted grimly, explaining that people are working such long hours just to keep up with all the little chores once done after work that are now condensed into a frantic weekend rush.

Lerntipp
Unbekannte Wörter beim ersten Lesen außer Acht lassen, dann vor dem zweiten Lesen die Aufgabe auf S.117 machen.

"Saturday is still a work day," said leisure researcher Harry Balzer. "It's just a different kind of work. People are spending more time in their cars doing multiple tasks. They are doing more chores with their kids but doing less shopping, spending less time preparing food and less time on themselves." ...

The classic multitask involves one of the most basic of all human activities: eating. Rather than waste time nourishing themselves, Americans prefer to grab a meal at a fast-food drive-by window and eat supper while driving home from work. ... " Consumers now see eating as something to be done while you do something else," Bobby Calder, a marketing professor at Northwestern University told the New York Times recently.

The Washington Post also lambasted the multitasking phenomenon recently: "We wake up in the morning, brush our teeth while reading the newspaper and taking in the Today show. We toss the twins into the Baby Jogger and run while listening to Morning Edition. We drive to work with a cup of coffee in one hand, a breakfast bar in the other while enjoying an audio book on the tape deck and yakking on the car's speaker phone," wrote the paper.

Such observations are no surprise to Harvard economist Juliet Schor, whose book "The Overworked American" has documented how technology, which was meant to increase leisure time, has had the opposite effect by tying humans to the relentless time cycle of the computer. According to Schor's studies, the average American worker now puts in 163 more hours annually than he did in the Sixties and works an astounding 300 more hours per year than his European counterpart.

Even champions of the hi-tech world have begun to bemoan the phenomenon, arguing that the haste of the modern world is having a negative effect on our patience, attention span and enjoyment of simple pleasures. ...

But even critics have no real solution to the alarming impact they chronicle and they tend to see these problems as part of the age-old dilemma about the price of progress. ... But younger folk, who grew up with mouse in hand and watching the mind-popping speed of MTV videos, are able to assimilate the glut of information and make sense of it in an almost intuitive manner. There's hope yet.

Andy Goldberg,
The Telegraph

19 Welche der folgenden Aussagen fasst den Text am besten zusammen?

a Faster is better.
b Americans are working more now, but the quality of life has also improved.
c Americans are doing more now, but that has not necessarily improved the quality of life.
d Modern technology now allows us to do more than one thing at a time.

Working with words

Unit 8

20 Ordnen Sie zu.

to enslave	mehrere Aufgaben gleichzeitig erledigen
to hype	Anhänger
multitasking	hochjubeln
assumption	Annahme
apostle	verdächtig
relentless	Prinzip
suspect	versklaven
tenet	vorschreiben
to dictate	unbarmherzig
to keep up	schwach
frantic	beklagen
to lambaste	(hier:) Ende
to toss	(hier:) drastisch reduzieren
feeble	grimmig, streng
demise	(hier:) mithalten
grimly	komprimieren
to lament	hektisch
to slash	ernähren
to condense	heftig kritisieren
to nourish	(hier:) anschauen
to take in	werfen, schmeißen
alarming	quasseln
haste	(hier:) arbeiten
to put in hours	erstaunlich
to yak	beklagen
astounding	Eile
patience	Geduld
mind-popping	Konzentrationsfähigkeit
impact	beunruhigend
to bemoan	Einfluss
attention span	erstaunlich

Lerntipp
Unterstreichen Sie oder notieren Sie Wörter in der Randspalte, die Sie wiederholen möchten.

Unit 8 — Working with words

21 Ordnen Sie die englischen Wörter von Übung 20 der passenden Kategorie zu.

noun	verb	adjective	adverb

2/28

22 Wo liegt die Hauptbetonung bei den folgenden Wörtern?

mul·ti·tasking con·dense
dis·con·cert·ing la·ment
as·sump·tion sus·pect
a·pos·tle as·tound·ing
en·slave be·moan
dic·tate pa·tience

Kontrollieren Sie nun Ihre Lösungen anhand der CD.

23 Wortverbindungen

Welches Wort passt *nicht* dazu?

a	to take in	1	a movie	2	a musical	3	television
b	to slash	1	the seat	2	prices	3	over
c	to keep up with	1	your work	2	your partner	3	your attention span
d	to put in	1	a lot of time	2	a lot of chores	3	a lot of preparation
e	to tie	1	a knot	2	a tie	3	a suspect
f	to lambaste	1	an opponent	2	an impact	3	an apostle

Kennen Sie weitere Ergänzungen, die zu den Verben passen?

Revision

24 Tragen Sie das passende Verb ein.

> slash ◆ take in ◆ dictate ◆ keep up ◆ toss ◆ put in ◆ condense

a He's too fast for me; I can't _____ with him.
b Computer World is closing and plans to _____ prices on all merchandise.
c Why don't we _____ a film tonight?
d It would be a help if you could _____ the information onto one page.
e _____ me a CD, will you?
f We can't _____ how they live their lives.
g I'd like to come but I have to _____ some time at the shop.

25 Wie lautet das Gegenteil?

a feeble   up-to-date
b grim   relaxed
c frantic   strong
d disconcerting   overpriced
e obsolete   reassuring
f competitive   cheerful

26 Streichen Sie die kursiv gedruckten Wörter, die nicht passen.

a I've got *much/some* disconcerting news for you.
b She doesn't have *much/some* luggage.
c You need *a lot of/a piece of* patience to deal with him.
d I've got to get *some/a lot of* information before making a decision.
e *Much/Some* knowledge of computers is recommended.
f I think there's *some/a piece of* furniture missing.
g Is there *any/much* traffic on the roads?

Unit 8

Unit 8

27 Stimmt das?

Lesen Sie die folgenden Behauptungen, hören Sie den Text auf der CD und kreuzen Sie die richtige(n) Lösung(en) an. Es geht um das gleiche Thema wie im Text auf S. 115–116.

2/29

The speaker …	true	false
a finds that she has less leisure time than she used to.	☐	☐
b doesn't think of herself as a workaholic.	☐	☐
c is currently working on an important project.	☐	☐
d leaves her notebook at the office where it belongs.	☐	☐
e is aware of the fact that working too much can cause problems.	☐	☐
f is certain that she will not continue to work so much.	☐	☐
g is unhappy with her present situation.	☐	☐

28 Wie sagt man's auf Englisch?

a Ich finde die Preise der Firma durchaus konkurrenzfähig.

___

b Was würden Sie (mir) empfehlen? – Es könnte nicht schaden, mit ihr zu sprechen.

___

c Du wirst einen Laptop für deine Arbeit benötigen.

___

d Wenn ich du wäre, würde ich die Preise vergleichen.

___

e Es hängt davon ab, wie viel Sie ausgeben können.

___

f Kann ich dich zurückrufen, wenn ich meine Hausarbeiten gemacht habe?

___

Wake up and smell the coffee!

Unit 9

Hier lernen Sie:

> wie Sie Zustimmung/ Ablehnung ausdrücken
> wie Sie eine Meinung erfragen und artikulieren
> Verlaufsform des Perfekts

Unit 9

Part 1

Listening

1 Pre-listening task

Setzen Sie die folgenden Diskussionsbeiträge in die richtige Reihenfolge.

A Well, I'm married and work, and my wife works, too. We've been sharing the household chores and taking care of the kids from the beginning. We're equal – but not the same – and I think we both benefit from that – no, I'd say we all benefit from that!

B That sounds just fine in theory, but it's the children who suffer in an arrangement like that. Who's home giving them the love and attention they need? A paid caregiver? Or are they left to themselves? It's no wonder that children are turning out the way they are, considering the lack of guidance they're getting! I think society as a whole is suffering as a result of the "gains" women have made.

C I couldn't agree more. The working world is set up by and for men, and men only. As long as we as a society do not bring about changes in the workplace, there will be no real equality, no genuine advancements.

D Get real! How are you supposed to help out with the housework, look after my kids and compete in the work force all at the same time?! I don't know about you, but there are only 24 hours in my day! I know it's not the politically correct thing to say, but I think things were better for everyone when women stayed home and took care of the house and the children.

E Right you are! Shorter work hours not just for women but for men, too, so that they can be home doing their fair share, and time off for Dad when the children are sick, things like that are needed.

F Wake up and smell the coffee! Women are out of the kitchen to stay and men had just better get used to the fact. The problem is that society in general – and men in particular – have not changed along with women. You make a valid point when you say that children suffer from lack of attention, but who said that men can't provide that attention? Why is it always assumed that women are responsible for the children, even when they work outside the home?

G Not "help with" the housework and the kids, but take responsibility for them, just like women have been doing all along. We're living in the 21st century, or haven't you heard? The days when you can relegate women to a fixed role are gone, and I, for one, am glad they are. Women are as capable as men – if not more so – in most fields, so why shouldn't they be out there competing with men?

Lerntipp
Heute schon Englisch gehört? Können Sie Radio- oder Fernsehprogramme in englischer Sprache hören oder sehen?

❓ Wie würden Sie den Umgangston der Diskussion beschreiben?

2 Hören Sie nun die Diskussion auf der CD und kontrollieren Sie Ihre Lösung.

3 Beantworten Sie folgende Fragen.

a How would you characterise the participants in the discussion?

	shy	moderate	outspoken
Speaker 1	☐	☐	☐
Speaker 2	☐	☐	☐
Speaker 3	☐	☐	☐
Speaker 4	☐	☐	☐

b How would you characterise the following expressions?

	polite	neutral	(too) direct
Get real!	☐	☐	☐
Wake up and smell the coffee!	☐	☐	☐
I couldn't agree more.	☐	☐	☐
Right you are!	☐	☐	☐
That sounds just fine in theory, but ...	☐	☐	☐
You still don't get it, do you?	☐	☐	☐

Welche dieser Ausdrücke möchten Sie im Gedächtnis behalten, welche nicht?

Unit 9

2/30
2/30

Unit 9 — Working with words

Lerntipp
Wenn Sie nicht sicher sind, ob Sie eine neue Vokabel anwenden könnten, schlagen Sie sie im Wörterbuch nach. Dort finden Sie zusätzliche Beispielsätze.

4 Zwei Übersetzungen in der folgenden Liste sind vertauscht worden. Welche?

to benefit	nützen, zugute kommen
to compete	am Wettbewerb teilnehmen
to look after	sorgen für, sich kümmern um
to take responsibility for something	Verantwortung für etwas übernehmen
to relegate	(hier:) festlegen
capable	fähig
field	Werbespot
to suffer	leiden
attention	Aufmerksamkeit
caregiver	(hier:) Tagesmutter, (allg.) Pflegepersonal
guidance	Führung
to consider	überlegen
to get used to something	sich an etwas gewöhnen
fact	Tatsache
valid	gültig
to set up	aufbauen
redistribution	Neuverteilung
to have something in common	etwas gemeinsam haben
to drift apart	(hier:) sich auseinanderleben
commercial break	Bereich
viewer	Zuschauer

5 Ordnen Sie dem Verb die passende Ergänzung zu.

a to put in   a price
b to quote   your homework
c to know   a deal
d to develop   your stuff
e to get   a strategy
f to do   a request

Language focus

Unit 9

6 Eine Diskussion führen

Folgende Elemente findet man oft in einer Diskussion. Ordnen Sie den Kategorien typische Wendungen (reihenweise) zu.

a Expressing an opinion
b Expressing agreement
c Expressing disagreement
d Expressing uncertainty
e Rephrasing something

1 I'm afraid I don't agree.	I think that depends on …	I doubt whether …
2 So do I.	Me, too.	Neither do I.
3 I think …	It seems to me that …	Don't you think …?
4 I suppose …	I'm not really sure.	Apparently …
5 I don't think that …	I don't really know.	It's difficult to say.
6 What I mean is …	What I'm trying to say is …	I guess you could say …
7 The only thing is …	That may be true, but …	Yes, but …
8 I see what you mean, but …	Well, actually, …	As a matter of fact …

7 Direct/indirect

Welche der Ausdrücke, mit denen man eine gegenteilige Ansicht äußert, sind direkt und welche indirekt?

8 True or false?

Hören Sie nun eine weitere Diskussion auf der CD. Welche der folgende Behauptungen treffen zu, wenn man diesen Dialog mit der Diskussion auf S. 123 vergleicht?

	true	false
a Es handelt sich im Gegensatz zur ersten Diskussion um ein Privatgespräch.		
b Meinungen werden hier weniger provokativ formuliert.		
c Die Gesprächspartner fallen einander manchmal ins Wort.		
d Die Gesprächspartner weichen auch hier nicht von ihren ursprünglichen Positionen ab.		
e Ausdrücke wie *I guess* und *actually* werden verwendet, um eine Aussage etwas abzuschwächen.		

! Man erreicht immer mehr in einer Diskussion, wenn man den Gesprächspartner nicht vor den Kopf stößt.

Unit 9

Bildung

Gebrauch

Grammar focus

The present perfect continuous tense

Die **Verlaufsform des Perfekts** *(the present perfect continuous tense)* wird mit dem Perfekt des Verbs *to be* und dem Partizip Präsens des Hauptverbs gebildet:

> I **have been sharing** the household chores from the beginning.

Die Verlaufsform des Perfekts wird für Handlungen und Situationen verwendet, die in der Vergangenheit begonnen haben und noch andauern:

> *The work week has been getting shorter here in Europe for decades now.*

Die Verlaufsform des Perfekts wird *nicht* bei Verben verwendet, die einen Zustand ausdrücken, wie z. B. *to be, to have, to know,* weil diese von sich aus eine gewisse Dauer implizieren:
   We've been married for about eight years.

Manche andere Verben, die ebenfalls eine Dauer implizieren, können entweder mit der einfachen oder mit der Verlaufsform gebraucht werden, ohne dass ein großer Unterschied in der Bedeutung wäre:
   The problem is that society in general – and men in particular – have not changed (oder: have not been changing) along with women.

Zur Erinnerung: Die *einfache* Form des Perfekts *(the present perfect simple tense)* wird verwendet, wenn es in erster Linie um die Auswirkung einer Handlung oder Situation auf die Gegenwart geht. Der Akzent liegt auf dem <u>Ergebnis</u>:

> *The problem is that society in general* **has** *not* **changed** *along with women.*
> *Where* **has** *the movement* **got** *us?*

Since oder for?

since + ein Zeit*punkt*:
   *It's been a couple of decades **since** women went out and demonstrated for their rights.*
Weitere Beispiele:
   I've been working here since 8.30 / Tuesday / last week / 1998 / I graduated from college.

for + ein Zeit*raum*:
   *The work week has been getting shorter here in Europe **for decades** now.*
Weitere Beispiele:
   I've been working here for an hour / a couple of days / three years / a long time.

Eine weitere Möglichkeit, den Zeitabstand auszudrücken, ist, die Präposition *from* zu benutzen, wie Sie im Dialog gehört haben:
   I **have been sharing** the household chores **from the beginning**.

From bedeutet wie *since* „von einem bestimmten Zeitpunkt an" und wird in dieser Bedeutung nur in bestimmten Ausdrücken verwendet.

Revision

Unit 9

9 Setzen Sie den passenden Ausdruck ein.

A: I don't think women should be _____ to the kitchen.

B: I don't _____ , but do you really think that's still the case?

A: _____ , I'm afraid that it is sometimes.

B: I think that's the way it _____ , but times have changed.

A: Sure, things have got better, but women are still the principle _____ .

B: I certainly can't _____ with you there.

A: It's time men _____ for children and senior citizens.

B: Really!

> Well
> used to be
> either
> relegated
> disagree
> caregivers
> took responsibility

10 *Since* oder *for*?

a	_____ a month	_____ you called
b	_____ we started work	_____ more than a decade
c	_____ ages	_____ 24 hours
d	_____ 2000	_____ the summer
e	_____ breakfast	_____ Christmas
f	_____ half past ten	_____ I met her
g	_____ half an hour	_____ May

127

Unit 9

11 *Present perfect simple* oder *continuous*?

Tragen Sie die passende Zeitform ein.

a I _____ ill for about a week.

b She _____ a cold since her birthday.

c They _____ with us since July.

d I _____ to the discussion since it began.

e He _____ with me on many points.

f How long _____ you _____ the children?

g We _____ looking for a new caregiver for my mother.

| be |
| have |
| live |
| listen |
| disagree |
| look after |
| consider |

12 Kreuzen Sie die passende(n) Reaktion(en) an.

a It seems to me that the business sector could do more.
  1 So do I.　　　　2 I suppose.　　　　3 Neither do I.

b Are you trying to say that women aren't capable of doing more?
  1 The only thing is …　2 That may be true, but …　3 What I mean is …

c Don't you think we'd all benefit from a change?
  1 I'm not really sure.　2 Yes, but …　　　　3 Apparently.

d How do you feel about that?
  1 I see what you mean.　2 It seems to me that …　3 What I'm trying to say is …

e That's a valid point.
  1 Me, too.　　　　2 I disagree.　　　　3 Well, actually, …

2/32–34

13 Arbeiten Sie nun die mündlichen Übungen A bis C zum Thema *present perfect continuous* durch. Die Anweisungen erhalten Sie auf der CD.

Part 2

Reading

14 **Pre-reading task**

How do our gender roles affect our physical and mental health? Write down several ways you can think of.

15 **Lesen Sie nun den folgenden Text.**

Unchanging men in changing times

The past fifty years have produced many changes in women's lives, in aging, and in longevity. But what has been happening for men? Very little, when compared to the changes in the lives of women. Although there has been no men's movement to compare with the women's movement, men's jobs have changed with the industrialization of society, and men are benefiting from an increased life span and better medical care. However, few people are seriously questioning men's roles, beliefs about masculinity and the addictive and aggressive behavior that damage men and shorten their lives as well as those of women.

Men have been much slower than women to recognize the benefits of changing old patterns and roles. Though some individual men are becoming more involved with the work of the home and the family, there is little evidence of any major societal change in men's roles. Women continue to do the bulk of the housework, child care, and elderly care.

An old-style masculinity is still alive and well and most men have not questioned the harm it does to their own well-being. The macho male image, as portrayed by numerous film and recording stars, is more popular than ever, promoting lifestyles and attitudes that don't lend themselves to care, nurturance, or longevity. Violence, disconnection, and delusions of invulnerability that lead to risk-taking are not the ingredients for a long life, yet these are the role models that little boys grow up with and that adult men measure themselves by.

From: Royda Crose, *Why Women Live Longer Than Men ... and what men can learn from them* (The book may be ordered directly from the author through her website at www.lifecycles.net.)

> *Disconnection* ist in unserer Gesellschaft offensichtlich weit verbreitet. Der Begriff bezeichnet so etwas wie das Gegenteil von „Anteilnahme". Man begegnet ihm inzwischen relativ oft.

16 **Welche der folgenden Behauptungen fasst den Text am besten zusammen?**

a Men have adapted in the business world but not in their private lives.
b Men would be more healthy and live longer if they examined their role in society.
c Both men and women would be more healthy and live longer if men examined their role in society.
d Men are disconnected and violent by nature.

Unit 9

Working with words

Lerntipp

Viele der Vokabeln in der Liste werden Sie nicht in Ihren aktiven Wortschatz aufnehmen wollen. Entscheiden Sie selbst, welche Sie sich merken möchten und schreiben Sie dazu Beispielsätze oder versuchen Sie, die Vokabeln zu diesem Thema nach den Kategorien "who", "where" und "when" zu gruppieren.

17 Ordnen Sie zu.

aging
longevity
to increase
belief
addictive
behaviour

Glaube
Benehmen
süchtig machend
Langlebigkeit
erhöhen
alternd

to damage
to shorten
to recognize
pattern
evidence
societal

kürzen
erkennen
schaden
gesellschaftlich
Muster
Beweis(material)

to continue
bulk
elderly
harm
well-being
to portray

darstellen
Wohlbefinden
Schaden
Hauptanteil
älter(er/e/es)
weitermachen

to promote
attitude
to lend themselves to
to nurture
violence

sich eignen zu
Gewalt
hegen
fördern, werben für
Einstellung

disconnected
delusion
invulnerability
risk
to measure

Irrglauben
messen
Risiko
Unverwundbarkeit
losgelöst

18 Welche Verben in der linken Spalte oben können *nicht* in der Verlaufsform des Perfekts verwendet werden?

19 Setzen Sie die fehlenden Formen ein.

	noun	verb	adjective	adverb
a	_____	_____	increased/increasing	increasingly
b	_____	to be addicted	_____	–
c	_____	_____	damaged/damaging	–
d	_____	_____	_____	measurably

20 Verbinden Sie die Antonyme.

a increase
b shorten
c damage
d well-being
e aged
f invulnerability
g disconnected

☐ promote
☐ decrease
☐ lengthen
☐ connected
☐ harm
☐ youthful
☐ non-addictive

21 Ein einziges Wort passt *nicht*; welches?

a to measure ➡ 1 your ability   2 your height   3 strength
b to promote ➡ 1 yourself   2 a cause   3 a product
c to shorten ➡ 1 your life   2 your stay   3 a dress
d to risk ➡ 1 your life   2 a fall   3 an increase
e to harm ➡ 1 your attitude   2 a cause   3 someone

22 Wo liegt die Hauptbetonung bei den folgenden Wörtern?

ag·ed
mea·su·ra·bly
well-be·ing
lon·gev·i·ty
com·mer·cial
re·spon·si·bil·i·ty

ad·dic·ted
in·creased
dam·a·ging
be·lief
rec·og·nise
vi·o·lence

dis·con·nec·ted
vul·ner·a·bil·i·ty
por·tray
be·hav·iour
ca·pa·ble
com·pete

Kontrollieren Sie anschließend Ihre Lösungen anhand der CD.

Unit 9

❓ Kennen Sie auch die Synonyme dieser Wörter?

❓ Sprechen Sie die Vokabeln laut nach. Wie beurteilen Sie Ihre Aussprache?

2/35

Unit 9 — Revision

23 Setzen Sie das passende Wort ein.

> promote ◆ portray ◆ guidance ◆ invulnerable ◆ addictive ◆ behaviour ◆ consider ◆ longevity ◆ risk

a I consider his _____ unacceptable; I think he lacks _____ .

b What is the secret of your _____ ? – Lots of sleep and no stress.

c I don't mean to _____ men as some kind of pre-historic cave-dwellers.

d She has done everything possible to _____ their well-being, hasn't she?

e I find chocolate almost _____ , don't you?

f Would you _____ going into a new field? – Actually, I've been thinking about it for quite some time.

g Young people often put themselves at _____ because they feel _____ .

cave-dweller = Höhlenbewohner

24 *Since* oder *for*?

a How long have you had a cold? – _____ about a week.

b We've been getting quite a lot of attention _____ we were on that TV show.

c I've been suffering from backache _____ a couple of months now.

d We've been drifting apart ever _____ that happened.

e He's been setting up the new company _____ the first of the year.

f How long have you been working for them? – _____ August.

g She has been competing in that kind of contest _____ years.

25 Wie sagt man's auf Englisch?

a Ich glaube, dass wir alle von der Frauenbewegung profitiert haben.
   _____

b Glaubst du nicht, dass Männer schon immer mehr Verantwortung übernommen haben?
   _____

c Es ist schwierig zu sagen.
   _____

d Ich verstehe, was du meinst, aber ich bezweifele, ob seine Haltung sich ändern wird.
   _____

e Ich passe seit zwei Jahren auf die Kinder auf. – Ich auch.
   _____

The Melting Pot

Unit 10

Hier lernen Sie:

› wie Sie über etwas berichten
› wie Sie etwas beschreiben
› adverbiale Ergänzungen

Unit 10

Part 1

Reading

1 **Ordnen Sie zu.**

In welchem Text erwarten Sie folgende Wörter?

> demography ◆ fondue ◆ alien ◆ pot ◆ ethnic ◆ minority ◆ stew ◆ immigrants ◆ stock ◆ assimilate ◆ fresh ◆ ethnicity ◆ culinary ◆ generation ◆ national identity ◆ weight ◆ English-speaking ◆ ingredients ◆ salad bowl ◆ core ◆ mixture ◆ bland ◆ lumpy

Text über Einwanderung	Text über Essen

Lerntipp
Prägen Sie sich eine „schwierige" Vokabel zusammen mit einem Bild ein. Je subjektiver, persönlicher das Bild, desto besser die Chance, dass Sie sich die Vokabeln merken.

Schlagen Sie die Wörter nach, bei deren genauer Bedeutung Sie nicht sicher sind.

2 Lesen Sie nun den folgenden Text.

Überprüfen Sie anschließend, ob die Antworten, die Sie in Übung 1 gegeben haben, richtig waren.

> Sicher gehen Sie jetzt etwas selbstbewusster an einen englischen Text heran! Haben Sie heute schon eine englischsprachige Zeitung oder Zeitschrift gelesen?

The ingredients are proving slow to melt in the American pot

Some time over the past generation, the great American immigrant fondue – that bland and featureless mass bubbling in the melting pot – has begun to look more like a lumpy stew.

My immigrant grandparents, born in Italy around the turn of the century, were fresh ingredients tipped into the pot nearly 100 years ago. By the time I was born, the mixture had returned to fondue.

But since then, and especially in the past three decades, there has been a wave of 20 million other immigrants, most from developing countries – the new American grandparents of the 21st century. Their arrival has sparked a battle of culinary metaphors (from melting pot to salad bowl to stew), but it has also called into question the core myth of American national identity: that all immigrants rapidly assimilate the same English-speaking, right-revering, Protestant-ethic-respecting norm.

Now, after the turn of yet another immigrant century – the one in which the Americans born of my grandparent's European stock will perhaps become the minority – technology, politics and demography have profoundly affected the process by which new Americans are formed. Suddenly, especially since the beginning of the 90s, ethnicity has begun to seem a matter of choice.

In the end, the sheer weight of Americanism – with its power to subdue alien cultures both at home and abroad – will probably ensure that assimilation becomes the norm of the future as well as the past. But at the moment, America's cultures are far more numerous than at any time in recent memory. For now, at least, we are closer to stew than fondue.

Patti Waldmeier, *The Financial Times*

3 Kreuzen Sie die richtige Antwort an.

a The text was written by an
  1 American 2 immigrant 3 Italian.

b The author compares immigrants of the third wave to
  1 a fondue 2 ingredients in stew 3 Protestants.

c What is the difference between the metaphors „fondue" and „stew"?
  1 In a fondue the ingredients blend together. 2 A fondue is European.

d Which one of the following statements is certain?
  1 There is a difference between the second and third wave of immigration to the US.
  2 The immigrants of the third wave will be assimilated just as those of the second wave.

Unit 10 — Working with words

Lerntipp
Diese Methode können Sie selbst anwenden, um Vokabeln zu wiederholen. Wählen Sie einige Adjektive und schreiben Sie alle Substantive eines Wortfeldes auf, die Ihnen dazu einfallen.

4 Brainstorming

Wie viele Lebensmittel bzw. Gerichte kennen Sie, zu denen die folgenden Adjektive passen?

bland *baby food,* _____.
lumpy *porridge,* _____.
fresh _____.

5 Tragen Sie das entsprechende Substantiv aus dem Text ein.

a to generate _____
b to immigrate _____
c to mix _____
d to arrive _____
e to identify _____
f to begin _____
g to weigh _____
h to assimilate _____

2/36

6 Wo liegt die Hauptbetonung bei den folgenden Wörtern?

de·mog·ra·phy   in·gre·di·ent
de·vel·op   Prot·es·tant
be·gin·ning   mix·ture
pro·cess   im·mi·grant
gen·e·ra·tion   a·broad
eth·ni·ci·ty   es·pe·cial·ly

7 to begin ...

In Verbindung mit einem anderen Verb bedeutet *to begin* bzw. *to start*, dass eine Handlung erst in Gang kommt.

> The melting pot **has begun**   to look more like a lumpy stew.
>   **has started**

136

Unit 10

Diesen Verben kann sowohl ein Verb in der *-ing*-Form als auch der Infinitiv mit *to* folgen. Es gibt keinen Bedeutungsunterschied.

> The melting pot has begun/started **to look** more like a lumpy stew.
> has begun/started **looking**

Nach der Verlaufsform folgt jedoch immer der Infinitiv des Hauptverbs:

> *Ethnicity* **is beginning to seem** *a matter of choice.*
> ~~Ethnicity is beginning seeming a matter of choice.~~

Streichen Sie jede nicht zulässige Form in den folgenden Sätzen.

a The snow is beginning *to melt/melting*.
b The soup started *to bubble/bubbling*.
c The sheer number of new Americans has begun *to call/calling* into question the feasibility of integration.
d Many have started *to revere/revering* the prime minister since her return to office.
e The weather is starting *to affect/affecting* our mood.
f Towards the end of the century the Spanish-speaking community began *to form/forming* political alliances.
g I was beginning *to think/thinking* you would never get here.

feasibility = Machbarkeit
to rever = verehren

Unit 10

Grammar focus

Gebrauch

Adverbiale Ergänzungen

Adverbiale Ergänzungen sind Wörter oder Phrasen, die z. B. Auskunft geben über die Fragen, wie, wo oder wann etwas geschehen ist:

- a That all immigrants **rapidly** assimilate is a myth.
- b My grandparents, born **in Italy** around the turn of the century, …
- c **By the time I was born**, the mixture had returned to fondue.

Adverbiale Ergänzungen können aus einem einzelnen Wort (in diesem Fall einem Adverb) (a), einem präpositionalen Ausdruck (b) oder einem ganzen Satzteil (c) bestehen.

Bildung

- Manche Adverbien (v. a. Adverbien der Art und Weise) werden durch Anhängen der Endung *-ly* an das Adjektiv gebildet. Betrachten Sie folgende Beispiele aus dem Text:

Adjektiv		Adverb
rapid		rapidly
sudden		suddenly
special	+ ly	especially
profound		profoundly
probable	-e + ly	probably

- Andere Adverbien haben eine eigene Form *(now, hard, fast)* oder bestehen aus mehreren Wörtern *(the turn of the century)*.

- Präpositionen leiten oft eine adverbiale Ergänzung ein *(at home and abroad, into the pot)*.

Satzstellung

Adverbiale Ergänzungen folgen in der Regel dem Hauptverb oder der Objektergänzung, wenn es eine gibt:

My grandparents, <u>born</u> **in Italy around the turn of the century**, …
I <u>ate lunch</u> **in a Chinese restaurant**.

Sie können aber zur Betonung auch z. B. am Satzanfang oder vor dem Hauptverb stehen:

Suddenly, … ethnicity has begun to seem a matter of choice.
Technology, politics, and … have **profoundly** <u>affected</u> the process …

Bei mehreren adverbialen Ergänzungen gilt die Reihenfolge: wie, wo, wann.

Revision

Unit 10

8 Tragen Sie die richtige Form des Adverbs ein.

a The newcomers are _____ finding their place.
b New Yorkers have _____ got used to hearing foreign languages.
c I'm _____ interested to hear about your trip.
d We _____ go out to eat Japanese when we're there.
e She learned the new language _____ .
f I couldn't understand because he spoke English _____ .
g How _____ does she speak German?

| slow |
| simple |
| real |
| usual |
| quick |
| poor |
| good |

9 Adjektiv oder Adverb? Kreuzen Sie die richtige Form an.

a The situation has *great/greatly* changed in the last few decades.
b *Ethnic/Ethnically* speaking, New York is a mirror of the world.
c The house was *fresh/freshly* painted.
d *Rapid/Rapidly* integration does not always take place.
e *New/Newly* arrived immigrants learn English in many ways.
f The mayor is *national/nationally* known.

mayor = Bürgermeister(in)

10 Bilden Sie Sätze mit den vorgegebenen Elementen.

Setzen Sie das Verb in die angegebene Zeitform.

a live/at the moment/we/in a small apartment/on the West side (present continuous)
_____

b in a friendly manner/answer/she/our questions (past)
_____

c plan to do/like real tourists/the city/we (present continuous for future)
_____

d open/a Mexican restaurant/near the bus stop/last year (past)
_____

e suddenly/realize/I/that/standing/she/next to me (past, past continuous)
_____

f speak/when I was a child/French/I/fluently/ (past)
_____

g hope to find/a new job/I/eventually/in another area (present)
_____

11 Arbeiten Sie nun die mündlichen Übungen A bis C zum Thema *adverbiale Ergänzungen* durch. Die Anweisungen erhalten Sie auf der CD.

2/37–39

Unit 10

Part 2

Listening

2/40

Flushing ist ein Stadtteil von Queens, das wiederum ein Stadtteil von New York City ist. Queens würde übrigens zu den größten Städten der USA gehören, wäre es nicht eingemeindet.

12 Flushing

Sie werden eine Fortsetzung des Textes aus Part 1 hören. Die Autorin erzählt von einem Spaziergang in Flushing, einem Vorort von New York.
Lesen Sie die folgenden Behauptungen, hören Sie den Text, und entscheiden Sie anschließend, ob die Behauptungen richtig oder falsch sind.

		true	false
a	The speaker comes from an immigrant family.	☐	☐
b	She feels very much at home in Flushing.	☐	☐
c	The speaker is not able to read many shop signs in Flushing.	☐	☐
d	There are products sold in shops in Flushing which she does not recognize.	☐	☐
e	The speaker had no trouble finding the public library in Flushing.	☐	☐
f	Blacks are the most likely people to speak English in Flushing.	☐	☐
g	Most newsagents in Flushing are South Asians.	☐	☐
h	The speaker ate at a restaurant where the menu was not in English.	☐	☐
i	The speaker ends her story with an anecdote which shows how quickly children are assimilated into a new culture.	☐	☐

Working with words

13 Aussprache: Wortbetonung

Wo liegt die Hauptbetonung bei den folgenden Wörtern?

as·sim·i·lat·ed   ad·min·is·ter   char·ac·ters   seg·re·gat·ed
oc·cu·pa·tion   re·peat·ed·ly   A·sian   Eu·ro·pe·an
ec·o·nom·ic   res·i·dents

Kontrollieren Sie anschließend das Ergebnis, indem Sie auf diese Wörter im Listening-Text achten.

14 Tragen Sie das passende Wort ein.

a That part of town isn't very colourful, in fact it's rather _____ .

b Not many "white-collar" workers live there, it's a _____ neighbourhood.

c The subway was _____ so I had to stand all the way home.

d The shop signs – Chinese and Korean – contain few western _____ .

e Some of the vegetables at the greengrocer's were _____ to the speaker.

f It was _____ in the city: 90° in the shade and humidity you could cut with a knife!

g I tried _____ to find someone who could speak English, but without success.

h Whites with European _____ are most likely to be immigrants from Russia.

i The only printed English in the Chinese restaurant was in the _____ .

---

features   characters   unrecognisable   drab   sweltering

repeatedly   working-class   fortune cookies   crowded

Unit 10

2/41

💡 Wenn Sie die Hauptbetonung richtig erkannt haben, können Sie sicherlich die Wörter perfekt aussprechen!

Unit 10

Lerntipp
Wie lernen Sie am besten? Sprechen, Hören, Schreiben und Lesen unterstützen sich gegenseitig.

15 Ordnen Sie nun die Wörter aus Übung 14 den folgenden Wortarten zu.

noun	adjective	adverb

16 Ordnen Sie den folgenden Verben aus dem Listening-Text die passende Ergänzung zu.

a to administer
b to search for
c to turn out to be
d to look for
e to point to
f to clamour
g to scold
h to answer back

☐ her five young children
☐ in English
☐ to learn English
☐ a dose of culture shock
☐ Russians
☐ the library
☐ in vain
☐ those with visibly European features

Kontrollieren Sie anschließend das Ergebnis, indem Sie auf diese Wortverbindungen im Listening-Text achten.

17 Kreuzen Sie jeweils die richtige Bedeutung des unterstrichenen Ausdrucks an.

a carefully segregated between Chinese and Korean
  1 sorgfältig unterhalten   2 feinsäuberlich getrennt

b I sought in vain for a black American.
  1 umsonst   2 in Eile

c He pointed to the library.
  1 zeigen auf   2 den Weg zeigen

d I searched for those with visibly European features.
  1 erkennbar   2 ansehnlich

e Five out of six vegetables are unrecognisable.
  1 nicht erkennbar   2 nicht bekannt

Language focus

Unit 10

Adverbiale Ergänzungen bei Erzählungen

Adverbiale Ergänzungen werden u. a. verwendet, um eine Erzählung zeitlich zu gliedern. Betrachten Sie folgende Beispiele im Text.

> <u>One recent sweltering day</u> I repeatedly asked passers-by for directions to the public library (which was within sight, had I only known it). I found no English-speakers among them.
> <u>First</u> I tried those closest (mainly Asian), <u>then</u> I searched for those with visibly European features, but they turned out to be Russians. I looked in vain for a black American (who, I thought, would surely share my language …). But most blacks in Queens are also immigrants, many of them Spanish-speaking.
> <u>In the end</u> I found an Indian newsagent (South Asians have created something of an economic monopoly in that business), and he pointed to the library. The staff says it is the busiest in the country – not least because of all those Flushing residents clamouring to learn English.
> <u>Later</u> I ate lunch in a Chinese restaurant (where the only printed English was in the fortune cookies), and watched as a Chinese woman scolded her five young children – only to hear them answering back in English, and throwing food with forks instead of chopsticks.

💡 Die zeitliche Gliederung einer Erzählung macht sie verständlicher.

18 Bringen Sie die folgenden Sätze in die richtige Reihenfolge.

- I hadn't seen her since graduation.
- Later on I thought about all the good times we had had at school and was glad I had remembered to give her my number.
- I immediately went over and said hello and she introduced me to her husband.
- Back then we sat next to each other in almost every course – we had the same major.
- A couple of days ago I was sitting in a wine bar in Soho when a friend of mine from university came in.
- I just hope she'll give me a ring before too long.
- Before I knew it, she sat down at a table where someone was already sitting.
- We chatted for about ten minutes or so, mostly just pleasantries, and then I had to leave.
- Anyway, when I saw her I waved, but she didn't see me.

major = Hauptfach

Unit 10

Revision

19 Tragen Sie die unterstrichenen Adverbiale im folgenden Text in die richtige Spalte ein.

straddle = (hier:) verbinden

Technology has made it possible to straddle two cultures in a way never possible before. Immigrants, especially those from Latin America and the Caribbean, can visit home <u>frequently</u>, and telephone <u>constantly</u>. So can Asians. Seoul runs tours to the homeland for Korean-American children, and Taipei sponsors what is known as the „Love Boat" to help Taiwanese-Americans find mates of their ethnicity.

Sheer numbers also play a role, especially in the case of Latino-Americans; <u>never before</u> has such a large immigrant group shared a common language, namely Spanish. <u>In some parts of the country</u>, including New York, Latino-Americans are the majority in their neighbourhood.

<u>In the end</u>, the biggest factor affecting the new American identity may be that the new immigrants are so different. The southern Europeans of the second wave of immigration <u>surely</u> differed <u>visibly</u> from the northern Europeans of the first wave. But the third wave immigrants differ <u>utterly</u>. And those differences could prove an insuperable barrier to the American mainstream.

insuperable = unüberwindlich

… Only time will tell whether the third wave of immigrants will settle, like the second, into the same old smooth fondue mix. But <u>in the meantime</u>, … the American grand-parents-to-be of the 21st century learn their Korean and play their salsa – on their way to becoming part of what sociologist Nathan Glazer calls „the <u>permanently</u> unfinished nation".

manner	time	frequency	place

20 Wie? Ordnen Sie zu.

a	**to sleep**	like the wind	f	**to fly**	like an idiot
b	**to drive**	like a fish	g	**to drink**	like a slave
c	**to eat**	like a madman	h	**to sleep**	like a bird
d	**to run**	like a horse/pig	i	**to work**	like a log
e	**to swim**	like a baby	j	**to act**	like a fish

Anhang

Hier finden Sie:

› Unterschiede britisches/amerikanisches Englisch
› Grammatik-Übersicht
› Lösungen
› Alphabetischer Wortschatz Englisch – Deutsch

Unterschiede britisches/amerikanisches Englisch

Aussprache

Allgemeines

Die wichtigste Regel sowohl für amerikanisches (AE) als auch für britisches Englisch (BE) ist: Ein Vokal in unbetonter Silbe wird zu einem Schwachlaut, der in der Lautschrift als [ə] dargestellt wird. Das heißt, ein Vokal verliert seinen eigentlichen Lautwert, wenn er nicht betont ist. Ein Beispiel:
apartment [əˈpɑːtmənt].

Das *a* am Wortbeginn und das *e* werden also nicht wie *a* und *e* ausgesprochen, da sie in unbetonter Silbe stehen. Ein weiteres Beispiel:
table [ˈteɪbl]   *vegetable* [ˈvedʒtəbl].

Das *a* in der Buchstabenkombination *-able* wird unterschiedlich ausgesprochen, je nachdem, ob es an betonter (wie im ersten Wort) oder unbetonter Stelle (wie im zweiten Wort) vorkommt. Bitte achten Sie daher auf die Betonung der Wörter, wenn Sie z. B. Übungen zur Betonung neuer Vokabeln machen. Übertreiben Sie die Betonung ruhig am Anfang, damit sich die unbetonten Vokale zwangsläufig abschwächen.

Die wichtigsten Unterschiede zwischen BE und AE

Auffallend ist, dass *a* vor allem vor *f, m, n* und *s* im AE ähnlich wie das deutsche *ä* [æ] ausgesprochen wird, im BE dagegen wie ein „dunkles" *a* [ɑ].
class, plant   BE: [ˈklɑːs, ˈplɑːnt]   AE: [ˈklæs, ˈplænt]

Ein kurzes *o* wird im AE fast wie deutsches *a* [ɑ], im BE dagegen wie ein sehr offenes *o* [ɒ] ausgesprochen.
clock, rock   BE: [ˈklɒk, ˈrɒk]   AE: [ˈklɑk, ˈrɑk]

Ein langes *o* ist im AE kein Diphthong oder langer Vokal wie im BE [əʊ], sondern ein geschlossenes *o* [o].
home, alone   BE: [ˈhəʊm, əˈləʊn]   AE: [ˈhom, əˈlon]

Im AE wird nach *d, l, n, s* der Vokal [u] nicht wie im BE mit vorausgehendem Gleitlaut [j] gesprochen. [ju] wird im AE nur nach *b, f, m* und *p* gesprochen.
news   BE: [ˈnjuːz]   AE: [ˈnuːz]
beautiful   BE: [ˈbjuːtəfʊl]   AE: [ˈbjuːdəfʊl]

Ein intervokalisches *t* bzw. *tt* wird im AE wie *d* ausgesprochen.
city, better   BE: [ˈsɪtɪ, ˈbetə]   AE: [ˈsɪdɪ, ˈbedər]

Ein *r* wird im AE immer gesprochen.
father, more   BE: [ˈfɑːðə, mɔː]   AE: [ˈfɑːðr, mɔːr]

Rechtschreibung

Einige Konsonantenverdoppelungen – vor allem bei *l* – entfallen im AE vor einer unbetonten Endung wie *-ed* (Vergangenheitsendung) oder *-er*.

BE: *travelled* AE: *traveled*
BE: *traveller* AE: *traveler*

Die Endung *-re* ist im AE meistens *-er*.
BE: *centre* AE: *center*

Die Endung *-our* wird im AE meistens *-or* geschrieben.
BE: *colour* AE: *color*

Die Endung *-mme* entspricht im AE *-m*.
BE: *programme* AE: *program*

Die Endung *-ise* wird im AE *-ize* geschrieben.
BE: *organise* AE: *organize*

Die Endung *-ce* wird im AE häufig *-se* geschrieben.
BE: *licence* AE: *license*

Grammatik

Grammatische Fachausdrücke und ihre Bedeutung

adjective	Adjektiv	Eigenschaftswort: ein *gutes* Buch
adverb	Adverb	Umstandswort: Sie spricht *schnell*.
apostrophe	Apostroph	Auslassungszeichen ('): *don't*
article	Artikel	Geschlechtswort: *der* Mann, *die* Frau, *das* Kind
consonant	Konsonant	Mitlaut: *b, k, l* usw.
demonstrative pronoun	Demonstrativpronomen	hinweisendes Fürwort: *Diese* Stadt ist schön.
direct object	Ergänzung im Akkusativ	4. Fall/Wenfall: Ich habe *den Wagen* gemietet.
genitive case	Genitiv	Bezitzfall/Wesfall: das Auto *des Mannes*
imperative	Imperativ	Befehlsform: *Kommen Sie!*
indefinite pronoun	Indefinitivpronomen	unbestimmtes Fürwort: *einige, jemand*
indirect object	Ergänzung im Dativ	3. Fall/Wemfall: Sie gab *ihm* das Ticket.
infinitive	Infinitiv	Grundform des Verbs: *gehen, kommen*
interrogative pronoun	Interrogativpronomen	Fragefürwort: *wer? wo?*
noun	Substantiv	Hauptwort: *Hotel, Strand*
object	Ergänzung	Satzergänzung: Er zahlte *das Taxi*.
past participle	Partizip Perfekt	Mittelwort der Vergangenheit: *geschrieben, gesungen, gekauft*
personal pronoun	Personalpronomen	persönliches Fürwort: *ich, du, er* usw.
plural	Plural	Mehrzahl: *die Kinder*
possessive pronoun	Possessivpronomen	besitzanzeigendes Fürwort: *mein, dein, unser* usw.
preposition	Präposition	Verhältniswort: *auf, in, von* usw.
reflexive pronoun	Reflexivpronomen	rückbezügliches Fürwort: er wäscht *sich*
relative pronoun	Relativpronomen	bezügliches Fürwort: das Geschenk, *das* ich gekauft habe
singular	Singular	Einzahl: *das Kind, die Frau*
subject	Subjekt/Nominativ	1. Fall/Werfall: *Der Reiseleiter* spricht Deutsch.
verb	Verb	Tätigkeitswort, Zeitwort: *schlafen, kommen*
vowel	Vokal	Selbstlaut: *a, o, u* usw.

Grammatik

Der Artikel

Der bestimmte Artikel (der/die/das) lautet im Englischen sowohl in der Einzahl als auch in der Mehrzahl **the**.

the car   das Auto
the cars   die Autos

the

Dem unbestimmten Artikel (ein/eine) entspricht im Englischen **a** bzw. **an**, wenn das folgende Substantiv mit einem Vokal beginnt.

a/an

a car   ein Auto
an apple   ein Apfel

Das Substantiv

1. Bildung des Plurals

Die Mehrzahl der meisten englischen Substantive wird durch Anhängen von -s an die Form des Singulars gebildet.
Bei Wörtern, die auf -o oder einen Zischlaut enden, wird in der Regel **-es** angehängt.
Substantive auf -y bilden den Plural auf **-ies**, wenn dem -y ein Konsonant vorangeht.

-s

-es
-ies

car	➡	car**s**
tomato	➡	tomato**es**
sandwich	➡	sandwich**es**
lady	➡	lad**ies**

Einige wichtige Ausnahmen:

man	➡	men
woman	➡	women
child	➡	children
foot	➡	feet
tooth	➡	teeth

2. Bildung des Genitivs

Zur Bezeichnung des Besitzes wird bei Personen **-'s** angefügt. Endet das Substantiv auf -s (einschließlich Mehrzahlformen), so wird nur ein Apostroph (') gesetzt.

-'s
-s'

the girl's glass   das Glas des Mädchens
the tourists' car   das Auto der Touristen

Bei Gegenständen und Mengenbezeichnungen wird der Genitiv mit **of** gebildet.

a glass of wine   ein Glas Wein
a quarter of a pound   ein Viertelpfund

149

Grammatik

Das Adjektiv

1. Steigerung

An kurze (ein- und zweisilbige) Eigenschaftswörter wird **-er** bzw. **-est** angehängt.

-er
-est

a small car	ein kleines Auto
a small**er** car	ein kleineres Auto
the small**est** car	das kleinste Auto

Eigenschaftswörter mit drei oder mehr Silben (auch einige mit zwei Silben) werden durch Voranstellung von **more** bzw. **most** gesteigert.

more
most

an interesting person	eine interessante Person
a **more** interesting person	eine interessantere Person
the **most** interesting person	die interessanteste Person

Einige Sonderformen:

good (gut)	better	best
bad (bad)	worse	worst
much/many (viel/-e)	more	most
little (wenig)	less	least

2. Vergleiche

Chris is **as big as** Susan.	... so groß wie ...
Scott **is bigger than** his brother.	... größer als ...

Adverbien

Die meisten Adverbien werden durch Anhängen der Endung **-ly** an das Adjektiv gebildet.

-ly

She speaks slow**ly**.	Sie spricht langsam.

Einige Sonderformen:

Adjektiv	**Adverb**
good (gut)	well
fast (schnell)	fast

Steigerung:
Adverbien auf **-ly** werden mit **more** und **most** gesteigert.

slowly	more slowly	most slowly

Grammatik

Das Pronomen

Personalpronomen

Subjekt		**Objekt** (Akkusativ/Dativ)	
I	ich	me	mich/mir
you	du / Sie	you	dich/dir / Sie/Ihnen
he	er	him	ihn/ihm
she	sie	her	sie/ihr
it	es	it	es/ihm
we	wir	us	uns
you	ihr / Sie	you	euch / Sie/Ihnen
they	sie	them	sie/ihnen

Zwischen „du" und „Sie" wird im Englischen nicht unterschieden.

Einige Beispielsätze:

He asked **me** ... **Er** fragte **mich** ...
She gave **me** the tickets. **Sie** gab **mir** die Karten.

Possessivpronomen

		alleinstehend	
my	mein(e)	mine	meiner(e/s)
your	dein(e) / Ihr(e)	yours	deiner(e/s) / Ihrer(e/es)
his	sein(e)	his	seiner(e/s)
her	ihr(e)	hers	ihrer(e/s)
its	sein(e)/ihr(e)	its	seiner(e/s)/ihrer(e/s)
our	unser(e)	ours	unserer(e/s)
your	euer(e) / Ihr(e)	yours	eurer(e/s) / Ihrer(e/s)
their	ihr(e)	theirs	ihrer(e/s)

Einige Beispielsätze:

It's **my** drink. Das ist mein Getränk.
It's **mine**. Das ist meins.

Reflexivpronomen

myself	ich/mich (selbst)
yourself	du/dich / Sie/sich (selbst)
himself	er/sich (selbst)
herself	sie/sich (selbst)
itself	es/sich (selbst)
ourselves	wir/uns (selbst)
yourselves	ihr/euch / Sie/sich (selbst)
themselves	sie/sich (selbst)

Grammatik

Einige Beispielsätze:

*I introduced **myself**.*	Ich stellte mich (selbst) vor.
*He bought the house **himself**.*	Er hat das Haus selbst gekauft.
*We helped **ourselves**.*	Wir bedienten uns.

Demonstrativpronomen

this	diese(r/s)	that	der/die/das dort/da
these	diese	those	die dort/da

Relativpronomen

	Personen	Sachen
Nominativ	who/that	which/that
Genitiv	whose	of which
Dativ	who/whom	to which
Akkusativ	(who/whom / that)	(that)

> ❗ *Whom*, eine alte Objektform, wird in der Regel nur noch in festen Redewendungen benutzt, z. B. in der schriftlichen Anrede: *To whom it may concern.*

Einige Beispielsätze:

*Do you know the man **who** is waiting over there?*	Kennst du den Mann, der dort drüben wartet?
*Here are the postcards (**that**) I bought.*	Hier sind die Postkarten, die ich gekauft habe.

Wenn *who* (seltener: *whom*), *which* oder *that* Objekt des Relativsatzes sind, können sie auch wegfallen. Aus diesem Grund sind sie in Klammern angegeben.

Interrogativpronomen

who?	wer?/wem?/wen?
whose?	wessen?
what?	was? (wie?)
(whom?)	wem?/wen?
which?	welche(r/s) …?/was für ein(e/s) …?
where?	wo?
when?	wann?
why?	warum?
how?	wie?

Grammatik

Die unbestimmten Pronomen *some* und *any*

Some und *any* bezeichnen unbestimmte Mengen.

Some benutzt man in bejahten Sätzen.

I'd like **some** coffee.	Ich hätte gerne (etwas) Kaffee.
I've bought **some** cheese.	Ich habe (etwas) Käse gekauft.

Any steht in verneinten Sätzen und in Fragen.

We have**n't** got **any** time.	Wir haben keine Zeit.
Have you got **any** German newspapers?	Haben Sie deutsche Zeitungen?

Some wird auch in Fragen verwendet, bei denen eine positive Antwort erwartet wird (z. B. bei Angeboten und Aufforderungen).

Would you like **some** more coffee?	Möchten Sie noch etwas Kaffee?

Das Verb

I. Hilfsverben

be (sein)

	bejaht	Gegenwart Kurzform	verneint	Kurzform
I	am	I'm	am not	'm not
you	are	you're	are not	aren't
he, she, it	is	he's, she's, it's	is not	isn't
we	are	we're	are not	aren't
you	are	you're	are not	aren't
they	are	they're	are not	aren't
		Vergangenheit		
I	was		was not	wasn't
you	were		were not	weren't
he, she, it	was		was not	wasn't
we	were		were not	weren't
you	were		were not	weren't
they	were		were not	weren't

💡 In der gesprochenen Sprache werden nur die Kurzformen verwendet, es sei denn, das Pronomen wird betont, z. B. am Anfang oder am Ende eines Satzes: *Are you German? – Yes, I am.*

Grammatik

have (haben)

	bejaht	**Gegenwart** Kurzform*	verneint	Kurzform
I	have	I've	do not have	don't have
you	have	you've	do not have	don't have
he, she, it	has	he's, she's, it's	does not have	doesn't have
we	have	we've	do not have	don't have
you	have	you've	do not have	don't have
they	have	they've	do not have	don't have

*nur als Hilfsverb

		Vergangenheit		
I, you, he, she, it, we, you, they	had	–	did not have	didn't have

do (tun, machen)

	Gegenwart bejaht	verneint	**Vergangenheit** bejaht	verneint
I, you we, you, they	do	do not / don't	did	did not / didn't
he, she, it	does	does not / doesn't		

II. Die modalen Hilfsverben

bejaht		verneint	
I can	ich kann	I cannot / can't	ich kann nicht
I could	ich konnte	I couldn't	ich konnte nicht
I should	ich sollte	I shouldn't	ich sollte nicht
I have to/must	ich muss	I don't have to	ich muss nicht
I had to	ich musste	I didn't have to	ich musste nicht

! *Must* hat keine Vergangenheitsform und kann auch nicht verneint werden. Also lieber gleich *have to*!

Die modalen Hilfsverben stehen immer zusammen mit einem Verb im Infinitiv. Sie haben keine -s-Endung und keine -ing-Form.

She **can take** a shower later.
We **couldn't exchange** the shoes.
I **have to leave** at 7.

III. Vollverben

1. Gegenwartsformen

Will man gegenwärtige Handlungen oder Zustände ausdrücken, verwendet man im Englischen entweder das *simple present* (die einfache Gegenwart) oder das *present continuous* (die Verlaufsform).

a. *Simple present*

Bildung

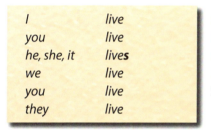

Das *simple present* ist mit dem Infinitiv identisch. Nur bei der 3. Person Einzahl wird an den Infinitiv ein **-s** angehängt.
Nach Zischlauten und nach -o wird bei der 3. Person Singular **-es** angehängt (*he watches, she goes*).

Verneinte Form

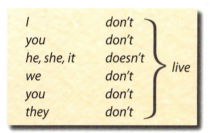

Sowohl die verneinte als auch die Frageform werden mit einer Form des Hilfsverbs *do* gebildet.

Frageform

Do you/Does he/she live …?

Das *simple present* gebraucht man

Gebrauch

- bei regelmäßigen Handlungen und Gewohnheiten: *I usually get up at 7 o'clock.*
- bei allgemeinen Wahrheiten: *I speak English.*

b. *Present continuous*

Die Verlaufsform bildet man nach dem folgenden Schema:
Form von **be** + **-ing**-Form des Hauptverbs

Bildung

I	am	
you	are	
he, she, it	is	reading
we	are	
you	are	
they	are	

Grammatik

Bildung der -ing-Form

work	➡	working	Infinitiv + -ing
study	➡	studying	Infinitiv + -ing
make	➡	making	Infinitiv auf -e + -ing
get	➡	getting	Infinitiv mit verdoppeltem Konsonant + -ing

Gebrauch

Für Handlungen, die sich zum gegenwärtigen Zeitpunkt abspielen, benutzt man das *present continuous*.

What are you doing? – I'm waiting for Tony.

2. Vergangenheitsformen

Im Englischen kann man vergangene Handlungen und Zustände u. a. mit dem *simple past* und dem *present perfect* wiedergeben.

Bildung

a. Simple past

Das *simple past* der regelmäßigen Verben wird durch Anhängen von **-ed** an den Infinitiv gebildet.

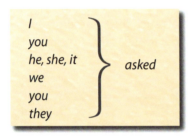

Einige Besonderheiten:

arrive	➡	arrived	+ -d
study	➡	studied	-y ➡ i + -ed
get	➡	getting	verdoppelter Konsonant + -ed

Viele Verben haben unregelmäßige Vergangenheitsformen. Sehen Sie sich dazu die Liste der unregelmäßigen Verben auf Seite 164–165 an.

Gebrauch

Will man eine Handlung oder einen Zustand beschreiben, die/der zu einem bestimmten Zeitpunkt in der Vergangenheit geschehen ist, verwendet man das *simple past*. Signalwörter fürs *simple past* sind z. B.:
yesterday, last year, on Monday.

I rented a car yesterday.
We returned from Boston on Wednesday.

b. Present perfect

Bildung

Das *present perfect* von regelmäßigen Verben bildet man mit dem Hilfsverb **have** + Partizip Perfekt + **-ed**. Das Partizip Perfekt entspricht bei den regelmäßigen Verben der Form des *simple past*.

I	have worked
you	have worked
he/she/it	has worked
we	have worked
you	have worked
they	have worked

Beachten Sie bitte auch die Liste der unregelmäßigen Verben auf Seite 160–161.

Wenn Handlungen in der Vergangenheit begonnen haben und in der Gegenwart noch andauern oder einen Gegenwartsbezug haben, gebraucht man das *present perfect*.

I've been here for ten days.
I'm hungry. **I haven't eaten** anything since breakfast.

Gebrauch

3. Zukunftsformen

Im Englischen gibt es mehrere Möglichkeiten, zukünftige Handlungen und Zustände auszudrücken. Dazu gehören:

Bildung und Gebrauch

a. *Present continuous*

Das *present continuous* drückt aus, dass eine Handlung für die Zukunft bereits fest geplant ist.
What are you doing tomorrow? – I'm taking the day off.

b. *be going to* + Infinitiv

I'm going to book the flight tomorrow.
We're going to have a cup of coffee.

Durch diese Form wird die gegenwärtige Absicht des Sprechers ausgedrückt. Außerdem verwendet man die *be-going-to*-Form zum Ausdruck von unmittelbar bevorstehenden Ereignissen.

It's five to five; the post office is going to close.

c. *will* + Infinitiv

Diese Form verwendet man zum Ausdruck eines spontanen Entschlusses.

I'll have the breakfast menu.
We'll take the double with bath.

Will verwendet man außerdem bei Vorhersagen und Annahmen über die Zukunft.

We won't have much time tomorrow.
I'm sure we'll find a hotel this evening.

Grammatik

d. Simple present

Diese Form verwendet man bei Zeitangaben in Fahr- und Terminplänen o.ä.

The train leaves at 8.05.

IV. Imperativ

Der Imperativ ist identisch mit dem Infinitiv. Die Verneinung wird mit *don't* gebildet.

Turn left.
Have a nice stay!
Don't do that!

V. Fragen

Fragen werden fast immer mithilfe von *do* oder eines anderen Hilfsverbs gebildet.

	Do	you	speak	German?
	Does	your son	speak	English?
	Did	you	like	the dessert?
	Can	you	help	me, please?
Where	did	you	go	on holiday/vacation?
How much	does	that	cost?	
How long	do	we	have to	wait?
	Are	you	–	from Germany?

VI. Verneinung

Ist im bejahten Satz ein Hilfsverb vorhanden, so wird bei der Verneinung **not** (Kurzform: **n't**) mit diesem Hilfsverb verbunden.

I can swim.   *I ca**n't** swim.*

Fehlt ein Hilfsverb, so wird nach folgendem Schema verneint:
don't/doesn't/didn't + Infinitiv

Carlo smokes.   *I **don't** (smoke).*
Peggy lives in Florida.   *Ellen **doesn't** (live in Florida).*
They drove to Virginia.   *We **didn't** (drive to Virginia).*

In Kurzantworten entfällt u. a. das Hauptverb:

<u>Does</u> *Peggy* <u>live</u> *in Flordia?*   *Yes, she* <u>does</u>.

VII. Die Zeitformen im Überblick

	einfache Form	Verlaufsform
Gegenwart	I work for a software company.	I'm working in sales at the moment.
Vergangenheit		
past tense	I worked for IBM until May.	I was working like crazy there.
present perfect	I've worked for three companies now.	I've been working here for two months.
past perfect	I had never worked in sales before.	I had been working in IBM.
Zukunft		
mit dem *present continuous*	I'm starting a training programme next month.	
mit *going to*	I'm going to start a training programme next month.	
mit *will*	I'll start a training programme as soon as I have time.	

Grammatik

Unregelmäßige Verben

Grundform	Präteritum	Partizip Perfekt	
be	was/were	been	sein
become	became	become	werden
begin	began	begun	beginnen
break	broke	broken	zerbrechen
bring	brought	brought	bringen
build	built	built	bauen
burn	burnt	burnt	brennen
buy	bought	bought	kaufen
can	could	–	können
catch	caught	caught	fangen
choose	chose	chosen	wählen
come	came	come	kommen
cost	cost	cost	kosten
cut	cut	cut	schneiden
do	did	done	tun, machen
drink	drank	drunk	trinken
drive	drove	driven	fahren
eat	ate	eaten	essen
fall	fell	fallen	fallen
feel	felt	felt	fühlen
fight	fought	fought	kämpfen
find	found	found	finden
fly	flew	flown	fliegen
forbid	forbid	forbidden	verbieten
forget	forgot	forgot	vergessen
forgive	forgave	forgiven	vergeben
get	got	got	bekommen
give	gave	given	geben
go	went	gone	gehen
grow	grew	grown	wachsen, werden
have	had	had	haben
hear	heard	heard	hören
hide	hid	hidden	verstecken
hold	held	held	halten
hurt	hurt	hurt	verletzen
keep	kept	kept	behalten
know	knew	known	kennen, wissen
lay	laid	laid	legen
lead	led	led	führen
learn	learnt	learnt	lernen
leave	left	left	(zurück-)lassen, verlassen

Grammatik

Grundform	Präteritum	Partizip Perfekt	
lend	lent	lent	leihen
let	let	let	lassen
lie	lay	lain	liegen
light	lit	lit	anzünden
lose	lost	lost	verlieren
make	made	made	machen
mean	meant	meant	bedeuten
meet	met	met	treffen
must	– / had to	– / had to	müssen
pay	paid	paid	bezahlen
put	put	put	legen, setzen
read ['riːd]	read ['red]	read ['red]	lesen
ride	rode	ridden	reiten
ring	rang	rung	läuten
run	ran	run	laufen
say ['seɪ]	said ['sed]	said ['sed]	sagen
see	saw	seen	sehen
sell	sold	sold	verkaufen
send	sent	sent	schicken
sew ['səʊ]	sewed ['səʊd]	sewn ['səʊn]	nähen
shake	shook	shaken	schütteln
show	showed	shown	zeigen
shut	shut	shut	schließen
sing	sang	sung	singen
sink	sank	sunk	sinken
sit	sat	sat	sitzen
sleep	slept	slept	schlafen
smell	smelt	smelt	riechen
speak	spoke	spoken	sprechen
spend	spent	spent	ausgeben
stand	stood	stood	stehen
steal	stole	stolen	stehlen
sting	stung	stung	stechen
swim	swam	swum	schwimmen
take	took	taken	nehmen
tell	told	told	sagen, erzählen
think	thought	thought	denken
throw	threw	thrown	werfen
wake	woke	woken	(auf-/er-)wachen
wear	wore	worn	tragen
win	won	won	gewinnen
write	wrote	written	schreiben

Lösungen

Unit 1

2

a false   b true   c true   d false   e true   f false   g true   h false

Tapescript

Sonia:	Are you waiting for a taxi?
Jim:	Yeah, for ten minutes, but I haven't seen one.
Sonia:	Where are you going?
Jim:	The Convention Center.
Sonia:	I'm going to the Marriott in center city. Is it OK if we share a cab?
Jim:	That's fine with me – if we ever find one! My name's Jim McMullen.
Sonia:	Hi, I'm Sonia Ricci.
Jim:	Nice to meet you, Sonia.
Sonia:	You know, it'd probably be a good idea to call for a cab. You never know how long we'll have to wait.
Jim:	You're right – I was just about to when you walked up.
Sonia:	Hi, I'd like the number of …
Jim:	Look, here comes one.
Sonia:	Never mind, operator. Thanks.
Jim:	The Marriott and the Convention Center.
	…
Sonia:	Are you in computers?
Jim:	Yeah, how did you know?
Sonia:	I'm going to the trade fair, too.
Jim:	Oh yeah? Who do you work for?
Sonia:	I'm a freelance communication trainer.
Jim:	Oh really?
Sonia:	In fact, that's why I'm here: I'm doing a workshop for INB reps tomorrow.
Jim:	Well, you're looking at one.
Sonia:	You're kidding?!
Jim:	No, I'm signed up for the workshop, too – but I don't remember seeing your name.
Sonia:	I'm filling in for Nancy Quinn – she was supposed to do it.
Jim:	That's right! … I met Nancy a couple of years ago; how is she?
Sonia:	She's fine – and expecting her second baby.
Jim:	Good for her! When's it due?
Sonia:	Any time now, I think. That's why she asked me to sub for her.
Jim:	Give her my best when you talk to her.
Sonia:	Will do. Oh, here we are. How much is it?
Jim:	Let me get this.
Sonia:	Thanks a lot, Jim. Well, it was nice to meet you. See you tomorrow!
Jim:	Same here. Bye now!

Lösungen

3

to be self-employed — selbstständig sein
to be scheduled — geplant sein

4

a to be signed up for
b to fill in/substitute for someone
c to be expecting a baby

5

a–2, b–1, c–2, d–1, e–2, f–2, g–2

6 + 7

a making a suggestion
5 Is it OK if we share a cab?
Yes.

b asking for something
1 I'd like the number of …
5 Would you mind giving me the number of …? ist zu höflich für die Situation.

c expressing an intention
1 I was just about to when you walked up.
2 I think I'll call a cab, too.

d giving a reason
3 (The baby is due any time now.) That's why she asked me to sub for her.

8

a Why don't we share a cab?
That's a good idea.
Sure, why not.
OK, fine.
Thanks, I'd like that.
No thanks, I'm not going that way.
Thanks, but I'll wait for my own.

b I'm a freelance consultant.
Oh, really, so am I.
That's very interesting.
What exactly do you do?

c Can you give me Robert's number?
Sure, it's …
Sorry, I don't have it.
Let me see, here it is.
I already have.

d The baby is due any time now.
That's great!
I didn't know that.
Are you sure?

e It was nice to meet you.
Same here.
It was nice to meet you, too.

Lösungen

9

present: a, f, i

10

a sales   b sub/fill in   c Will do.   d signed up   e are expecting, due   f Anytime.   g Let me get this

11

a am waiting   b are … going   c is filling in   d are doing   e 's calling   f 're … sharing
g Are … signing up

12

a	1	To center city.	2	I'm calling a cab.		
b	1	Same here.	2	That's a good idea.	3	Is it OK if we share one?
c	1	No, I'm not.	2	How did you know?		
d	1	IBN.				
e	1	Same here.	3	Nice to meet you too.		

13   Mündliche Übungen

A

Ändern Sie die Aussage des Satzes. Ersetzen Sie den entsprechenden Satzteil durch den Ausdruck, der jeweils angegeben wird. Beispiel:

1 I'm leaving for the trade fair on Tuesday.   the reps
2 *The reps are* leaving for the trade fair on Tuesday.   tomorrow night
3 The reps are leaving for the trade fair *tomorrow night*.   we
4 *We're* leaving for the trade fair tomorrow night.   the convention
5 We're leaving for *the convention* tomorrow night.   he
6 *He's* leaving for the convention tomorrow night.   in a couple of hours
7 He's leaving for the convention *in a couple of hours*.   go to
   He's *going to* the convention in a couple of hours.

B

Setzen Sie die folgenden Sätze ins *present continuous*. Verwenden Sie dabei die Ausdrücke, die Sie nach jedem Satz hören werden.

8 We usually share a room when we travel.   in Madrid
   We're sharing a room in Madrid.
9 I work as a freelance communications trainer.   at the fair
   I'm working as a freelance communications trainer at the fair.
10 I registered for the seminar.   later today
   I'm registering for the seminar later today.
11 She filled in for me last week.   again tonight
   She's filling in for me again tonight.
12 We took a cab to the convention center.   in an hour
   We're taking a cab to the convention center in an hour.

Lösungen

13 He's already done his workshop.   tomorrow afternoon
    He's doing his workshop tomorrow afternoon.
14 I went to the trade fair as a sales rep.   next week
    I'm going to the trade fair as a sales rep next week.

C
Antworten Sie auf die folgenden Fragen mithilfe der Hinweise, die Sie nach jedem Satz hören werden.

15 Are you waiting for the bus?   no / take a cab
    No, I'm taking a cab.
16 Are you going to the convention center?   no / tomorrow morning
    No, I'm going there tomorrow morning.
17 Is Nancy Quinn filling in for Peter?   no / Laura Stanton
    No, Laura Stanton is filling in for him.
18 Is she calling a cab?   no / come with us
    No, she's coming with us.
19 Is Lew Samuels doing a seminar at the fair?   no / Ken Jamesson
    No, Ken Jamesson is doing one.
20 Are they talking to him now?   no / at 10:30
    No, they're talking to him at 10:30.
21 Are you quitting your job at IBN?   no / stay until the end of the year
    No, I'm staying until the end of the year.

16

c   There is rarely just one way to say something in English.

17

to point out	to direct one's attention to
incredible	unbelievable
practically	(here:) almost
lifetime	the span of time you live
stock phrase	fixed expression
conventional	usual
a remark	comment
to consist of	to be made up of
to make up	to invent
to describe	to give an account in words
to represent	to portray
to determine	to obtain definite knowledge
to generate	to create
a study	an investigation
it is safe to say	it can be assumed
rarely	seldom
pattern	arrangement, model
to adhere to	to keep to, to respect
to put together	to assemble
to get a feel for	to develop a sense for

Lösungen

18

noun	verb	adjective	adverb
lifetime	to point out	incredible	practically
stock phrase	to consist of	conventional	rarely
remark	to make up		
a study	to describe		
pattern	to represent		
	to determine		
	to generate		
	to adhere to		
	to put together		
	to get a feel for		

19 Stock phrases:

Have a nice weekend. See you later. Give me a call. Let's do lunch. Are you serious?
You've got to be kidding! I don't think so. Good luck. Can I help you? May I be of assistance?
Help yourself! Be careful! Never mind! Give him/her my best. Take care! What the heck!

20

See you later.	+	I'll see you after a while.
Let's do lunch.	+	How about having lunch sometime?
Are you serious?	+	I can't believe that!/You've got to be kidding!
Can I help you?	+	May I be of assistance?

21

a Do you mind if I call you?
   How about if I call you?
   Is it OK if I call you?
   Why don't I call you?

b There are patterns of language that must be adhered to; that's why you must get a feel for the way English is used.
   As there are patterns of language that must be adhered to, you must get a feel for the way English is used.
   Because there are patterns of language that must be adhered to, you must get a feel for the way English is used.
   Because there are patterns of language that must be adhered to, so you must get a feel for the way English is used.

c We were going to make a reservation this week.
   We wanted to make a reservation this week.
   We were thinking about making a reservation this week.

22

a point out   b consist of   c rarely   d describe   e generated   f adhere to   g practically

Lösungen

23

a   The two women are shaking hands. / The two women are greeting each other.
b   A woman is checking in at the airport.
c   It looks like a man is renting a car.
d   People are queuing up / standing/waiting in line.

24

a   3   That's fine with me.
b   3   Sure, no problem.
c   1   Good for you!
d   3   That's why I asked you to come.

25

a   Why don't we share a cab? / How about sharing a cab?
b   I'm going to the trade fair/convention center. – Really? Me, too.
c   When are they expecting the baby? – Any time (now).
d   I was just about to register/sign up when you came up/arrived.
e   He's a freelance sales rep; that's why he's here.
f   I'd like the number of Jim McMullin.
g   It was nice to meet you.

Unit 2

b   What are you doing this afternoon?
d   Have you got any plans for this afternoon?
e   What's going on this afternoon? (most colloquial)
f   What are you going to do this afternoon?

2

a true   b true   c true   d false

3

a–1, 3, b–1, 3, 4

Tapescript
Cary: What are you going to do this afternoon?
Matt: What do you mean?
Cary: I mean, have you got any plans?
Matt: It depends; what are you thinking about?
Cary: I asked you first.

167

Lösungen

Matt: Well, I hadn't really thought about it. I guess I should start my taxes; April first isn't that far off. Or I might catch up on my work. There was a pile of stuff on my desk when I got back to the office.
Cary: I thought you were gonna give your taxes to Sam. (= going to)
Matt: Yeah, I forgot about that. I better give him a call.
Cary: Glad I reminded you of it!
Matt: What was it you had in mind?
Cary: Well, I was wondering if you could give me a hand with the housework. I really need to work on my seminar for next week, and if I have to do everything myself, I won't get to it.
Matt: I wish I could, but …
Cary: I'll bet!
Matt: Like I said, I really need to get caught up at the office.
Cary: Well then, I guess the washing just won't get done.
Matt: Do I have any clean shirts?
Cary: How should I know?
Matt: I think I wore my last dress shirt yesterday.
Cary: Oh, that's interesting.
Matt: OK, I'll do the wash. But then I'm outta here. (=out of)
Cary: Do you think you could stop at the store while you're out? The refrigerator's almost empty.
Matt: Couldn't we just eat out?
Cary: All weekend? Besides, we're both working on Monday and Tuesday.
Matt: OK, *you* make up the list and *I'll* do the shopping.
Cary: Now you're talking!
Matt: I can see I'm gonna get a lot done at the office. Anything else?!
Cary: Well, actually, there is one other thing: you could pick up my gray suit at the cleaner's.
Matt: What exactly are you gonna be doing all this time?
Cary: That reminds me, …

4

to remind someone of something   jemand an etwas erinnern
besides   außerdem

5

a   to be sorry about something   to be glad about something
b   to fall behind with something   to catch up on something
c   to get a call   to give someone a call
d   to stop doing something   to get started on something

6 + 7

a   asking about someone's plans
    2   I mean, have you got any plans?
    3   What are you doing this afternoon?
b   asking someone to do something
    4   I was wondering if you could give me a hand.

Lösungen

c giving a reason
   4 I really need to get caught up at the office.
d conceding
   3 OK, *you* make up the list and *I'll* do the shopping.
   None of the other alternatives are possible.

8

a Do you think you could give me a hand with the ironing?
   Sorry, I'm afraid I can't. I ...   You've got to be kidding!? (familiar)
   I wish I could, but ...
b Have you got any plans for tonight?
   I'm not sure. I'm thinking about going to ...
   I hadn't really thought about it.
   I'll probably go to bed early.
   It depends; what have you got in mind?
   I might catch up on my work.
c Would you mind stopping at the chemist's while you're out?
   No, not at all.   Sure, no problem. (familiar)
d OK, if you cook, I'll do the washing up.
   Now you're talking! (familiar) Great!
e Have we got enough food for the weekend?
   Why don't you go have a look? (familiar) How should I know?! (familiar)
   I think so. I'm pretty sure we do.

9

a depends   b catch up   c wonder   d give you a hand   e wish   f give ... a call   g reminds

10

a Vorhersage   b spontane Entscheidung   c Plan   d Plan   e Vorhersage   f spontane Entscheidung
g Plan

11

a yes   b yes   c no   d yes   e no

12

a 2 I asked you first.
b 1 It depends.   3 What exactly do you want me to do?
c 3 I was thinking of eating out.
d 2 Now you're talking!
e 1 I wish I could, but ...

Lösungen

13

Stan is going to do his taxes.
Jack is going to do the wash.
Ursula is going to catch up on her work at the office.
Astrid is going to do the shopping.
Elene is going to pick something up at the cleaner's.

14 Mündliche Übungen

A
Verneinen Sie die folgenden Sätze.
1. I think he'll help you.
   I don't think he'll help you.
2. I think we're doing something this afternoon.
   I don't think we're doing anything this afternoon.
3. I think he's gonna to do my taxes for me.
   I don't think he's gonna to do my taxes for me.
4. I think I'll give them a call.
   I don't think I'll give them a call.
5. I think they're gonna t̶o̶ go to the office.
   I don't think they're gonna t̶o̶ go to the office.
6. I think I'll wear a dress shirt
   I don't think I'll wear a dress shirt.
7. I think she's stopping at the store.
   I don't think she's stopping at the store.

B
Sagen Sie, was Sie unternehmen möchten. Verwenden Sie dabei die Verlaufsform des Präsens und die vorgegebenen Wörter.

8. What are you doing later? — going shopping
   I'm going shopping.
9. What are you doing this afternoon? — work on my taxes
   I'm working on my taxes.
10. What are you doing this weekend? — catch up on the laundry
    I'm catching up on the laundry.
11. What are you doing for vacation? — go to Spain
    I'm going to Spain.
12. What are you doing on Wednesday? — do a seminar
    I'm doing a seminar.
13. What are you doing tonight? — meet a friend
    I'm meeting a friend.
14. What are you doing for dinner? — go out
    I'm going out.

Lösungen

C

Sagen Sie, was Sie unternehmen möchten. Verwenden Sie dabei die Konstruktion mit *going to* bzw. die gesprochene Form *gonna*. Verwenden Sie wieder die vorgegebenen Wörter.

15 What are you gonna do this morning? — clean the refrigerator
    I'm gonna clean the refrigerator.
16 What are you gonna do later on? — pick up my suit
    I'm gonna pick up my suit.
17 What are you gonna do for money? — get a job
    I'm gonna get a job.
18 What are you gonna do at the end of the year? — move to the States
    I'm gonna move to the States.
19 What are you gonna do when he calls? — ask him over
    I'm gonna ask him over.
20 What are you gonna do for transportation? — call a cab
    I'm gonna call a cab.
21 What are you gonna do on Sunday? — just take it easy
    I'm just gonna take it easy.

17

the wife

18

to be shocked	to be very surprised
to finish lunch	to end the midday meal
to pop in	to go to someone's home unexpectedly
to offer to do something	to ask if you can do something for someone
to be annoyed	to be a little irritated
to rip up	to remove
to add	to say one more thing
to respond	to answer
to avoid	to try not to let something happen
to sand	to make smooth
pickup truck	small truck with open loading area
to unload	to take off/out of
to pick up after someone	to gather the things someone leaves lying around
to haul	to carry
to collect	to gather up
to come over	to visit
to feel guilty about something	to think something is your fault
to mop	to clean with water (usually the floor)
subject	topic
a shocker	something that is shocking (slang)
it's not her business	it doesn't concern her

Lösungen

19

normal housework
to pick up after someone
to mop

renovation
to sand
to rip up
to unload
to haul

20

to make an effort, to make a meal

21

a He's always writing letters to the newspaper.
b They're constantly popping in at the wrong time.
c I'm always trying to avoid the subject.
d She's constantly reminding me about the housework.
e I'm always feeling guilty about something.
f We're constantly offering to help.
g He's always repairing something around the house.

22

making plans
finishing lunch
picking up after
unloading
suggesting
popping in

persuading
mopping
catching up on
ripping up
wondering
avoiding

23

a Ralph and his brother are going to unload the pickup truck.
b We're going to collect the newspapers and bring them to the recycling centre.
c I'm not doing the dishes!
d I'm going to the subject when I see them.
e Sarah's parents are coming over later for dinner.
f I think I'll pop in and say hello.
g I'm not going to pick up after my daughter any more.

24

a 1 I think so. 3 I'm pretty sure they are.
b 1 Can't it wait? 3 You've got to be kidding!?
c 2 I'll bet!
d 1 Because it's late. 2 Maybe I will. 3 I wish I could, but …
e 1 No, thanks. 3 Well, actually, there is something …

172

Lösungen

25

a Do you think you could help me with the dishes?
b I'm sorry, I can't. I'm ...
c That's none of your business.
d I'm going to the cinema/watching TV/...
e That would be great. / No, thanks.
f I don't mind giving you a hand.

26

Tapescript

Craig   Hey, Keith, how's it going?
Keith   Can't complain, how about you?
Craig   Good, good. Say, I wanted to ask a favour. Are you doing anything on Saturday?
Keith   This coming Saturday?
Craig   Yeah.
Keith   Um, I don't think so, why?
Craig   I was wondering if you could give me a hand at the recycling centre.
Keith   I wish I could, old buddy, but I've got some errands to do.
Craig   It doesn't have to be all day – just a couple of hours in the morning.
Keith   I don't know ...
Craig   Come on, you'll have the whole afternoon to get your errands done.
Keith   Couldn't you ask Frank?
Craig   I already have; he's gonna be away. What do you say?
Keith   Oh, ok, but just until noon.
Craig   That's the spirit!
Keith   When are you picking me up?
Craig   Picking you up?!

Unit 3

a 2 plan the day   b 2 no   c 1 stay home   d 3 bed linens

a true   b true   c false   d true   e true   f false

Tapescript

A: So what do you feel like doing?
B: I don't know. What do you want to do?
A: I asked you first.
B: Well, how about breakfast in bed?
A: Sure; let me know if you need any help.

Lösungen

B: On second thought, ...
A: We could go to my parents'.
B: Any other suggestions? _(tedn)_
A: How about going to the Matisse exhibition?
B: At the art museum?
A: Yeah.
B: What, and stand in line for an hour to get in? No, thanks.
A: Well, what do you suggest?
B: How about going out for brunch?
A: Out to brunch?
B: Yeah.
A: I'd rather eat here and go somewhere else.
B: Come on ...
A: Where do you want to go?
B: Um ... how about Harry's?
A: We were just there a couple of weeks ago, weren't we?
B: You're right.
A: Why don't we try the Green Bean instead? _anstelle_
B: That's over by eh ... on the other side of town, isn't it?
A: It's not that far. I'll bet it won't take us more than fifteen minutes. There won't be much traffic. _wette_
B: But it means looking for a parking space. That'll take longer than driving there.
A: You know what: they have another location. I'll check the phone book to see where it is.
B: And I'll get us some o.j.   _Orange juice_
   ...
A: Here it is: Point Vedra Beach.
B: Wuo; that's even further away! _noch weiter_
A: OK, so forget the Green Bean.
B: Any other suggestions?
A: I'm looking.
B: Does Elliott's do breakfast?
A: Umm, Elliott's ... Elliott's: "Elliott's on the square: breakfast, lunch and dinner."
B: Is that alright with you?
A: Sure.
B: Elliott's it is then!
A: I'll call and see if we need a reservation.
B: Good idea!

3

a 1 too far   3 difficulty parking
b 3 Elliott's

4 + 5

A: So what do you feel like doing?
B: I don't know. What do *you* want to do?

A: I asked you first.
B: Well, how about breakfast in bed?
A: Sure; let me know if you need any help.
B: On second thought, …
A: We could go to my parent's.
B: Any other suggestions?
A: How about going to the Matisse exhibition?
A: At the art museum?
B: Yeah.
B: What, and stand in line for an hour to get in? No, thanks.
A: Well, what do you suggest?
B: How about going out for brunch?

a agreed with   b agree that   c agree on   d do … agree that   e agree on   f did … agree with
g agree on

Man sagt auch: *to disagree with someone, to disagree on something* und *to disagree that,* aber nicht *to disagree to something*.

8

Welches Gespräch passt zu welchem Bild?
a–1, b–2, c–3

Tapescript
1
A: OK, who's for going to the beach?
B: I don't know; what's the weather supposed to be like?
A: I don't know; I haven't seen the weather forecast.
C: It doesn't look all that sunny out.
A: OK, anybody have any other ideas?
D: Well, as long as it doesn't rain we could still do something outdoors.
A: For example?
B: What about driving down to the mountains and hiking?
C: It's a little late to get started; by the time we get there it will be afternoon.
D: Yeah.
B: I've got an idea: why don't we drive out to the lake? If the weather stays nice we can go swimming. If not, we can just go for a walk or something.
C: Yeah, that's it!
A: Who wants to drive?
C: Why don't we take the train?
A: Sure, why not?
B: It's all the same to me.

Lösungen

D: OK, it's the train then. Shall we pack a lunch or eat there?
C: Why don't we eat there? Otherwise we'll get a late start.
A: That's ok with me.
B: Me too.
C: We don't have anything to take anyway.
A: OK, let's get going.
B: I'm with you.
D: We're outta here!
C: OK!

2

A: Can we try to come to a decision about where we're going? We've got to make reservations or we'll never get what we want.
B: Well, what do you suggest?
A: I don't know; I haven't been home for over a year …
B: Yeah, but we said you'd go alone the next time. We wanted to do something else together.
A: Yeah, well … So what do you want to do?
B: What do I want to do? … Go backpacking.
A: I hope you don't mean camping, too?
B: Not necessarily.
A: And where were you thinking about?
B: What about Scotland?
A: Do you really think it's the right time of the year?
B: Well, it certainly won't be beach weather, but I'm sure it'll be fine for sightseeing and stuff.
A: We don't really know that, do we?
B: Um …
A: Why don't you call a travel agent?
B: I've got a better idea: I'll check it out on the Internet; I'm sure you can find the average temperatures there somewhere.
A: OK, but I'm still not sure that's what I want to do.
B: Let me just check the Web and see what's what.
A: Wouldn't you rather go to Greece?
B: Well, actually, no.

3

A: So, what do you feel like doing tonight?
B: I don't know. What are our options?
A: Well, we could get a bite to eat and then go see a film.
B: Umm …
A: You're not hungry?
B: No, going out to eat sounds good, but the weather is too nice to waste at the cinema.
A: That's true …
C: We could come back here and just veg out.
B: I've got a better idea: why don't we see if we can get tickets to the jazz concert in the park?
C: I heard that Sammy Waller is going to be there.
A: And I heard that it's completely sold out.
C: I've got it: how about hiring bikes and riding out to the lake for dinner?

A: Sounds good to me!
B: Where can we rent bikes?
A: Um, there's a place around the corner.
C: Now that you mention it, I've seen the bikes standing out front.
A: I'll run down there and reserve a couple.
B: Don't bother: I only need a couple of minutes to get ready.
C: Me too. That way we can go down there together and leave from there.
A: OK, I'll wait for you down in reception.
B: OK, we'll be down it ten minutes.
A: That's ok, take your time.
C: OK.

9

Dialog 2

10

It doesn't look all that sunny.	i
It's a little late to get started.	i
I've got a better idea …	d
What, and stand in line for an hour?	i
I'd rather …	d
How about …?	d
(Yeah) Well, …	i
Do you really think it's the right time of the year?	i
We wanted to do something else together.	d
Umm …	i
Let's … instead.	d

11

B: Um … how about Harry's?
A: We were just there a couple of weeks ago, <u>weren't we</u>?
B: You're right.
A: Why don't we try the Green Bean instead?
B: That's over by eh … on the other side of town, <u>isn't it</u>?

12

A: So what do you feel like doing ?
B: I don't know. What do you want to do?
A: Um, I don't know.
B: Well how about going shopping?
A: Sure; let me know when you get back.
B: I thought we could do something together.
A: We could go over my parents'.
B: Any other suggestions?

Lösungen

C: Why don't we call for pizza?
A: Sure, why not?
B: It doesn't matter to me.
D: OK, I'll get one large plain and one with sausage.
C: Hey, wait a minute. Why not get one veggie?
A: That's ok with me.
B: Me too.
C: I meant one veggie and one with sausage.
A: OK, is everyone in agreement?
B: Yeah, that's fine with me ...

13

g   Why don't we wait and see?   I guess not.

14

a   That was fun, wasn't it?
b   They can come, can't they?
c   She's very nice, isn't she?
d   We haven't been there before, have we?
e   You're Toni's friend, aren't you?
f   You work with Gerry, don't you?
g   You're not going, are you?
h   He'll call, won't he?
i   You didn't wait, did you?

15

a   She <u>can't</u> come, can she?
b   The food <u>was</u> good, wasn't it?
c   I <u>can</u> call and make a reservation, can't I?
d   They<u>'ve</u> been there before, haven't they?
e   We <u>hadn't</u> really thought about it, had we?
f   She<u>'ll</u> drive, won't she?
g   It<u>'s</u> been a nice party, hasn't it?

16 Mündliche Übungen

A

Verwandeln Sie die Aussagen in Fragen. Verwenden Sie dabei ein *question tag*. Jede Aussage enthält eine Form des Verbs *to be*.

1   She's in California.
    She's in California, isn't she?
2   Joe's Mexican.
    Joe's Mexican, isn't he?

3 I'm not late.
  I'm not late, am I?
4 They're here.
  They're here, aren't they?
5 The Green Bean's on the other side of town.
  The Green Bean's on the other side of town, isn't it?
6 You aren't from here.
  You aren't from here, are you?
7 I'm early.
  I'm early, aren't I?

B
Verwandeln Sie die Aussagen in Fragen. Verwenden Sie dabei ein *question tag*. Jede Aussage enthält ein Modalverb.
8 They can't go.
  They can't go, can they?
9 You'll have to wait.
  You'll have to wait, won't you?
10 Tina couldn't get a reservation.
  Tina couldn't get a reservation, could she?
11 Saul would prefer meeting us there.
  Saul would prefer meeting us there, wouldn't he?
12 She won't give you an answer.
  She won't give you an answer, will she?
13 You can't remember her name.
  You can't remember her name, can you?
14 It won't help.
  It won't help, will it?

C
Verwandeln Sie die Aussagen in Fragen. Verwenden Sie dabei ein *question tag*. Jede Aussage enthält weder das Verb *to be* noch ein anderes Hilfsverb; verwenden Sie also eine Form des Hilfsverbs *to do* im *question tag*.
15 They like to skate.
  They like to skate, don't they?
16 You have the tickets.
  You have the tickets, don't you?
17 He likes Mexican food.
  He likes Mexican food, doesn't he?
18 Tom made breakfast.
  Tom made breakfast, didn't he?
19 Linda suggested that.
  Linda suggested that, didn't she?
20 Paul parks there all the time.
  Paul parks there all the time, doesn't he?

Lösungen

D

Verwandeln Sie die Aussagen in Fragen. Verwenden Sie dabei ein *question tag*. Die Aussagen enthalten entweder *to be* oder *to have* als Hilfsverb.

21 They're not coming.
   They're not coming, are they?
22 We're going to drive.
   We're going to drive, aren't we?
23 She isn't taking the train.
   She isn't taking the train, is she?
24 Al's waiting to hear the weather forecast.
   Al's waiting to hear the weather forecast, isn't he?
25 You've never heard of them.
   You've never heard of them, have you?
26 You're getting started a little late.
   You're getting started a little late, aren't you?
27 It's going to be fun.
   It's going to be fun, isn't it?
28 You've been backpacking.
   You've been backpacking, haven't you?

E

Verwandeln Sie die Aussagen in Fragen. Verwenden Sie dabei ein *question tag*. Aufgepasst: In dieser Übung enthalten die Aussagen alle möglichen Verben!

29 We could eat there.
   We could eat there, couldn't we?
30 You don't have any suggestions.
   You don't have any suggestions, do you?
31 There's a bike store around the corner.
   There's a bike store around the corner, isn't there?
32 Kay likes jazz.
   Kay likes jazz, doesn't she?
33 You've heard of Sammy Waller.
   You've heard of Sammy Waller, haven't you?
34 It sounds good.
   It sounds good, doesn't it?
35 They'll call us.
   They'll call us, won't they?

17

a–3, b–1, c–7, d–10, e–2, f–6, g–4

19

b   Venice is unlike most other places in California – or America for that matter!

20

Words referring to people
adults, old people, body builders, senior citizens, drifters, drug addicts, hopeful moviemakers, aging hippies, surfers, lawyers, dentists, real estate brokers, accountants, workaholics, natives

Words referring to leisure-time activities
playing volleyball, running, rolling on skates, riding bikes, skateboards, surf boards, flying kites, drinking milk, eating quiche lorraine, playing checkers, work out, perform on the paddle tennis courts

21

demented	crazy
to work out	to train
pen	fenced in area
to line up	to wait in an orderly fashion
beach community	place to live near the sea
checkers	a board game
the latter	the last one mentioned
boardwalk	pavement made of wood
to perform	to give a show
to long for	to miss
to wonder	to ask yourself
to be attached to	to be fond of

22

noun	verb	adjective	adverb
beach community	to work out	demented	
checkers	to line up		
pen	to perform		
the latter	to wonder		
boardwalk	to be attached to		
	to long for		

23

cross country skiing | horseback riding | ice skating / speed skating | mountain climbing

Lösungen

hiking biking / cycling weight lifting / working out ping pong / table tennis

athletics / track and field football / soccer wrestling fencing

24

fly a kite
play volleyball
go swimming
ride a bike
play checkers
see/go to a film
sail a boot

take/go for a walk
go to an exhibition
have/go for brunch
go camping
go backpacking
go out to eat
surf the net

25

a 2 I'don t know.   3 We could go to brunch.
b 1 Fine.   2 That's OK with me.   3 You've got to be kidding!?
c 3 Good idea!
d 1 Greece.
e 3 Well, actually, no.

26

a He's looking forward to coming, isn't he?
b We've already seen that film, haven't we?
c It's going to rain, isn't it?
d The service was excellent, wasn't it?
e They can't afford it, can they?
f Seeing them again will be fun, won't it?
g You want her to succeed, don't you?

Lösungen

27

Musterdialog

A   Hello?
B   Hi, it's me.
A   What do you feel like doing tonight?
B   I don't know, what do you want to do?
A   Why don't we go out to eat something?
B   I'd rather eat at home. Why don't we go to a film later on?
A   I think the weather is too nice to go to the cinema, why don't we do something outside?
B   OK; what were you thinking about?
A   Why don't we have a look in the paper? I'll call you later.
B   That's OK with me. Talk to you later.
A   Bye bye.

Unit 4

d   b   e   a   c

a true   b true   c true   d true   e true   f false   g false

Tapescript

Karen: And how about you – have you ever been to California?
Nancy: Once – back when I was seeing David. He was working for a hotel chain at the time and got like a discount at other hotels, so we wanted to take advantage of that.
Karen: Where did you go?
Nancy: San Francisco and Los Angeles.
Karen: How did you like it?
Nancy: Well, it was a trip!
Karen: It's not the Cotswolds, that's for sure.
Nancy: I liked San Francisco, but L.A. was sort of strange.
Karen: How do you mean?
Nancy: You know, like everything's so spread out, people in their cars all the time; you hardly ever see people walking anywhere, do you?
Karen: Not unless they're like out for a "power walk".
Nancy: Right! On the one hand they get in their cars to go to the supermarket down the street and on the other they've got this thing with fitness; it's crazy.
Karen: Did you go to Venice?
Nancy: Yeah. How crazy is that place?
Karen: About as crazy as they get!
Nancy: Tell me about it! I lived there for a couple of months.
Karen: That's funny – you seem normal enough …

Lösungen

Nancy: I got out in time!
Karen: I thought you said you lived in West Hollywood?
Nancy: I did, but before I found my own apartment I was sharing a flat with a friend in Venice.
Karen: You mean after you broke up with David?
Nancy: Yeah.
Karen: What happened there anyway?
Nancy: I don't know, we just hadn't been getting along, so we decided to call it quits.
Karen: Do you ever hear from him?
Nancy: We used to keep in touch, but I haven't heard from him in a while now.
Karen: So, you lived in Venice: Bet you were out rollerblading with the rest of the loonies.
Nancy: Actually, I was – and I loved every minute of it!
Karen: Yeah?
Nancy: Yeah, it s fun.
Karen: I guess I should try it. So what else did you do in California?
Nancy: What else did we do? Well, we went to Disneyland. That was brilliant or – at least I thought so. David didn't even want to go, but he was a good sport about it – and even ended up having a great time.
Karen: They never know what they want!
Nancy: Yeah, really!
Karen: Did you do the studio tours in Hollywood?
Nancy: Yeah, they were OK. The thing I liked the most was Sea World in San Diego.
Karen: Oh, me too. I was there a couple of times.
Nancy: I could have stayed all day.
Karen: I know ...
Nancy: I'll never forget what happened that day.
Karen: What?
Nancy: Well, you know how the killer whales swim around the side of the pool and splash the people sitting in the front rows?
Karen: Uhuh.
Nancy: Well, David got completely soaked.
Karen: He didn't!?
Nancy: He did! And he had just got finished saying: "I think we should move."
Karen: You're kidding!?
Nancy: No, it was hilarious!
Karen: Wish I could have seen that!
Nancy: So later on we looked for a place to dry off; something a little secluded.
Karen: Uhuh.
Nancy: We found this little park nearby – just what the doctor ordered.
Karen: Yeah.
Nancy: So he took off his clothes to let them dry out and before you could say "indecent exposure" a police car pulled up.
Karen: You're kidding? What happened?
Nancy: David is like standing there wringing out his shorts with the rest of his clothes hanging in the tree and these two cops get out.
Karen: He's standing there naked in the middle of the park?
Nancy: Nooo, we were over by some bushes.

Karen:	Oh.
Nancy:	You should've heard David when he saw the cops: "Oh f…!!"
Karen:	So then what happened?
Nancy:	Well, we explained the situation and they turned out to be pretty nice about it.
Karen:	He didn't get arrested?
Nancy:	No, they just, um, told him to put his clothes back on.
Karen:	So he walked around the rest of the day in soggy clothes?
Nancy:	Well, actually, they dried out pretty quickly.
Karen:	So, you almost landed in the poky?
Nancy:	Certainly one of the highlights of our trip!
Karen:	(laugh)
Nancy:	Oh, I didn't realise how late it was. I'd better be going.
Karen:	Oh, yeah, I have things to do, too.
Nancy:	OK, well, it was nice to see you. Let's not make it so long the next time.
Karen:	Right!

3

to be a good sport about something	etwas locker nehmen
to pull up	vorfahren

4

a to get wet/drenched — to get soaked
b to drive up — to pull up
c (the opposite of *to get wet*)(2x) — to dry out, to dry off
d to end (a relationship) — to call it quits
e to be apprehended by the police — to get arrested

5 + 7

Introduction	d	What?
Background information	e	Uhuh. / Oh, right. / Yeah.
The plot	b	You re kidding?
Highpoint	a	No! / Really?
Comment	c	Wow! / I can imagine!

6

actually, anyway

8

a (I'll) Bet you were out rollerblading with the rest of the loonies. – Actually, I was – and (I) loved every minute of it!
b How crazy is that place? – (It's) About as crazy as they get!
c It was hilarious! – (I) Wish I could have seen that!
d We found this park nearby – (it was) just what the doctor ordered.

Lösungen

9

simple past, past perfect

10

a eine

Sätze wie: *Right! On the one hand they get in their cars to go to the supermarket down the street and on the other they've got this thing with fitness; it's crazy* oder *Well, you know how the killer whales swim around the side of the pool and splash the people sitting in the front rows?* beschreiben Situationen, die immer so sind und nicht einmalige Handlungen in der Vergangenheit.

11

a was rooming, met   b kept   c got   d was   e were drying out, pulled up
f did ... get arrested   g got along

12

a We went to L.A.   b Yes, I did.   c Yes, I have.   d Well, we explained the situation.
e Yes, it was pretty funny.   f No, I haven't.   g Once, when we were in New York.

13

a Paul was having breakfast between 7.00 and 7.30.
b He was reading the paper between 7.45 and 8.15.
c He was shopping between 8.30 and 9.10.
d He was waiting for a friend between 9.15 and 9.30.
e He was having a cup of coffee between 9.30 and 10.15

14

a Do you know Liz?   No, I've never met her before.
b How long have you lived there?   Since 1999.
c When did you see the film?   I haven't seen it yet!
d Where is your jacket?   I think I left it at the cinema.
e When are you leaving?   As soon as we've finished packing.
f What happened?   I think I've broken my thumb.
g Are you new here?   Yes, we've just moved from London.

15

a Larry doesn't really know what he's doing, does he?
b First you have to arrange for transportation. – I see.
c And then she put it on her head! – You're kidding?!
d Actually, I don't really care!
e Do you know what I mean? – Yes, go on.
f I'd like you to come to the picnic. – Really?
g They've got this thing about fitness. – Tell me about it!

Lösungen

16 Mündliche Übungen

A

become	became	has become
buy	bought	has bought
catch	caught	has caught
drink	drank	has drunk
drive	drove	has driven
eat	ate	has eaten
fly	flew	has flown
forbid	forbid	has forbidden
get	got	has got
hear	heard	has heard
hurt	hurt	has hurt
know	knew	has known
leave	left	has left
make	made	has made
see	saw	has seen
sleep	slept	has slept
spend	spent	has spent
take	took	has taken
understand	understood	has understood
write	wrote	has written

B

Wenn Sie von einem Ereignis in der Vergangenheit sprechen, das zu einem bestimmten Zeitpunkt geschehen ist, müssen Sie im Englischen das *simple past* verwenden.
Setzen Sie das Verb in den folgenden Sätzen in diese Zeitform. Verwenden Sie dabei die Zeitadverbiale, die Sie nach dem Satz hören.

1 Have you ever been arrested? when you were in California
  Were you arrested when you were in California?
2 I've already dried off. in an hour
  I dried off in an hour.
3 Have you already told them about your objections? this morning
  Did you tell them about your objections this morning?
4 That's been the highlight of our trip. last year
  That was the highlight of our trip last year.
5 He's already had his say. last night
  He had his say last night.
6 We've given her lots of encouragement. when she was young
  We gave her lots of encouragement when she was young.
7 Have you already broken the news to her? when she came home
  Did you break the news to her when she came home?

Lösungen

C
Beim Gebrauch des *past tense* muss der Zeitpunkt des Geschehens nicht immer im Satz erwähnt werden; oft wird er schon aus dem Zusammenhang klar. Setzen Sie das Verb in den folgenden Sätzen ins *simple past*.

8 He's very abusive.
   He was very abusive.
9 They've bungled the plan.
   They bungled the plan.
10 They're calling it quits.
   They called it quits.
11 I feel obliged to go.
   I felt obliged to go.
12 She's getting out of the car.
   She got out of the car.
13 He doesn't meddle in other peoples' business.
   He didn't meddle in other people's business.
14 She tells me everything.
   She told me everything.

D
Setzen Sie auch in den folgenden Sätzen das Verb ins *simple past*.

15 That expression is commonly used.
   That expression was commonly used.
16 What do you mean?
   What did you mean?
17 We don't interfere in their lives.
   We didn't interfere in their lives.
18 He keeps in touch.
   He kept in touch.
19 She's a good sport about it.
   She was a good sport about it.
20 We often stroll along the beach.
   We often strolled along the beach.
21 I get along with her just fine.
   I got along with her just fine.

E
Setzen Sie das Verb in den folgenden Sätzen ins *past continuous*. Auch hier denkt der Sprecher an einen bestimmten Zeitpunkt in der Vergangenheit.

22 What are you whispering about?
   What were you whispering about?
23 I'm just speaking my mind.
   I was just speaking my mind.
24 Is he gossiping again?
   Was he gossiping again?
25 My sister is rooming with a girl from Spain.
   My sister was rooming with a girl from Spain.
26 What are you alluding to?

What were you alluding to?
27 You're splashing me!
You were splashing me!
28 He's taking advantage of the situation.
He was taking advantage of the situation.

F

Verwandeln Sie die folgenden Aussagesätzen in eine Frage. Verwenden Sie dabei das Pronomen, das Sie nach dem Satz hören.

29 I got along well with him.   you
Did you get along with him?
30 We lived in Santa Monica.   they
Did they live in Santa Monica?
31 We kept in touch.   you
Did you keep in touch?
32 I objected to the story.   she
Did she object to the story?
33 He was a good sport about it.   she
Was she a good sport about it?
34 They called it quits.   he
Did he call it quits?
35 I felt obliged to speak my mind.   you
Did you feel obliged to speak your mind?

19

b Although the word in question has become commonplace in spoken English, it is seldom written.

20

to feel obliged	sich verpflichtet fühlen
objection	Einwand, Bedenken
commonly used	gebräuchlich, alltäglich
let alone	geschweige (denn)
verbatim	Wort für Wort
to allude to something	eine Andeutung machen
intercourse	Geschlechtsverkehr
contempt	Abscheu
account	Bericht
frankness	Offenheit
malevolence	Bosheit
convention	Brauch
to interfere	sich einmischen
to meddle	sich einmischen
to bungle	verpfuschen
to mishandle	schlecht behandeln
mean	gemein

Lösungen

encouragement	Ermutigung
to stroll	spazieren
to curse	verdammen
suppose	annehmen
enduring	bleibend, fortdauernd
abusive	beleidigend

21

	noun	verb	adjective	adverb
a	frankness	to be frank	frank	frankly
b	abuse	to be abusive	abusive	abusively
c	encouragement	to encourage	encouraging	encouragingly
d	shock	to shock	shocking	shockingly

22

a	divulge	disclose
b	tell	narrate
c	break the news	report
d	have your say	speak your mind
e	rant and rave	rattle on
f	improvise	speak off the cuff
g	gossip	spread rumours
h	chat	converse

23

a	narrate	descriptive
b	leak	indiscreet
c	broadcast	wide audience
d	whisper	softly
e	gossip	unsubstantiated
f	speak your mind	open
g	rattle on	unending
h	improvise	spontaneous

24

al·<u>lude</u>	in·ter·<u>fere</u>	in·<u>de</u>·cent
ver·<u>ba</u>·tim	a·<u>bu</u>·sive	<u>dis</u>·count
ma·<u>lev</u>·o·lence	con·<u>ven</u>·tion	ob·<u>jec</u>·tion
mis·<u>han</u>·dle	en·<u>cour</u>·age·ment	con·<u>tempt</u>

Lösungen

25

a thought better　b feel obliged　c stroll　d interfering　e bungled　f verbatim　g mean

26

a lived, have not been　b tried, went　c have ... seen, saw　d did ... go, 've never been
e have ... met, didn't ... meet　f called, was

27

a was, had seen　b had ... left, arrived　c had ... been, let　d had ... bought, came out　e liked, had ... had
f had ... dried out, began　g promised, did

28

a　3 About as crazy as they get.
b　2 Really!　　　　　3 Right!
c　1 Actually, ...　　　3 To tell you the truth, ...
d　1 You don't say!?　2 Does she?　3 You're kidding?!
e　3 What?

29 Wie sagt man's auf Englisch?

a　Do you still keep in touch?　　　– No, not since we called it quits.
b　Venice is a weird city.　　　　　– Tell me about it!?
c　Do you get along with her?　　　– Yes, we've been rooming together for five years.
d　I used to work for a hotel chain.　– Really?
e　Did he get arrested?　　　　　　– Yes, and he spent the night in the poky.

30

a　I was living in Sydney when I met my wife.
b　I was standing there talking to a colleague when Susan walked in.
c　Driving home from work that day I got an idea.
d　She called that night while I was watching TV.

Tapescript

Leon:　I was living in Sydney when I met my wife.
Nate:　Oh really?
Leon:　Yeah, she was working in the same company as I was, but in another department. Anyway, one day I was standing there talking to a colleague when Susan walked in.
Nate:　And the colleague introduced you?
Leon:　That's right.
Nate:　So, then what happened?
Leon:　Well, that was that, at least at first. Driving home from work that day I got an idea.
Nate:　What was that?
Leon:　Well, we were supposed to go on a company picnic the following week.

Lösungen

Nate: Uhuh.
Leon: We had to arrange our own transportation. I asked her if she needed a ride.
Nate: And she did?
Leon: Well, she had planned to go with a couple of friends from the office, but their car was pretty full, so she said she'd let me know.
Nate: I can't stand the suspense!
Leon: She called that night while I was watching TV. And since I wasn't doing anything I asked her if she wanted to go out.
Nate: And the rest is history.
Leon: You got it, mate!

Unit 5

1

a–G/E, b–G/E, c–G/E, d–G/E, e–G, f–G, g–G/E

2

Bitte um Hilfe

a true   b true   c true   d true   e false   f false   g true

Tapescript
Phil: Hello?
Tommy: Hey Phil, how's it going?
Phil: Not bad. How about yourself?
Tommy: Can't complain.
Phil: Work going OK? The last time I talked to you, you said you were having a problem with your boss.
Tommy: He's history and I'm still hanging in there.
Phil: Good for you! Still seeing Tina?
Tommy: Am I still seeing Tina? As a matter of fact, we're moving in together.
Phil: You're kidding: you and Tina!?
Tommy: That's right, old buddy and that's why I'm calling. What are you doing on Saturday in two weeks?
Phil: It depends. If you're having a house warming, I'm free. If you're moving, I've got plans.
Tommy: No, seriously.
Phil: Who's not serious? You remember the last time I helped you move? I couldn't stand up straight for a month.
Tommy: I don't need your back this time, just your technical expertise.
Phil: In what area?
Tommy: You know, installing light fixtures, hooking up the stereo, stuff like that.
Phil: I don't have to install the kitchen or redo the plumbing?
Tommy: Not unless you want to.
Phil: In your dreams, pal.
Tommy: Just kidding. The kitchen's already there and, as far as I know, the plumbing's fine. I've also got a moving company this time.

Phil:	Good move.	
Tommy:	Did I mention that Tina is making her famous chili?	
Phil:	Count me in.	
Tommy:	I thought that would convince you.	
Phil:	Is anyone else going to help?	
Tommy:	Nelson – and Fitz said he'd try to make it.	
Phil:	Why don't you give Pete a call?	
Tommy:	That's a good idea; I think I will.	
Phil:	When did you say it was?	
Tommy:	Saturday the 19th.	
Phil:	You're not getting started at the crack of dawn, are you?	
Tommy:	I told the others about 10 o'clock.	
Phil:	I think I can handle that. You want to tell me where the place is?	
Tommy:	Oh yeah, it's in Wynnwood. 473 Dulles Drive.	
Phil:	4-7-3 Dulles Drive. Ok, I got it.	
Tommy:	Thanks old buddy, I appreciate it.	
Phil:	Don't mention it.	
Tommy:	Well, I've got to get moving; I'm picking Tina up at the airport.	
Phil:	Tell her I said hello.	
Tommy:	Will do. Take care.	
Phil:	You too. See you.	
Tommy:	Bye. And thanks again.	

3

in your dreams!   das hättest du wohl gern!
count me in   ich bin dabei

4

a   to gripe/grumble   to complain
b   to date someone   to see someone
c   to install   to hook something up
d   to deal with something   to handle something

5

move away from the old neighbourhood
move in to a new apartment
move out of your house
move in together with someone

Lösungen

6

Gespräch 2

Tapescript

1

Sally:	Hello?
Nina:	Hi Sally, it's Nina. How are you?
Sally:	Hi Nina, good. I've been meaning to call you. *beabsichtigen zu tun*
Nina:	Oh, really? How com?
Sally:	You remember I told you my parents were coming? Well, on Tuesday we're going out to dinner and I wanted to ask you if you would watch the kids.
Nina:	This coming Tuesday?
Sally:	Yeah, are you doing anything?
Nina:	Well, not really; it's just that I've been working late lately. *länger*
Sally:	If it's a problem I could ask …
Nina:	No, no, that's alright.
Sally:	You're sure?
Nina:	No, really.
Sally:	Because I could always get my sister-in-law – it's just that she's done it a couple of times lately. *or ask*
Nina:	Hey, it's no problem. What time do you want me?
Sally:	Is 6.30 too early?
Nina:	No, that's OK.
Sally:	I'll order pizza, so you won't have to cook.
Nina:	Sounds like a plan to me.
Sally:	Thanks, Nina.
Nina:	You're welcome.
Sally:	Now what was it you called about?
Nina:	Umm, what did I call you about? … What did I call about? Oh, this is embarrassing! *peinlich*
Sally:	That's alright, dear, you're just having a "senior moment".
Nina:	I think you're right! Jeez, I'll have to call you back.
Sally:	No problem. I'll be here for a while.
Nina:	Sorry, Sal.
Sally:	No problem. And thanks for saying you'd baby-sit.
Nina:	You're welcome. Bye.
Sally:	Bye.

2

Sally:	Hello?
Nina:	Hi Sally, it's me again.
Sally:	Do you remember what you called for?
Nina:	Yeah, I wanted to ask if I could borrow your power drill.
Sally:	Jim's drill?
Nina:	Yeah, I'm putting up some shelves. *Regale*
Sally:	I think that's OK; when do you need it?
Nina:	Is it alright if I come over now?
Sally:	Um, Jim's not here right now and I don't know if I'll be able to find it. Sometimes he has it in his car.

Nina:	Oh …
Sally:	He said he wouldn't be long. How about if I call you when he gets back?
Nina:	That's fine.
Sally:	We're going to go out after that.
Nina:	Um…
Sally:	I'll put it on the side porch befor we go out. *Veranda*
Nina:	OK, great.
Sally:	That way you can pick it up anytime.
Nina:	Thanks a lot, Sal.
Sally:	Hey, I owe you one. *Schulde*
Nina:	You scratch my back … *eine Hand wäscht die andere*
Sally:	Hey, I gotta run. The natives are restless.
Nina:	OK. Take care. *Rest d. Familie*
Sally:	You too. Bye.
Nina:	Bye.

What goes around will come around

3

Lynn:	Hello?
Carl:	Hey Lynn, it's Carl. What's up?
Lynn:	Not much. And you?
Carl:	Well, things are kind of crazy at the moment.
Lynn:	Oh yeah?
Carl:	Yeah, we're in the middle of inventory at work and two of my assistants are out sick.
Lynn:	Boy, not good, huh?
Carl:	You can say that again!
Lynn:	I will if you want, but I don't think it will help.
Carl:	Very funny. Seriously, I'll tell you why I'm calling.
Lynn:	Why do I have the feeling I don't want to know?
Carl:	No, really …
Lynn:	Shoot.
Carl:	I wanted to know if you could do me a favor and come in for a couple of hours tomorrow.
Lynn:	Tomorrow?
Carl:	Yeah, any time is OK with me.
Lynn:	Actually, Carl, I'd really like to help you out, but I'm leaving for Toronto tomorrow.
Carl:	Darn it! You were my last hope.
Lynn:	I'm really sorry.
Carl:	I guess I'll just have to get used to the idea of not getting finished on time.
Lynn:	I just read an article on stress management I can send you.
Carl:	I haven't got time to read it, but thanks.
Lynn:	Chill out, Carl.
Carl:	That's easy for you to say.
Lynn:	I know.
Carl:	Well, OK, I gotta get back to work now.
Lynn:	Sorry, Carl, I wish I could help.
Carl:	No problem, thanks anyway.

Lösungen

Lynn:	Sure – and relax.
Carl:	When this is over.
Lynn:	You're hopeless.
Carl:	Have a good trip.
Lynn:	Thanks. Talk to you when I get back.
Carl:	OK, bye.
Lynn:	Bye.

7

neutral
How about ...?
Can you ...?
Would you ...?

polite
Could you ...?
Would you mind ...?
Do you think you could ...?
I was wondering if you could ...

very polite (Die Grenze hier ist fließend.)
I wanted to ask if you could ...
I would really appreciate it if you would ...
I was wondering if you could possibly ...

8

a
I'd really like to help, but I'm leaving for Toronto tomorrow.

b
1 Sorry, but I make it a point not to work on the weekend.
4 I wish I could, but I'm already doing something.
5 I'm really sorry, but I really need the day off.

9

a complain   b want to   c need   d mention   e convince   f handle   g appreciate

10

a He said he couldn't complain.
b He asked what I was doing on Saturday.
c She asked what time I wanted her to come.
d He said he had a moving company.
e She said she would order pizza.
f He said he thought he could handle that.
g She said she was having a "senior moment".

Lösungen

11

a If you're having a housewarming, I'm free.
b Do you remember the last time I helped you move?
c I couldn't stand up straight for a month.
d Do I have to install the kitchen?
e Not unless you want to.
f Count me in!
g Who else is going to help?

12

a He encouraged me to call someone else.
b She suggested making chili.
c He asked me to come at 10.
d He asked me to say hello to Tina.
e She recommended relaxing.
f She proposed sending him an article on stress management.
g She promised to call when she got back.

13

a 1 Sure.   2 I'll have to call you.   3 Sorry, I'm doing something already.
b 2 I'd be happy to.   3 You're outta luck!
c 1 No, not at all.   2 When?   3 Sure, no problem!
d 1 Forget it!   2 You're kidding, right?   3 I'm using it myself.
e 1 Um, I'll have to think about that.   3 I'm really sorry, but …

14 Mündliche Übungen

A

Geben Sie die Äußerungen, die Sie gleich hören werden, in der indirekten Rede wieder. Verwenden Sie dabei den Satzanfang, den Sie gleichfalls hören.

1 I'm seeing Robert.   She said she …
   She said she was seeing Robert.
2 We get up at the crack of dawn.   She said they …
   She said they get up at the crack of dawn.
3 I can't convince them.   She told me …
   She told me she couldn't convince them.
4 We're redoing the kitchen.   She said they …
   She said they were redoing the kitchen.
5 I can't convince her.   She said she …
   She said she couldn't convince her.
6 We're moving in together.   She told me …
   She told me they were moving in together.
7 I need your expertise.   She said she …
   She said she needed my expertise.

Lösungen

B

Geben Sie die Fragen, die Sie gleich hören werden, in der indirekten Rede wieder. Verwenden Sie dabei den Satzanfang, den Sie gleichfalls hören.

8 Are you still seeing Tina?   He asked if ...
   He asked if I was still seeing Tina.
9 Remember the last time we moved?   He asked if ...
   He asked if I remembered the last time they moved.
10 Is Tina making her famous chili?   He asked if ...
   He asked if Tina was making her famous chili.
11 You're not getting started at the crack of dawn, are you?   He asked if we ...
   He asked if we were getting started at the crack of dawn.
12 How come?   He asked ...
   He asked how come. / He asked why.
13 Is 6:30 too early?   He asked if ...
   He asked if 6:30 was too early.
14 What's up?   He asked ...
   He asked what was up.

C

Geben Sie die Befehle, die Sie gleich hören werden, in der indirekten Rede wieder. Verwenden Sie dabei den Satzanfang, den Sie gleichfalls hören.

15 Relax!   She told me ...
   She told me to relax.
16 Hang in there!   She told me ...
   She told me to hang in there.
17 Stop complaining!   She told me ...
   She told me to stop complaining.
18 Stand up straight!   She told me ...
   She told me to stand up straight.
19 Don't do that!   She told me not ...
   She told me not to do that.
20 Don't touch that stuff!   She told me not ...
   She told me not to touch that stuff.
21 Chill out!   She told me ...
   She told me to chill out.

D

Geben Sie die Vorschläge, die Sie gleich hören werden, in der indirekten Rede wieder. Verwenden Sie dabei den Satzanfang, den Sie hören.

22 Why don't you give Ulla a ring?   He suggested ...
   He suggested giving Ulla a ring.
23 Let's move in together!   He suggested ...
   He suggested moving in together.
24 Why don't you hook up the light fixture?   He suggested ...
   He suggested hooking up the light fixture.
25 Let's redo the place!   He suggested ...
   He suggested redoing the place.

Lösungen

26 How about making chili? He suggested ...
He suggested making chili.
27 Why don't we get started? He suggested ...
He suggested getting started.
28 How about asking Tony? He suggested ...
He suggested asking Tony.

E
Geben Sie die Äußerungen, die Sie hören werden, in der indirekten Rede wieder. Verwenden Sie dabei den Satzanfang, den Sie gleichfalls hören.

29 Did you give him the new address? She asked if ...
She asked if I had given him the new address.
30 Did you tell him it's the 19th? She asked if ...
She asked if I had told him when it was.
31 Did you thank him? She asked if ...
She asked if I had thanked him.
32 Have you invited them to the housewarming? She asked if ...
She asked if I had invited them to the housewarming.
33 Have you checked the plumbing? She asked if ...
She asked if I had checked the plumbing.
34 Have you convinced him to help out? She asked if ...
She asked if I had convinced him to help out.
35 Has she promised to make chili? She asked if ...
She asked if she had promised to make chili.

17

b English can't seem to find the right word to describe people in relationships.

18

to lack	fehlen
much less	schon gar nicht
to capture	(hier:) einfangen
blissful	(glück)selig
cohabitation	Zusammenwohnen
to blend	mischen
reference	Verweis
residency	wohnhaft sein
shading	Schattierung
care	Sorge
hint	Hinweis
dash	Prise
to cry out for	(hier:) schreien nach
precise	präzise
to rush in	sich darauf stürzen
to fill a gap	eine Lücke füllen

Lösungen

pretender	Bewerber/in
to earn a thumbs up	angenommen, akzeptiert werden
coy	kokett
to be at issue	zur Debatte stehen
to fail	unterlassen
to convey	vermitteln
intimation	Andeutung
mate	(hier:) Lebensgefährte/in

19

noun	verb	adjective	adverb
cohabitation	to lack	blissful	much less
reference	to capture	precise	
residency	to blend	coy	
shading	to cry out for		
care	to rush in		
hint	to fill a gap		
dash	to earn a thumbs up		
pretender	to be at issue		
intimation	to fail		
mate	to convey		

20

de·scribe
op·po·site
co·ha·bi·ta·tion
ref er·ence
e·mo·tion·al
per·ma·nence

can·di·date
eu·phe·mis·tic
pre·cise
in·ti·ma·tion
con·tra·ry
ev·i·dent

21

a 3 cohabitation   b 2 a gap   c 3 a candidate   d 2 sexuality   e 3 a hint   f 3 a reference
g 1 residency

22

a
He called and asked if I could give him a hand …
I told him I could only stay for an hour or so, …
Marge called and said she wouldn't be able to make it tonight.

b
Could you give me a hand?
I can only stay for an hour.
I won't be able to make it tonight.

Lösungen

23

a "Sure, count me in." — He **assured** me he would come.
b "Good move." — He **thought** it was a good idea.
c "How's it going?" — He **inquired** how I was doing.
d "Things are crazy at the moment!" — He **complained** about his workload.
e "I don't need your back." — He **promised** me I wouldn't have to carry anything.
f "No, really, work is going OK." — He **insisted** that things were going well at work.
g "I'll leave it on the side porch." — He **explained** where I could find it.

24

a true   b true   c true   d false   e true

Tapescript
I'm not married, but I'm not single either. And I'm also no spring chicken. So what do I call my "significant other"? In the old days this problem didn't exist: you went out with someone for a while, then you got engaged and then you got married. It was all fairly straightforward. When you introduced the other person you said: "This is my boyfriend/girlfriend, fiancé/fiancée" and then: "This is my husband/wife." It's not that simple any more. There are a lot more grey areas than there used to be. Nowadays you can live with someone for years without any mention of marriage. As a result of divorce you have people in their forties dating: do you call your "significant other" your "boyfriend" or "girlfriend"? Doesn't the term conjure up teenage infatuation? And what about same-sex couples?
Let's look at some of the options: "friend" seems to work in some languages, but in English it just means "friend", no more and no less. The term "significant other" is trying too hard. I sometimes use it, but even when I'm speaking you can hear the quotation marks. "Partner" sounds more like business than pleasure. And lover, the expression commonly used by gay couples, almost sounds too intimate for general use.
There are, of course, ways of getting around the problem. You can always resort to just names when introducing that special person and skip the part about "my" this or that. Depending on the particular situation however, a bit of explanation may be required, as most of the terms in existence to describe relationships outside the mainstream are in some way unsatisfactory. I guess the language just hasn't kept up with changing lifestyles.

25

a How's it going? – I can't complain.
b Could you give me a hand tomorrow? – Sorry, I wanted to work tomorrow.
c I wish I could, but I told her, that I would stay here.
d You said you had problems at work. – Yes, I remember.
e I'm really sorry, but I need a day off.
f She said she would make her famous chili.

Lösungen

26

a She said she was leaving for Toronto tomorrow.
b She said she had just read an article on stress management.
c She said she would try to make it.
d She said she would talk to me when I got back.
e She said she was leaving.

Unit 6

1

Mit welcher der folgenden Formulierungen haben Sie die besten Erfolgschancen?
I'd like to exchange these shoes.

Mit welcher die schlechtesten?
Exchange these shoes, will you?

Welche sind zu höflich?
Would you be so kind as to exchange these shoes?
Would it be possible for you to exchange these shoes?

Welche Formulierung passt überhaupt nicht?
I like exchanging these shoes.

2

a false   b false   c true   d true   e true

Tapescript

Customer:	Hello.
Salesperson:	Hello, can I help you?
Customer:	Yes, I'd like to exchange these shoes. I bought them here a couple of months ago and the heel is coming off one of them already.
Salesperson:	Do you have your receipt?
Customer:	No, I don't. I threw it away once I started wearing them.
Salesperson:	You just want to exchange them?
Customer:	Yes.
Salesperson:	Well, let's see if I have them in your size. These were on sale; I don't think I've got them in all sizes.
Customer:	They're an eight. I don't mind another colour.
Salesperson:	Eight, eight – seven and a half, eight and a half. I hate to tell you this, but we're out of eights.
Customer:	Oh, great!
Salesperson:	You'll have to go to the refund department and try getting your money back.
Customer:	Try?
Salesperson:	I don't think they're going to want to give you a refund if you can't prove the shoes were bought here. Tell them you just wanted to exchange them, but we don't have your size.

202

Customer:	OK, thanks. Where is the returns counter?
Salesperson:	It's on the third floor.
Customer:	Thanks for your help.
Salesperson:	You're welcome. Oh, tell them to give me a call if there's a problem.
Customer:	Thanks.
	...
Customer:	Hello, I bought these shoes here recently and one of the heels is coming off one of them already. I wanted to exchange them for a new pair, but you don't have them in my size any more. The salesperson told me to come here for a refund.
Employee:	Do you have your receipt?
Customer:	No, as I told the salesperson, I threw it away when I started wearing them.
Employee:	Did you pay cash or charge them?
Customer:	I paid cash.
Employee:	Can I see the shoes, please? ... When did you say you bought them?
Customer:	I don't know exactly; about three months ago, I guess.
Employee:	The best I can do is give you a store credit. I need an article number in order to get the price. Do you mind waiting till I call downstairs?
Customer:	No, no.
	...
Employee:	OK, mam. These were reduced last month, so I'll have to give you the sale price since you can't prove when you bought them.
Customer:	That's fine. How much is that?
Employee:	Nineteen ninety-five.
Customer:	Oh, that was a good sale; I think I paid 29.95!
Employee:	I'm sorry, I have no other choice.
Customer:	I know, that's OK.
	...
Employee:	OK, if you'll just sign here. ... And here's your credit.
Customer:	Thank you.
Employee:	You're welcome. Have a nice day.
Customer:	Same to you.

to come off   sich lösen
to prove   beweisen

a   to toss out   to throw away
b   to run out of something   to be out of something
c   to put something on your credit card to charge something
d   to be on sale   to be reduced

Lösungen

5

Professional Services	General Services	Entertainment	Travel services
acupuncture	bike + skate rentals	live music venue	real estate agency
attorney	beauty salon	movie theater	AAA
chiropractor	massage	comedy club	car rentals
dentist	tanning studio	dining out	accommodations
doctor	guided tours	playhouse	airline reservations
financial planner			

6

staff	product	location
fast	long-lasting	well-lit
cheerful	strong	well laid out
helpful	environmentally friendly	accessible
knowledgeable	good quality	conveniently located
accessible	well-built	spacious
courteous	reasonable	
friendly	flexible	
well-informed		
discreet		
reasonable		
patient		
flexible		
articulate		
polite		

7

a Die Behauptungen, die zutreffen:
1 All three situations involve a customer complaint.
4 All three customers are satisfied with the outcome of their conversations.
5 The language used in all three complaints is non-confrontational, that is, both customer and service employee want to resolve the problem in a way that is acceptable to both parties.
6 The tone of the dialogues is <u>polite</u>.

Tapescript
1

Laura:	Hello, can you help me?
Salesperson:	Yes.
Laura:	I bought this a couple of days ago and when I put it on for the first time I noticed this hole.
Salesperson:	Has it been washed?
Laura:	No.
Salesperson:	I don't think it's actually a hole; it looks like the seam has come apart. Have you got your receipt?

Laura:	No, I don't; I threw it out when I got home. I tried it on and it fit ok, so I didn't think I'd need it.
Salesperson:	Did you want to exchange it? Have you looked to see if we have another one?
Laura:	Yes, I've already checked; you don't have another one in my size, at least not in this colour.
Salesperson:	OK, well, I can only give you a store credit without the receipt.
Laura:	I'd prefer a cash refund; I'm just here on vacation and I'll be leaving in a couple of days.
Salesperson:	OK, just let me get the information from the tag on one of the other sweaters like it. Then I'll have to get the refund approved by the manager.
Laura:	Thanks, I appreciate it.
Salesperson:	You're welcome.

2

Karen:	... my name is Karen Hallowell. How may I help you?
Thomas:	Hello, my name is Thomas Stivick. I applied for a credit card ten days ago and still haven't received it.
Karen:	Normally it takes about three weeks for an application to be processed.
Thomas:	I know, but I'm only in the United States for a month and I told the person who helped me that I needed it as soon as possible. She promised to put a rush on it.
Karen:	What was your name again?
Thomas:	Thomas Stivick.
Karen:	Could you spell your last name for me, please?
Thomas:	S-t-i-v-i-c-k.
Karen:	I'm sorry, Mr. Stivick, but I don't see your name in the computer. Are you sure this is the credit card you applied for?
Thomas:	Positive.
Karen:	Do you know the number you called?
Thomas:	This one.
Karen:	Do you know the name of the person you spoke to?
Thomas:	No, I don't.
Karen:	Did you receive a pre-approved application in the mail?
Thomas:	Yes, I did.
Karen:	OK, well, the only thing I can do at this point is to take your information again and see that you application is processed immediately.
Thomas:	I'm not sure there's any point. I wanted to rent a car next week – that's what I need the credit card for.
Karen:	Well, assuming there's no problem with your application we can Fed Ex your card to you and you should have it by the beginning of next week.
Thomas:	Well, I guess I have no other choice, but I'd sure like to know what happened to my first application.
Karen:	I'll look into that, but I think you'll get your card sooner if we start over again.
Thomas:	OK.
Karen:	OK, what's your permanent address, Mr. Stivick? ...

3

Receptionist:	Reception, how can I help you?
Guest:	Hi, I'm in room 315 and the air conditioning is so loud I can't sleep. I turned it off, but there's no way to open the window. Could you send someone up to open it?
Receptionist:	I'm sorry, sir, but that's not possible. The windows don't open: fire regulations.

Lösungen

Guest:	Well, what am I supposed to do? It's impossible to sleep with it on.
Receptionist:	Have you tried turning it down?
Guest:	It was on the lowest setting. Besides, it was dripping on the floor.
Receptionist:	I'll send someone up to take a look at it in the morning.
Guest:	Are there any rooms without air conditioning?
Receptionist:	No, I'm sorry. All our rooms have air conditioning.
Guest:	But it's not even that hot outside and it was freezing in here.
Receptionist:	It's possible that the thermostat wasn't working correctly. I'll send someone from maintenance up. If we can't get if fixed immediately, would you be willing to move to another room?
Guest:	Now?
Receptionist:	Well, I think it will get pretty stuffy in your room if the air conditioning is turned off. On second thought, why don't I just move you now?
Guest:	OK, I guess that would be better than waiting for someone and then waiting to see if he can fix the air conditioning.
Receptionist:	I have a room on your floor, just a couple of doors down. Would that be OK?
Guest:	I guess so.
Receptionist:	I'll send someone up right away to help you move, Sir.
Guest:	Why don't you give me about ten minutes to get dressed and packed.
Receptionist:	Sure, take your time, Sir.

Dear Madam or Sir,

My wife and I stayed at your hotel from 29 June to 1. July and we (a) <u>wanted to tell</u> you that although we (b) <u>enjoyed staying</u> at the Wellington Inn once we did get a room, we think there is room for improvement at the reception.

When I called and made our reservations the person I spoke to (c) <u>promised to hold</u> our room until 9 o'clock as we knew we would be arriving late. Well, although we (d) <u>managed to arrive</u> on time, we were first told our room had been given to someone else. Apparently the person I had spoken to had (e) <u>forgotten to make</u> a note of my request to hold the room. The gentleman who was at the desk (f) <u>invited us to have</u> a drink in the lounge while he (g) <u>tried to straighten</u> things out. We would have preferred to go/going to our room as we had had a long drive, but (h) <u>agreed to give</u> him some time. We had hardly (i) <u>finished ordering</u> when he came and told us he had (j) <u>managed to find</u> us a double. The only problem was that it was on the street side and was quite loud. I categorically (k) <u>refused to be put</u> in a room no one else wanted! We (l) <u>continued to sip/sipping</u> our drinks while Mr. Singh (m) <u>tried again to work</u> something out. I give him a lot of credit for keeping his cool under the circumstances – I was not an easy guest!) After another ten minutes he returned and asked us if we (n) <u>minded staying</u> in two single rooms – just for the one night. We agreed and were moved into a lovely double the next day.

Certainly this was not a major catastrophe, but I think you (o) <u>need to look</u> at the way reservations are handled at your hotel so that this type of thing doesn't happen again. After a tiring trip the last thing you need is this kind of hassle. The incident was especially unfortunate since we were otherwise pleased with the accommodations and staff, who (p) <u>made us feel at home</u> whenever possible.

I (q) <u>hope to have been</u> of service to you and (r) <u>look forward to staying</u> at your hotel in the future.
Sincerely,
Jason and Amy Crenshaw

Lösungen

9

verb + -ing
enjoy doing something
finish doing something
(not) mind doing something
look forward to doing something
can't stand doing something

verb + to + infinitive
want to do something
promise to do something
manage to do something
forget to do something
try to do something
agree to do something
refuse to do something
need to do something
hope to do something

verb + -ing or verb + to + infinitive

prefer doing something
continue doing something
hate doing something
start doing something
stop doing something

prefer to do something
continue to do something
hate to do something
start to do something
stop to do something
   (Bedeutungsunterschied!)

verb + pronoun + to + infinitive
invite someone to do something
tell doing something

verb + pronoun + infinitive
make someone do something

10

Tapescript
a The salesperson told me to wait here for a refund.
   (verb + pronoun + *to* + infinitive)
b I'm a person who hates to wait. / I'm a person who hates waiting.
   (verb + *ing* or verb + *to* + infinitive)
c I threw the receipt away once I started wearing the shoes. (verb + *ing*)
d I really can't stand having to wait at the end of a long day. (verb + *ing*)
e We stopped assuming our reservations would be processed properly and started asking for a confirmation by fax. (verb + *ing* / verb + *ing* or verb + *to* + infinitive)
f I stopped to write down the name of the store. (verb + *to* + infinitive)

11

Die Verbkonstruktion **verb + *to* + infinitive** kommt am häufigsten vor, am seltensten kommt die Konstruktion **verb + pronoun + infinitive** vor.

12

a exchange   b came off   c Did ... pay cash   d Are out of   e prove   f are reduced   g sign

Lösungen

13

a told b made c don't mind d wants e can't stand f didn't mind g made

14

b I stopped to see what was on sale.
a I stopped looking for sales.

15

a to ask b asking c to come d relaxing e to send f to say g to call

16

a 1 I'm just looking, thank you.   3 I'd like to return this.
b 3 Have you got your receipt?
c 1 Thanks.   2 Thanks, I appreciate it.
d 3 I'd prefer a cash refund.
e 3 You're welcome.

17

Folgende Adjektive haben eine ähnliche Bedeutung:
idiosyncratic   one-of-a-kind
eccentric   quirky
Was haben sie mit diesem Thema zu tun? Sie beschreiben, was verloren geht, wenn alles vereinheitlicht wird.

19

a Uniformity brings convenience, but it also leads to monotony.

20

merchandise	**personnel**	**facility**
cereals	stock boy	aisle
detergents	checkout clerk	
pet food	company bigwig	
bottled water		
raisins		
green beans		
black olives		
kitchen utensils		

Lösungen

21

to decide	to make up one's mind
to rearrange	to put in a new place
to replace	to substitute
I'll be damned	(exclamation)
way	method
to display	to show
homogenization	uniformity
to be convinced	to be sure of something
hardware store	shop where tools are sold
to discover	to find out
nestled	sheltered
foothills	beginning of the mountains
patina	coating
nooks and crannies	hidden areas
eatery	restaurant
to peruse	to look slowly
to be in a hurry	to have little time
oxford cloth	type of material

22

cour·te·ous	u·ni·for·mi·ty	ac·u·punc·ture
re·ar·range	ho·mo·ge·ni·za·tion	chi·ro·prac·tor
re·place	pe·ruse	con·ve·nient·ly lo·cat·ed
damned	nooks and cran·nies	ac·ces·si·ble
sur·prise	pat·i·na	spa·cious
con·vinced	flex·i·ble	rea·so·na·ble
en·vi·ron·men·tal·ly friend·ly	real es·tate a·gen·cy	dis·creet
hard·ware store	ac·com·mo·da·tions	po·lite
nes·tled	knowl·ed·gea·ble	ar·tic·u·late

23

a	quirky	personality
b	idiosyncratic	way of doing things
c	cruel	surprise
d	creaking	floors
e	mind-numbing	uniformity
f	unique	opportunity
g	well-worn	sofa
h	handmade	toys

Lösungen

24

a decided b replace c convince d peruse e being in a hurry f rearrange g displays

25

a are contained b is taxed. d are sold e has been reduced g were displayed

26

a be redeemed b be used c be replaced d be made e be used f be presented g be redeemed

27

a is required b be approved c are based d was inspired e are prepared f be sent
g be delivered

28

a The manager was told that his contract would not be renewed.
b The Green Onion was named one of the ten best restaurants in the city (by Urban Magazine).
c The shop was closed six months ago for renovations.
d The last one was sold yesterday.
e It was designed Donna Karan.
f My appointment had to be postponed.
g The bread is baked on the premises.

29

a I'd like to return these pants/trousers.
b Would you mind waiting over there?
c I hope to see you again soon.
d They invited us to meet them after shopping.
e I hate to have to wait.
f I started to wear it/them recently.
g She told me I had to go to the third floor.

30 Mündliche Übungen

A

Setzen Sie die folgenden Sätze ins *past tense*.
1 Everything is rearranged.
   Everything was rearranged.
2 The cereals have been moved to where the detergents used to be.
   The cereals were moved to where the detergents used to be.
3 I understand the idiosyncratic way that things are displayed.
   I understand the idiosyncratic way that things were displayed.
4 A cruel little game is being played on me.
   A cruel little game was being played on me.

Lösungen

5 The town is nestled in the foothills.
The town was nestled in the foothills.
6 The shirts are shipped in boxes.
The shirts were shipped in boxes.
7 The store has been rudely rearranged.
The store was rudely rearranged.

B

Setzen Sie die folgenden Sätze ins *future tense*.

8 Returns are not accepted without a receipt.
Returns will not be accepted without a receipt.
9 The package was delivered this morning.
The package will be delivered this morning.
10 The appointment has to be cancelled.
The appointment will have to be cancelled.
11 The car must be returned to this location.
The car will have to be returned to this location.
12 The fitness studio wasn't opened this year.
The fitness studio won't be opened this year.
13 The clothes were designed by Calvin Klein.
The clothes will be designed by Calvin Klein.
14 Proof of purchase is required.
Proof of purchase will be required.

C

Setzen Sie die folgenden Sätze ins *present perfect*.

15 The dining hours were extended to midnight.
The dining hours have been extended to midnight.
16 The personal trainers were recruited from the local university.
The personal trainers have been recruited from the local university.
17 The shoes were reduced.
The shoes have been reduced.
18 The broken part was replaced.
The broken part has been replaced.
19 The last one was sold yesterday.
The last one has been sold.
20 The comedy club was reopened last month.
The comedy club has been reopened.
21 The return was approved by the manager.
The return has been approved by the manager.

D

Setzen Sie die folgenden Sätze ins Passiv. Die Zeitform bleibt dieselbe.

22 They cancelled the airline reservations.
The airline reservations were cancelled.
23 He charged the sweater.
The sweater was charged.

Lösungen

24 They've rearranged the grocery store.
The grocery store has been rearranged.
25 They have homogenized everything.
Everything has been homogenized.
26 They are going to replace the manager.
The manager is going to be replaced.
27 They won't accept the coupons.
The coupons won't be accepted.
28 She sold the tanning studio.
The tanning studio was sold.

Unit 7

2

a call prospective customers
b make appointments
c visit clients at their home
d give advice
e arrange financing
f do paperwork

Tapescript

Jake:	So, how did the interview go?
Barbara:	Well, pretty well, I think. I'll know in a couple of days.
Jake:	Are they interviewing others?
Barbara:	They didn't say so, but I got that impression.
Jake:	So tell me about the job. Is it something you think you'd enjoy doing?
Barbara:	I think so: I'm certainly going to take it if they offer it to me.
Jake:	Uhuh.
Barbara:	It's basically a sales job, partially on commission. I'd be working out of the office, but would probably be spending a good amount of time visiting customers.
Jake:	Selling what?
Barbara:	Furniture and other home furnishings, especially window treatments.
Jake:	Window treatments?
Barbara:	Yeah, you know, curtains, sheers, valances – stuff like that.
Jake:	Sheers? You lost me right after curtains.
Barbara:	Sheers are a type of curtain that are transparent; they cover the window and you usually keep them closed.
Jake:	I got ya. And what exactly are valances?
Barbara:	Valances are those things above windows that hide the curtain rods. Sometimes they're covered with the same material as the curtains, ya know?
Jake:	Like the ones Aunt Kit has?
Barbara:	Right.
Jake:	Anyway, you were telling me about the job.

Barbara:	Well, I'd have to call prospective customers and get them to agree to an appointment.
Jake:	Are we talking tele-marketing here?
Barbara:	Not exactly; the company gives me a list of names – mostly people that have bought from them before – and after that you're on your own. Once you've got an appointment you go out and talk to them, try to interest them in something, give them some decorating advice. The company has a really nice line of furniture, mostly custom-made.
Jake:	My kind of stuff, huh?
Barbara:	In your dreams!
Jake:	Do you get a discount?
Barbara:	I didn't ask, but I wouldn't be able to afford it even if I did get a discount.
Jake:	Pricey stuff, huh?
Barbara:	Top of the line. Anyway, if they decide to buy, you process their orders, suggest possible financing if they need it, and that's basically it.
Jake:	Sounds pretty good; what about benefits?
Barbara:	Well, I'd get the usual health benefits and vacation, plus a company car.
Jake:	What do you mean, you would?
Barbara:	Well, if I get the job.
Jake:	Oh yeah, well, if they know anything about anything, you'll get it.
Barbara:	Thanks for the vote of confidence. We'll see what happens!

3

to spend time	Zeit verbringen
to process an order	eine Bestellung bearbeiten

4

advise, help, wait on	a customer
make, keep, postpone, confirm, cancel, reschedule	an appointment
place, process, confirm, expedite, cancel	an order

5 (Lösungsvorschlag)

put together a resume
get recommendations
check the want ads
apply for a job / send in your resume
go for an interview
fill out an application
hear from the prospective employer
get the job / get a rejection
get a promotion / get demoted
get transferred
quit / get sacked/fired
look for a new job

Lösungen

secretary, headhunter, circus performer

Tapescript

1
It was my first day on the job, so one of my colleagues showed me the ropes. First she took me around and introduced me to the others in the department. After that she showed me my duties: First of all, I have to take incoming calls and put them through to the right people. Then I'm responsible for keeping track of the boss' appointments. Of course I have to do the correspondence and filing and generally organise the office. One thing I don't have to do is make coffee; there's a cafeteria open most of the day that takes care of that.
One of my other main responsibilities is travel planning: making hotel and plane reservations, making sure that members of the department have their travel documents on time and that we get the best rates from our travel agency. I'm also in charge of planning the odd conference during the year. Beyond that, I have to keep an eye on people's holidays, you know, co-ordinate them so that everyone's not away at the same time. And, well, I think that's about it, but then I think that's quite enough, don't you?

2
What do I do? Well, it seems like I spend most of my time on the phone with people; I'm either interviewing some or getting information about someone else. Of course sometimes I'm out drumming up business – talking to heads of personnel departments, finding out what kind of people they need and also learning about new developments in order to anticipate their needs in the future. But then it's back on the phone – networking, keeping up your contacts is everything in this business.

3
I guess you'd say I have an unusual job, but it seems like the most normal thing in the world for me: it's what my parents do and it's what I've known all my life. Of course it involves a lot of travel, and that has it's drawbacks, but it also means that you get to see new places and meet a lot of new people.
What do I do most days? Well, if we're not packing up or setting up, I'm usually training, and that takes up the best part of the day. And then of course there are the shows – that's what it's all about, that's what I live for.

real estate agent	driving instructor	sales assistant
travel agent	mechanic	photographer
undertaker	building contractor	university lecturer
electrician	police officer	public health inspector
maintenance engineer	headhunter	advertising executive
social worker	buyer	circus performer
interior decorator	medical technician	computer programmer
secretary	food-service employee	financial consultant

checking to see if the other person understands
Do you know what I mean?
Am I making myself clear?
Are you following me?
Do you understand what I'm saying?

signalling that you don't follow
Excuse me? / Pardon me?
What was that?
Sorry, I don't understand.
Sorry, I didn't get that.
Could you repeat that, please?

rephrasing something
What I'm trying to say is …
What I mean is …
It's a kind of / sort of …
It's used for …

expressing that you don't know how to say something
How do you say … in English?
I don't know the word in English.
I don't know what you call it in English.
What's the word for … in English?

9

a If you apply, you could get the job.
b If the stuff wasn't so pricey, I might buy something.
c If I get the job, I'll have to move.
d If the interview has gone better, I might have had a chance.
e If I knew what happened, I would be in a better position to help you.
f If I got a discount, I would reconsider.
g If you had dressed appropriately, you would have made a better impression.

10

a expanded   b sweat   c had reminded   d hadn't been   e got   f don't get   g thought

11

a at   b at   c in   d on   e to   f of   g in   h from   i to   j for

12

a spent   b will last   c consisted   d visited   e wasn't   f processed   g decorated

13

a colleagues   b department   c calls   d appointments   e correspondence   f responsibilities
g travel agency   h conference   i holidays

Lösungen

14 Mündliche Übungen

A
Vervollständigen Sie die *if*-Sätze, die Sie gleich hören werden, nach dem vorgegebenen Muster.

1. If you make a good impression, ...   get the job
   If you make a good impression, you'll get the job.
2. If I need your advice, ...   ask for it
   If I need your advice, I'll ask for it.
3. If I can't get anyone, ...   call you
   If I can't get anyone, I'll call you.
4. If you need help, ...   give you a hand
   If you need help, I'll give you a hand.
5. If you want, ...   pick you up
   If you want, I'll pick you up.
6. If you can't come,   they understand
   If you can't come, they'll understand.
7. If you have to go, ...   we clean up
   If you have to go, we'll clean up.

B
Vervollständigen Sie die *if*-Sätze, die Sie gleich hören werden, nach dem vorgegebenen Muster. Wiederholen Sie dabei keine Informationen, die bereits im ersten Satz mitgeteilt wurden.

8. I don't know if they're going to offer me the job.   take it
   If they do, I'll take it.
9. I don't know if they're going to invite me for an interview.   go
   If they do, I'll go.
10. I don't know if the products are good.   sell
    If they are, they'll sell.
11. I don't know if the order has been processed.   do it right away
    If it hasn't, I'll do it right away.
12. I don't know if she's going to ask me to help.   will
    If she does, I will.
13. I don't know if I get a discount.   be happy
    If I do, I'll be happy.
14. I don't know if they know anything about anything.   you get the job
    If they do, you'll get the job.

C
Sagen Sie, was Sie machen müssten, wenn Sie eine neue Stelle bekämen. Verwenden Sie dabei die Hinweise, die Sie hören.

15. If I got the job, ...   have to call prospective customers
    If I got the job, I'd have to call prospective customers.
16. If I got the job, ...   make my own appointments
    If I got the job, I'd have to make my own appointments.
17. If I got the job, ...   advise clients
    If I got the job, I'd have to advise clients.
18. If I got the job, ...   visit customers at their homes
    If I got the job, I'd have to visit customers at their homes.

Lösungen

19 If I got the job, ...   do a lot of paperwork
    If I got the job, I'd have to do a lot of paperwork.
20 If I got the job, ...   go to trade fairs
    If I got the job, I'd have to go to trade fairs.
21 If I got the job, ...   arrange financing for the clients
    If I got the job, I'd have to arrange financing for the clients.

D
Welche Ratschläge würden Sie geben? Verwenden Sie die Hinweise, die Sie hören.
22 If I were you, ...   go on holiday
    If I were you, I'd go on holiday.
23 If I were you, ...   ring the office
    If I were you, I'd ring the office.
24 If I were you, ...   cancel the appointment
    If I were you, I'd cancel the appointment.
25 If I were you, ...   ask for a company car
    If I were you, I'd ask for a company car.
26 If I were you, ...   redecorate the office
    If I were you, I'd redecorate the office.
27 If I were you, ...   ask about the health benefits
    If I were you, I'd ask about the health benefits.
28 If I were you, ...   try to make a good impression
    If I were you, I'd try to make a good impression.

E
Setzen Sie die folgenden Sätzen in die Vergangenheit.
29 If I had to move, I would.
    If I had had to move, I would have.
30 If I got the financing, I'd buy it.
    If I had got the financing, I would have bought it.
31 If I cancelled the order, I'd get my money back.
    If I had cancelled the order, I would have got my money back.
32 If the health benefits were better, I'd consider the job.
    If the health benefits had been better, I would have considered the job.
33 If your sales were better, you'd get a promotion.
    If your sales had been better, you would have got a promotion.
34 If I made an appointment, I wouldn't have to wait.
    If I had made an appointment, I wouldn't have had to wait.
35 If you gave me the order, I'd process it as quickly as possible.
    If I had given me the order, I would have processed it as quickly as possible.

17

c   Worrying gets in the way of success.

Lösungen

18

to sweat	(hier:) to worry
in a snit	angry
Chill out!	Take it easy!
consultant	advisor
to catch up with someone	(hier:) to speak to
to counsel	to give advice
corporate executive	head of a company
lighten up	relax
to expand	to grow
small stuff	things that aren't important
co-worker	colleague
annoying	disturbing
to remind	to cause to remember
despite	in spite of
to get in the way	to hinder
ludicrous	ridiculous
stride	step
demanding	asking a lot
to drive someone nuts	to get on someone's nerves
to be caught up in something	to be occupied with something
roughly	approximately
to get mad	to get angry
anxiety	fear
worth	value
deadline	date something must be finished
to spin your wheels	to waste your time
source	origin

19

pricey	furniture, hotel, restaurant, material
transparent	motives, seat covers, piece of clothing, material
prospective	job, employer, buyer, order, partner
custom-made	furniture, seat covers, piece of clothing, material

20

a sweat   b remind   c did ... get mad   d spinning your wheels   e driving me nuts   f 's caught up in
g get in the way

Lösungen

21

a to catch up with a friend
b to remind someone to do something
c to sweat an interview
d to expand your business
e to be caught up in your work
f to drive someone nuts with an annoying habit
g to spin your wheels at a job

22

a If she asks me, I'll go.
b If I needed money, I'd ask you for it.
c If I can't get anyone, I'll give you a ring.
d If you need help, I'll give you a hand.
e If you want me to, I'll pick you up.
f If you can't come, we'll understand.
g If you have to go, we'll clean up.

23

a 1 Sure.   3 What I said was …
b 2 I think so.   3 I'm not sure.
c 1 I think it's …   2 Neither do I.
d 3 What I meant was …
e 2 I see.   3 I know what you mean.
f 2 I see.   3 I know what you mean.

24

a–3, b–3, c–1, d–1, e–1, f–1, g–1

25

a If I were you, I'd order new curtains.
b Do you know what I mean? – I think so.
c If they give me a company car, I'll take / I'm going to take the job.
d If I had made an appointment, I'd have to postpone it now.
e Stop it, you're driving me nuts.
f May I remind you that she's a pretty demanding co-worker.

Lösungen

Unit 8

2

a true   b true   c true   d false   e false   f true   g false

Tapescript

Andrew:	Hey Diana!
Diana:	Hi, Andrew. Don't see you around these parts too often.
Andrew:	No, I've been working over in Rockledge lately, not to mention travelling a lot.
Diana:	What have you been doing over in Rockledge?
Andrew:	Working with a project team over there. We're developing a marketing strategy for the new magazine.
Diana:	Sounds interesting. How far along are you?
Andrew:	Oh, we're just about finished. I'll be back in my office here starting next week, which brings me to why I'm here. I thought maybe you could give me some advice.
Diana:	About what?
Andrew:	Well, as I said, I've been travelling a lot more and I think it's time I got a notebook.
Diana:	So you can take your data with you?
Andrew:	Well, not only that: I want to be able to get my e-mail wherever I am. It's kind of inconvenient not having access.
Diana:	I know what you mean. What kind of notebook did you have in mind?
Andrew:	That's what I wanted to talk to you about; you're the expert. I'd either buy the wrong thing – or the next day something new would come out and what I bought would become totally obsolete.
Diana:	Well, if you let that stop you, you'll never get one. There's always something new on the horizon.
Andrew:	I guess you're right. What would you recommend?
Diana:	Well, it depends; what do you need it for besides e-mail?
Andrew:	Um, well, I want to keep my accounts with me.
Diana:	So you'll need spreadsheets?
Andrew:	Yeah.
Diana:	What about access to the server and applications here?
Andrew:	Yeah, definitely.
Diana:	Well, you're probably going to need almost as much RAM as you've got on your desktop computer.
Andrew:	Is that possible?
Diana:	Sure, it's just a matter of cost. What's your budget?
Andrew:	Well, I don't know yet; I thought I would get an idea of what I need and how much that costs before I put in a request.
Diana:	Well, my guess is you're going to need between two and three thousand.
Andrew:	That much?
Diana:	Well, I could talk to our supplier; I might be able to get you a deal.
Andrew:	Do you think you could get them to quote a price? It'd be a good idea to get something in writing.
Diana:	You know what: why don't you give them a call yourself? That way you can tell them exactly what you need.

Andrew:	Good idea. Do you have a name and number for me?
Diana:	Sure. Let me see … I have it right here: Tom O'Connell. 555 3952.
Andrew:	What's the name of the place?
Diana:	The Hardware Store.
Andrew:	Is this a serious outfit?
Diana:	Believe me, this guy know his stuff – and the prices are competitive.
Andrew:	OK, I'll give him a call and see if he can fax me some info.
Diana:	And mention my name.
Andrew:	Will do. Thanks a lot, Diana.
Diana:	Not at all; glad to help. … If I were you I'd think about how much you want to spend.
Andrew:	Um, do you think it would be a good idea to check the price somewhere else after they give me a quote?
Diana:	I find they're the best around price-wise, but, sure, it can't hurt to shop around. Just be sure you're comparing exactly the same model.
Andrew:	Right. Is it alright if I get back to you after I've done my homework?
Diana:	Sure, no problem.
Andrew:	Great, talk to you later then.
Diana:	Bye, bye.
Andrew:	Bye.

to recommend   empfehlen
to shop around   Preise vergleichen

a   to put in   a request
b   to quote   a price
c   to know   your stuff
d   to develop   a strategy
e   to get   a deal
f   to do   your homework
g   to mention   someone's name
h   to have   access

5

phrasal verb   quote
Adjektiv   lately
Verb/Substantiv   recommend

Lösungen

6

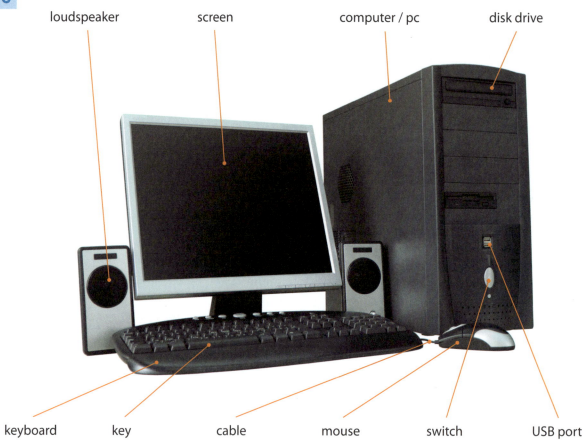

loudspeaker, screen, computer / pc, disk drive, keyboard, key, cable, mouse, switch, USB port

7

asking for advice
I thought maybe you could give me some advice.
What would you recommend?
That's what I wanted to talk to you about; you're the expert.
Do you think it would be a good idea to ...?

advising
I find that ...
That way you can ...
If I were you I'd ...
Well, you're probably going to need ...
What kind of notebook did you have in mind?
Why don't you ...?
My guess is you're going to need ...
It can't hurt to ...

8

It's just a matter of cost.　　Is that possible?
　　　　　　　　　　　　　Is this a serious outfit?

9

I'd either buy the wrong thing – or the next day something new would come out and what I bought would become totally obsolete.

222

10

Dialog 2

Tapescript

1

Rita:	Jamie, have you met Linda?
Jamie:	No, I don't think so. Hi, Linda.
Linda:	Hi Jamie.
Rita:	Linda is from Chicago.
Jamie:	Oh, really? What do you do there?
Linda:	I work for a school book publisher.
Jamie:	Oh, that's interesting. What do you do?
Linda:	I'm an editor.
Jamie:	Really? My daughter majored in English and Spanish and is doing her student teaching now, but she'd really like to get into the publishing business. How would she go about that?
Linda:	Do you mean educational publishing, like what I do?
Jamie:	Yes.
Linda:	Well, it's pretty difficult to get into the business right out of school. Most educational publishers want teaching experience.
Jamie:	So she should look for a job in the school system?
Linda:	I would. And then after a couple of years, if she's still interested, she can apply to some of the better-known companies.
Jamie:	Is there somewhere she can get a list of textbook companies?
Linda:	If she does a search on the net she'll find them.
Jamie:	Oh, that's a good idea.
Linda:	It certainly has made getting the information you need easier.
Jamie:	I guess; I don't have much experience with it myself.
Rita:	Jamie, can you give me a hand over here?
Jamie:	Well, thank you for your advice. It's been very nice talking to you.
Linda:	You're welcome. Same here.
Jamie:	See you later, I hope.
Linda:	Bye.

2

Al:	Hello?
Bettina:	Hi Al, it's Bettina. How are you?
Al:	Can't complain. And you?
Bettina:	Really good.
Al:	Glad to hear it! Say, did I see you over in Chestnut Street last week – on Tuesday, I think?
Bettina:	Tuesday? No, I don't think so. I was nearby, but not in Chestnut Street.
Al:	You know, now that I think about it, it was probably Locust Street.
Bettina:	OK, that sounds more like it. Yeah, that was probably me you saw.
Al:	I was driving by on my way to my dentist's …
Bettina:	You have a dentist near there?
Al:	Yeah, in Pine. Why?
Bettina:	I've been looking for one near work. Is he any good?

Lösungen

Al: It's a she, and she's great.
Bettina: Fantastic, can you give me her number?
Al: Uh, I'll have to call you back. I have to look for it.
Bettina: That's alright. What's her name; I can look it up in the phone book.
Al: Bowen, Margaret Bowen.
Bettina: Great, thanks a lot.
Al: Glad to help.
Bettina: Now I'll tell you why I called …

3

Harry: Hey Beau, you've been to Tampa before, haven't you?
Beau: Yeah, why?
Harry: Well, we're planning to visit Anita's parents there in May and I was wondering if you could give us some advice on what to do when we're there. You know, places to go, things to see, places to eat and so forth.
Beau: Well, how long are you going to be there?
Harry: About a week, I guess.
Beau: Well, I would certainly recommend Busch Gardens.
Harry: What's that?
Beau: It's a theme park, kind of a combination safari park and amusement park.
Harry: Sounds pretty neat.
Beau: It is, especially for the kids.
Harry: Good rides?
Beau: The best.
Harry: Great! Anything else?
Beau: Well, there's the aquarium, and the beach in Clearwater is nice.
Harry: How far is that?
Beau: Clearwater?
Harry: Yeah.
Beau: About half an hour from Tampa. Depends of course on where you're staying.
Harry: What about restaurants?
Beau: Well, I don't remember any names – Emily might. There were a couple of good ones. Why don't you just ask Anita's parents?
Harry: Well, I guess we could, but I think their tastes are a little more conservative than ours.
Beau: What you ought to do is get hold of one of those local papers, the kind you get for free at the entrance to supermarkets and places like that.
Harry: Yeah, I know what you mean. Good idea. I'll make it a point to look for one as soon as we get there. Thanks for the tip.
Beau: Hey, glad to be of service.
Harry: Say hello to Emily for me.
Beau: Will do, and say hello to Anita.
Harry: You bet.
Beau: Take care.
Harry: You, too, bye.
Beau: Bye-bye.

Lösungen

11

a Well, you're probably going to need almost as much RAM as you've got on your desktop computer here.
b Well, my guess is you're going to need between two and three thousand.
c You know what: why don't you give them a call yourself?
d I find they're the best around price-wise, but, sure, it can't hurt to shop around.

12

info(rmation), homework

13

a knows   b mention   c check   d do   e put   f get   g have

14

a 2 We're just about finished.   3 Not very far.
b 2 I know what you mean.
c 1 It depends.   2 For you?
d 1 That's true.   2 I guess you're right.
e 1 No problem.   2 Glad to help.   3 Not at all.

15

a She knows her stuff; I'll ask her for information.
b I thought she could give me some advice.
c Have they done their homework yet?
d The news isn't good.
e Have I (already) mentioned that the equipment is new?

16 Mündliche Übungen

A

Hören Sie die folgenden Sätze. Sind die Substantive, die vorkommen, zählbar?

1	We had a lot of fun.	*fun* is not countable
2	Do you have access to them?	*access* is not countable
3	What was her request?	*request* is countable
	She made a request.	
4	She gave me a lot of help.	*help* is not countable
5	Do you think you can get me a deal?	*deal* is countable
	We made the two best deals possible.	
6	I need to get some sleep.	*sleep* is not countable
7	The price is much too high.	*price* is countable
	Did you shop around and compare prices?	

Lösungen

B
Die folgenden Sätze enthalten nicht zählbare Substantive. Deuten Sie eine größere Menge an, indem Sie den Ausdruck *a lot of* verwenden.

8 She gave me some good advice.
She gave me a lot of good advice.
9 We have some homework for next week.
We have a lot of homework for next week.
10 There's still some luggage in the lobby.
There's still a lot of luggage in the lobby.
11 You're going to need some money.
You're going to need a lot of money.
12 I'll need some more information.
I'll need a lot more information.
13 My job requires some travel.
My job requires of lot of travel.
14 You have to have patience to work with him.
You have to have a lot of patience to work with him.

C
Auch die folgenden Sätze enthalten nicht zählbare Substantive. Deuten Sie eine große Menge an, indem Sie das Wort *much* verwenden.

15 I don't think he has equipment.
I don't think he has much equipment.
16 Have you done any housework since you've been home?
Have you done much housework since you've been home?
17 So far he hasn't asked for any help.
So far he hasn't asked for much help.
18 I don't have access to them.
I don't have much access to them.
19 I don't have any office furniture.
I don't have much office furniture.
20 I can't give you advice in that area.
I can't give you much advice in that area.
21 I haven't heard any news.
I haven't heard much news.

19

c Americans are doing more now, but that has not necessarily improved the quality of life.

20

to enslave	versklaven
to hype	hochjubeln
multitasking	mehrere Aufgaben gleichzeitig erledigen
assumption	Annahme
apostle	Anhänger

relentless	unbarmherzig
suspect	verdächtig
tenet	Prinzip
to dictate	vorschreiben
to keep up	(hier:) mithalten
frantic	hektisch
to lambaste	heftig kritisieren
to toss	werfen, schmeißen
feeble	schwach
demise	(hier:) Ende
grimly	grimmig, streng
to lament	beklagen
to slash	(hier:) drastisch reduzieren
to condense	komprimieren
to nourish	ernähren
to take in	(hier:) anschauen
alarming	beunruhigend
haste	Eile
to put in hours	(hier:) arbeiten
to yak	quasseln
astounding	erstaunlich
patience	Geduld
mind-popping	erstaunlich
impact	Einfluss
to bemoan	beklagen
attention span	Konzentrationsfähigkeit

21

noun	verb	adjective	adverb
multitasking	hype	suspect	grimly
apostle	enslave	relentless	
assumption	dictate	feeble	
tenet	lament	frantic	
demise	slash	astounding	
haste	keep up	alarming	
patience	condense	mind-popping	
attention span	nourish		
impact	lambaste		
	take in		
	toss		
	yak		
	put in hours		
	bemoan		

Lösungen

22

mul·ti·<u>task</u>ing
dis·con·<u>cert</u>·ing
as·<u>sump</u>·tion
a·<u>pos</u>·tle
en·<u>slave</u>
dic·<u>tate</u>

con·<u>dense</u>
la·<u>ment</u>
<u>sus</u>·pect
as·<u>tound</u>·ing
be·<u>moan</u>
<u>pa</u>·tience

23

a 3 television   b 3 over   c 3 your attention span   d 2 a lot of chores   e 3 a suspect
f 2 an impact

24

a keep up   b slash   c take in   d condense   e toss   f dictate   g put in

25

a feeble   strong   d disconcerting   reassuring
b grim   cheerful   e obsolete   up-to-date
c frantic   relaxed   f competitive   overpriced

26

a I've got some disconcerting news for you.
b She doesn't have much luggage.
c You need a lot of patience to deal with him.
d I've got to get some / a lot of information before making a decision.
e Some knowledge of computers is recommended.
f I think there's some / a piece of furniture missing.
g Is there any / much traffic on the roads?

27

a true   b true   c true   d false   e true   f false   g false

Tapescript

I'm one of those people you read about in the paper all the time – you know, multitasking yuppie workaholics, the ones whose lives are dictated by their work and wouldn't know what to do with themselves if they had an afternoon off. Well, I may look like one of that species to others, but I don't feel like one. It's true that I don't have a lot of free time any more, but that's only temporary. I do have a life outside the office – although you wouldn't know it recently. Yes, I do take my notebook home with me in the evening, and work is a large part of my life, but once this big project I'm working on is over, I'm going to leave it at the office where it belongs. I, for one, couldn't keep up this pace indefinitely. Even I find it disconcerting that I work this much, and I know it's had a negative impact on my relationship, and I find that somewhat alarming, but as I said, I don't plan to continue like this – at least that's what I keep telling myself. What can I say? I like my work and yes, sometimes it gets a little frantic, but for the moment, I wouldn't have it any other way.

28

a   I find the prices pretty competitive.
b   What would you advise? – It couldn't hurt to talk to her.
c   You'll need a notebook for your work.
d   If I were you, I'd shop around/compare prices.
e   It depends on how much you can spend.
f   Can I call you back when I've done my chores/housework?

Unit 9

1 + 2

A–1, **D**–2, **G**–3, **B**–4, **F**–5, **C**–6, **E**–7

Tapescript
MODERATOR:
Thank you for tuning in to this edition of Give and Take. My name is Roger Burrows and tonight we're going to talk about the status of feminism in today's society. It's been a couple of decades since women went out and demonstrated for their rights. What we're asking tonight is: where has the movement got us, is it still relevant and if so, where will it take us next? My guests in the studio tonight are people just like you. They've got an opinion and they're here to express it. So, without further ado, let's open the mikes. Let me ask this gentleman in the first row: Sir, I'm guessing you're about 35 Is that right?
SPEAKER 1:
Yes, that's close enough.
MODERATOR:
So you grew up in the age of the feminist movement, you've been influenced by it one way or another all your life, I assume. Tell us a little about yourself and how you feel about the topic.
SPEAKER 1: (man)
Yes, well, I'm married and work, and my wife works, too.
MODERATOR:
Excuse me, how long have you been married?
SPEAKER 1: (man)
Um, we've been married for about eight years, and we've been sharing the household chores and taking care of the kids from the beginning. We're equal – but not the same – and I think we both benefit from that – no, I'd say we all benefit!
MODERATOR:
Sir?
SPEAKER 2: (man)
Get real! How are you supposed to help out with the housework, look after the kids and compete in the work force all at the same time?! I don't know about you, but there are only 24 hours in my day! I know it's not the politically correct thing to say, but I think things were better for everyone when women stayed home and looked after the house and the children.
MODERATOR:
I think the woman over here would like to say something.

Lösungen

SPEAKER 3: (woman)
Not "help out with" the housework and the kids, but take responsibility for them, just like women have been doing all along. We're living in the 21st century, or haven't you heard? The days when you can relegate women to a fixed role are gone, and I, for one, am glad they are. Women are as capable as men – if not more so – in most fields, so why shouldn't they be out there competing with men?

SPEAKER 2:
That sounds just fine in theory, but it's the children who suffer in an arrangement like that, isn't it. Who's home giving them the love and attention they need? A paid caregiver? Or are they left to themselves? It's no wonder that children are turning out the way they are, considering the lack of guidance they're getting! I think society as a whole is suffering as a result of the "gains" women have made.

SPEAKER 3:
Wake up and smell the coffee! Women are out of the kitchen to stay and men had just better get used to the fact. The problem is that society in general – and men in particular – have not changed along with women. You make a valid point when you say that children suffer from lack of attention, but who said that men can't provide that attention? Why is it always assumed that women are responsible for the children, even when they work outside the home?

MODERATOR:
The woman in the last row.

SPEAKER 4: (woman)
I couldn't agree more. The working world is set up by and for men, and men only. As long as we as a society do not bring about changes in the workplace, there will be no real equality, no genuine advancement.

SPEAKER 3:
Right you are! Shorter work hours not just for women, but for men, too, so that they can be home doing their fair share, and time off for Dad when the children are sick – things like that are needed.

SPEAKER 2:
And who's going to pay for all these benefits? The work week has been getting shorter for decades now, but we're finally beginning to realise that you have to compete globally, and we can't compete if we're all home taking care of the kids, can we?

SPEAKER 3:
You still don't get it, do you? We're not talking about less work, we're talking about a redistribution of the existing work. It just doesn't make sense that the worlds of a husband and wife are so often so different. What have they got in common? It's no wonder they drift apart after a while, is it?

MODERATOR:
I'm afraid we're going to have to interrupt for a commercial break, but don't go away, we'll be opening up our lines to our viewers at home.

a How would you characterise the participants in the discussion?

	shy	moderate	outspoken
Speaker 1		x	
Speaker 2			x
Speaker 3			x
Speaker 4		x	

Lösungen

b How would you characterise the following expressions?

	polite	neutral	(too) direct
Get real!			x
Wake up and smell the coffee!			x
I couldn't agree more.	x		
Right you are!		x	
That sounds just fine in theory, but …		x	
You still don't get it, do you?			x

4

| field | Bereich |
| commercial break | Werbespot |

5

a	to put in	a request
b	to quote	a price
c	to know	your stuff
d	to develop	a strategy
e	to get	a deal
f	to do	your homework

6

a	Expressing an opinion	3
b	Agreement	2
c	Disagreement	1 7 8
d	Uncertainty	4 5
e	Rephrasing something	6

7

Direct: I disagree. / I'm afraid I don't agree. / I beg to differ!
Indirect: Yes, but … / That may be true, but … / I see what you mean, but …

8

a true   b true   c true   d false   e true

Tapescript
A: But do you really think there needs to be a law forcing people to wear a helmet? Don't you think that's something that should be left up to the individual?
B: I don't know. Look at all the injuries caused by people not wearing helmets.
A: Accidents happen all the time though. Helmets don't stop accidents.
B: True, but they do prevent a lot of injuries.
A: Well, I don't know if they prevent injuries …
B: I guess I should have said reduce the seriousness of the injuries.

Lösungen

A: I understand what you're saying, but I think in the final analysis, people have to take responsibility for their own actions.
B: I agree in theory ...
A: But ...?
B: Except that a lot of times it's others who have to bear the responsibility.
A: What do you mean?
B: Well, a long time ago I was hitchhiking – back in my youth – and a young woman picked me up who was just coming back from visiting her husband in hospital. He was being treated there for major head injuries incurred in a motorcycle accident. She started telling me about how it had affected their lives. She said that if he was ever able to come home she would be his nurse, his caregiver rather than his wife 'cause he had permanent brain damage. And how it was really difficult for their little daughter 'cause she couldn't understand why her father didn't recognise her. ... Ever since then I've thought differently about the subject.
A: I hadn't really thought about it like that. I guess you have a point.
B: To be honest, I've been telling that story for the last ten years and I haven't heard any really good arguments against helmets – or against laws making you wear them.
A: Actually, the only ones I can think of aren't really good ones: laziness and vanity, I guess.
B: I think you're absolutely right!

9

A: I don't think women should be **relegated** to the kitchen.
B: I don't **either**, but do you really think that's still the case?
A: **Well**, I'm afraid that it is sometimes.
B: I think that's the way it **used to be**, but times have changed.
A: Sure, things have got better, but women are still the principle **caregivers**.
B: I certainly can't **disagree** with you there.
A: It's time men **took responsibility** for children and senior citizens.
B: Really!

10

a for a month   since you called
b since we started work   for more than a decade
c for ages   for 24 hours
d since/for 2000   for the summer
e since breakfast   since Christmas
f since half past ten since I met her
g for half an hour   since May

232

Lösungen

11

a have been
b has had
c have been living
d have been listening
e has disagreed
f have ... been looking after
g have been considering

12

a 2 I suppose.
b 3 What I mean is ...
c 1 I'm not really sure.   2 Yes, but ...
d 2 It seems to me that ...
e 2 I disagree.   3 Well, actually, ...

13 Mündliche Übungen

A
Verwandeln Sie den Satz, den Sie gleich hören werden, und benutzen Sie dabei die Hinweise, die im Anschluss gegeben werden. Achtung: Das zu verändernde Element wechselt ständig; es gilt also: Am Ball bleiben!

1 I've been living here for two years.   February
   I've been living here since February.
2 I've been living here since February.   we
   We've been living here since February.
3 We've been living here since February.   work
   We've been working here since February.
4 We've been working here since February.   from the start
   We've been working here from the start.
5 We've been working here from the start.   months
   We've been working here for months.
6 We've been working here for months.   she
   She's been working here for months.
7 She's been working here for months.   the beginning of the year
   She's been working here the since beginning of the year.

B
Dasselbe Prinzip noch einmal! Verwandeln Sie den Satz, den Sie gleich hören werden, und benutzen Sie dabei die Hinweise, die im Anschluss gegeben werden.

8 His attitude has been changing for a while now.   our discussion
   His attitude has been changing since our discussion.
9 His attitude has been changing since our discussion.   beliefs
   His beliefs have been changing since our discussion.
10 His beliefs have been changing since our discussion.   behaviour
   His behaviour has been changing since our discussion.

Lösungen

11 His behaviour has been changing since our discussion.   disconnected
His behaviour has been disconnected since our discussion.
12 His behaviour has been disconnected since our discussion.   weeks
His behaviour has been disconnected for weeks.
13 His behaviour has been disconnected for weeks.   her
Her behaviour has been disconnected for weeks.
14 Her behaviour has been disconnected for weeks.   she started working here
Her behaviour has been disconnected since she started working here.

C
Auf die Frage, wie lange Sie beispielsweise schon in Köln leben, können Sie folgende Antworten geben: seit Februar, oder: seit 2 Jahren. Einmal nennen Sie den Zeitpunkt, einmal den Zeitraum, immer benutzen Sie „seit". Das Englische dagegen hat für jeden der Fälle ein anderes Wort. Es heißt: *since February*, aber *for 2 months*. Probieren Sie es mal aus: Beantworten Sie die Fragen mit der vorgegebenen Zeitangabe.

15 How long have you been drifting apart?   July
Since July.
16 How long have you been competing?   1999
Since 1999.
17 How long have you been considering moving?   a couple of years
For a couple of years.
18 How long have you been discussing the point?   an hour
For an hour.
19 How long have you been looking after the kids?   school ended
Since school ended.
20 How long have you been promoting the cause?   a long time
For a long time.
21 How long have you been suffering from their behaviour?   last year
Since last year.

16

c   Both men and women would be more healthy and live longer if men examined their role in society.

17

aging	alternd
longevity	Langlebigkeit
to increase	erhöhen
belief	Glaube
addictive	süchtig machend
behaviour	Benehmen
to damage	schaden
to shorten	kürzen
to recognize	erkennen
pattern	Muster
evidence	Beweis(material)
societal	gesellschaftlich

to continue	weitermachen
bulk	Hauptanteil
elderly	älter(er/e/es)
harm	Schaden
well-being	Wohlbefinden
to portray	darstellen
to promote	fördern, werben für
attitude	Einstellung
to lend themselves to	sich eignen zu
to nurture	hegen
violence	Gewalt
disconnected	losgelöst
delusion	Irrglauben
invulnerability	Unverwundbarkeit
risk	Risiko
to measure	messen

18

recognize, lend ... to, nurture

19

	noun	verb	adjective	adverb
a	increase	to increase	increased/ increasing	increasingly
b	addiction	to be addicted	addicting	–
c	damage	to damage	damaged/damaging	damagingly
d	measure	to measure	measurable	measurably

20

a	increase	decrease
b	shorten	lengthen
c	damage	promote
d	well-being	harm
e	aged	youthful
f	invulnerability	vulnerability
g	disconnected	connected

21

e to harm   1 your attitude

Lösungen

22

ag·ed
mea·su·ra·bly
well-be·ing
lon·gev·i·ty
com·mer·cial
re·spon·si·bil·i·ty

ad·dic·ted
in·creased
dam·ag·ing
be·lief
rec·og·nise
vi·o·lence

dis·con·nect·ed
vul·ner·a·bil·i·ty
por·tray
be·hav·ior
ca·pa·ble
com·pete

23

a behaviour, guidance   b longevity   c portray   d promote   e addictive   f consider
g risk, invulnerable

24

a for   b since   c for   d since   e since   f since   g for

25

a I think we have all profited from the women's movement.
b Don't you think that men have taken on more responsibility?
c It's difficult to say.
d I know what you mean, but I doubt whether his behaviour will change.
e I've been looking after the children for two years. – Me, too.

Unit 10

1 + 2

Text über Einwanderung
demography
alien
ethnic
minority
immigrants
assimilate
ethnicity
generation
national
English-speaking
identity

Text über Essen
fondue
pot
stew
stock
fresh
culinary
weight
ingredients
salad bowl
core
mixture
bland
lumpy

Lösungen

3

a 1 an American
b 2 ingredients in stew
c 1 In a fondue the ingredients blend together.
d 1 There is a difference between the second and third wave of immigration to the US.

4

bland   gelatin, …
lumpy   pudding, soup, …
fresh   fruit, vegetables, bread, …

5

a generation   b immigration, immigrant   c mixture   d arrival   e identity   f beginning   g weight
h assimilation

6

de·mog·ra·phy   in·gre·di·ent
de·vel·op   Prot·es·tant
be·gin·ning   mix·ture
pro·cess   im·mi·grant
gen·e·ra·tion   a·broad
eth·ni·ci·ty   es·pe·cial·ly

7

a The snow is beginning to melt/~~melting~~.
e The weather is starting to affect/~~affecting~~ our mood.
g I was beginning to think/~~thinking~~ you would never get here.

8

a slowly   b simply   c really   d usually   e quickly   f poorly   g well

9

a greatly   b ethnically   c freshly   d rapid   e newly   f nationally

237

Lösungen

10

a At the moment we're living in a small apartment on the West side.
b She answered our questions in a friendly manner.
c We are planning to do the city like real tourists.
d Last year a Mexican restaurant opened near the bus stop.
e I suddenly realized that she was standing next to me.
f I spoke French fluently when I was a child.
g Eventually I hope to find a new job in another area.

11 Mündliche Übungen

A

Ergänzen Sie die Sätze, die Sie hören, mit dem vorgegebenen Adverb.

1 Things have begun to change. — suddenly
  Things have suddenly begun to change.
2 The fondue in the melting pot has become more like a stew. — recently
  The fondue in the melting pot has recently become more like a stew.
3 The number of immigrants is increasing. — rapidly
  The number of immigrants is rapidly increasing.
4 Many immigrants have not been assimilated. — yet
  Many immigrants have not yet been assimilated.
5 The new immigrants have affected American society. — profoundly
  The new immigrants have profoundly affected American society.
6 Immigrants come from developing countries. — usually
  Immigrants usually come from developing countries.
7 The new immigrants will be assimilated. — probably
  The new immigrants will probably be assimilated.

B

Ergänzen Sie die Sätze, die Sie hören, mit der vorgegebenen adverbialen Ergänzung.

8 My grandparents moved here from Ireland. — at the turn of the century
  My grandparents moved here from Ireland at the turn of the century.
9 They came with other family members. — on a ship
  They came with other family members on a ship.
10 They settled in Philadelphia. — before my father was born
  They settled in Philadelphia before my father was born.
11 There were already a lot of Irish immigrants in the city. — at that time
  There were already a lot of Irish immigrants in the city at that time.
12 They moved to the suburbs. — a generation later
  They moved to the suburbs a generation later.
13 Do you know where your family was? — around the turn of the century
  Do you know where your family was around the turn of the century?
14 That kind of information is often lost. — in the course of time
  That kind of information is often lost in the course of time.

Lösungen

C
Ergänzen Sie die Sätze, die Sie hören, mit den vorgegebenen adverbialen Ergänzungen.

15 My parents have been living in Florida. — happily, for seven years
    My parents have been living happily in Florida for seven years.
16 Spanish-speaking people have become a large minority. — gradually, in the last decades
    Spanish-speaking people have gradually become a large minority in the last decades.
17 My family is from Italy. — originally
    My family is originally from Italy.
18 The vast wave of immigrants — probably, in the coming years will continue.
    The vast wave of immigrants will probably continue in the coming years.
19 I've been considering moving. — for some time, to California
    I've been considering moving to California for some time.
20 We've lived abroad. — in one place or another, always
    We've always lived abroad in one place or another.
21 I'm going to Mexico. — probably, next week
    I'm probably going to Mexico next week.

12

a true   b false   c true   d true   e false   f false   g true.   h false   i true

Tapescript

To an assimilated American of my generation, this drab working-class town of Flushing administers a big dose of culture shock: among the people on the crowded pavement, not the least sound of English can be heard, and few western characters are found on the shop signs, carefully segregated between Chinese and Korean. At the greengrocer's, five out of six vegetables are unrecognisable.

One recent sweltering day I repeatedly asked passers-by for directions to the public library (which was within sight, had I only known it). I found no English-speakers among them.

First I tried those closest (mainly Asian), then I searched for those with visibly European features, but they turned out to be Russians. I looked in vain for a black American (who, I thought, would surely share my language). But most blacks in Queens are also immigrants, many of them Spanish-speaking.

In the end I found an Indian newsagent (South Asians have created something of an economic monopoly in that business), and he pointed to the library. The staff says it is the busiest in the country – not the least because of all those Flushing residents clamouring to learn English.

Later I ate lunch in a Chinese restaurant (where the only printed English was in the fortune cookies), and watched as a Chinese woman scolded her five young children – only to hear them answering back in English, and throwing food with forks instead of chopsticks.

13

as·sim·i·lat·ed	ad·min·is·ter	char·ac·ters	seg·re·gat·ed	oc·cu·pa·tion
re·peat·ed·ly	A·sian	Eu·ro·pe·an	ec·o·nom·ic	res·i·dents

Lösungen

14

a drab   b working-class   c crowded   d characters   e unrecognisable   f sweltering   g repeatedly   h features   i fortune cookies

15

noun	adjective	adverb
characters	drab	repeatedly
features	working-class	
fortune cookies	crowded	
	unrecognisable	
	sweltering	

16

a to administer a dose of culture shock
b to search for those with visibly European features
c to turn out to be Russians
d to look for in vain
e to point to the library
f to clamour to learn English
g to scold her five young children
h to answer back in English

17

a 2 feinsäuberlich getrennt   b 1 umsonst   c 1 zeigen auf   d 1 erkennbar
e 1 nicht erkennbar

18

A couple of days ago I was sitting in a coffee shop on Seventh Avenue when a friend of mine from mine from college came in. I hadn't seen her since graduation. Back then we sat next to each other in almost every course – we had the same major. Anyway, when I saw her I waved, but she didn't see me. Before I knew it, she sat down at a table where someone was already sitting. I immediately went over and said hello and she introduced me to her husband. We chatted for about ten minutes or so, mostly just pleasantries, and then I had to leave. Later on I thought about all the good times we had had at school and was glad I had remembered to give her my number. I just hope she will give me a call before too long.

19

manner	time	frequency	place
surely	In the end	frequently	In some parts of the country
visibly	in the meantime	constantly	
utterly		never before	
	permanently		

240

20

to sleep like a baby
to drive like a madman
to eat like a horse
to run like the wind
to swim like a fish

to fly like a bird
to drink like a fish
to sleep like a log
to work like a slave
to act like an idiot

Wortschatz

A

abusive beleidigend 4
access Zugang 8
account Bericht, auch: Kundenakten 4, 8
actually eigentlich 2
addictive süchtig machend 9
adhere to beachten 1
administer a shock einen Schrecken einjagen 10
advice Rat 8
affect beeinflussen 10
aging alternd 3
agree on sich einigen auf 3
agree to sich einigen über, zustimmen 3
agree with einverstanden sein mit 3
aisle Gang 6
alarming beunruhigend 8
alien fremd, ausländisch 10
allude to something eine Andeutung machen 4
annoying lästig, nervig 7
answer back eine freche Antwort geben 10
anxiety Angst 7
apostle Anhänger 8
appointment Termin 7
around these parts (etwa:) in dieser Gegend 8
article Artikel 6
assumption Annahme 8
astounding erstaunlich 8
at the crack of dawn bei Tagesanbruch 5
attention Aufmerksamkeit 9
attention span Konzentrationsfähigkeit 8
attitude Einstellung 9

B

backpacking mit dem Rucksack wandern 3
based on aufgrund von 1
basically grundsätzlich 7
be a good sport about something etwas locker nehmen 4
be able to afford something sich etwas leisten können 7
be at issue zur Debatte stehen 5
be attached to an jemandem/etwas hängen 3
be caught up in something mit etwas sehr beschäftigt sein 7
be convinced überzeugt sein 6
be in a hurry es eilig haben 6
be out of something etwas nicht vorrätig haben 6
be reduced herabgesetzt/reduziert sein 6
be scheduled geplant sein 1
be supposed to do something für etwas vorgesehen sein 1
be/make sure pass(en Sie) auf 8
beach community Badeort 3
behaviour Benehmen 9
belief Glaube 9
bemoan beklagen 8
benefit nützen, zugutekommen 9
bigwig Bonze 6
black olives schwarze Oliven 6
blend mischen 5
blissful (glück)selig 5
boardwalk Gehweg aus Holzplanken 3
bottled water Mineralwasser 6
brilliant toll 4
bubble (hier:) köcheln 10
bulk Hauptanteil 9
bungle verpfuschen 4

C

cab Taxi 1
call into question in Frage stellen 10
call it quits sich trennen, (eine Beziehung) beenden 4
cancel stornieren 7
capable fähig 9
capture (hier:) einfangen 5
care Sorge 5
caregiver (hier:) Tagesmutter 9
carry (hier:) transportieren 10
case Fall 1
catch up with someone jemanden erreichen 7
cereals Frühstücksflocken 6
certainly bestimmt 7
characters Charaktere, Schriftzeichen 10
charge something etwas mit Kreditkarte bezahlen 6
checkers Damespiel 3
checkout clerk Kassierer 6
Chill out! Nimm's leicht!, Bleib cool! 7

Wortschatz

chores Hausarbeit(en) 7
clamour for fordernd nach etwas rufen 10
cohabitation Zusammenleben, Zusammenwohnen 5
come off sich lösen 6
commercial break Spot, Werbung im Fernsehen 9
commonly used gebräuchlich, alltäglich 4
company car Firmenwagen 7
compete am Wettbewerb teilnehmen 9
competitive konkurrenzfähig, marktgerecht (Preise) 8
complain sich beklagen/beschweren 5
condense komprimieren 8
confirm bestätigen 7
conjure up heraufbeschwören 5
consider betrachten, ansehen 9
consist of bestehen aus 1
consultant Berater 7
contempt Abscheu 4
continue weitermachen 9
convention Brauch 4
convention center Messe(gelände) 1
conventional konventionell 1
convey vermitteln 5
convince überzeugen 5
core Kern 10
corporate executive Geschäftsführer 7
counsel jemanden beraten 7
count me in! (etwa:) ich bin dabei! 5
counter Theke 6
co-worker Mitarbeiter 7
coy kokett 5
crowded überfüllt 10
cry out for (hier:) schreien nach 5
culinary kulinarisch 10
curse verdammen 4
curtains Vorhänge 7
customer Kunde 7
custom-made nach Maß angefertigt 7

D

damage schaden 9
dash Prise 5
deadline Abgabetermin 7
deal ein (gutes) Geschäft 8

decide entscheiden 6
decorate (hier:) einrichten 7
delusion Irrglauben 9
demanding anspruchsvoll 7
demented wahnsinnig 3
demise (Ver-)Fall, Untergang 8
demography Demographie 10
describe beschreiben 1
description Beschreibung 1
despite trotz 7
detergents Waschmittel 6
determine feststellen 1
develop a strategy eine Strategie entwickeln 8
dictate vorschreiben 8
disconnected losgelöst 9
discount Rabatt 4
discover entdecken 6
display ausstellen, zeigen 6
distinct (hier:) verschiedenartig 6
do you mind …? macht es Ihnen etwas aus …? 6
dose Dosis 10
drab farblos 10
drift apart (hier:) sich auseinanderleben 9
drive someone nuts jemanden verrückt machen 7
drug addict Drogenabhängige(r) 3
dry off trocken werden, trocknen lassen 4
dry out trocknen 4
due fällig 1

E

earn a thumbs up angenommen/akzeptiert werden 5
eatery Lokal 6
eccentric exzentrisch 6
elderly älter(er/e/es) 9
encouragement Ermutigung 4
enduring bleibend, fortdauernd 4
English-speaking englischsprachig 10
enjoy genießen 7
enslave versklaven 8
ensure sichern, sicher gehen 10
errands Besorgungen 2
ethic Ethik 10
ethnicity Ethnizität 10

243

Wortschatz

evidence Beweis(material) 9
exchange tauschen, umtauschen 6
exhibition Ausstellung 3
expand erweitern 7
expect (a baby) (ein Kind) erwarten 1
expedite beschleunigen 7

F

facility Anlage, Einrichtung 6
fact Tatsache 9
fail unterlassen 5
feasibility Machbarkeit 10
features Gesichtszüge 10
feeble schwach 8
feel obliged sich verpflichtet fühlen 4
field Bereich 9
fill a gap eine Lücke füllen 5
fill in for someone jemanden vertreten 1
financing Finanzierung 7
flabbergasted verblüfft 4
foothills Vorgebirge 6
form bilden 10
fortune cookies Glückskekse 10
frankness Offenheit 4
frantic hektisch 8
freelance freiberuflich 1

G

generate erzeugen 1
get a feel for ein Gefühl entwickeln für 1
get along with someone sich mit jemandem verstehen 4
get arrested verhaftet werden 4
get in the way verhindern 7
get mad sich ärgern 7
get out (of a car) aussteigen 4
get soaked klatschnass werden 4
get used to something sich an etwas gewöhnen 9
get your money back sein Geld zurückerstattet bekommen 6
good move! (etwa:) gute/kluge Entscheidung! 5
gradually allmählich 10
green beans grüne Bohnen 6
guidance Führung 9

H

habit Gewohnheit 7
handle something (hier:) mit etwas umgehen können 5
hang in there (etwa:) hartnäckig bleiben, sich behaupten 5
hardware store Eisenwarengeschäft 6
harm Schaden 9
hassle Ärger 6
haste Eile 8
have something in common etwas gemeinsam haben 9
health benefits Leistungen zur Gesundheitsfürsorge 7
heel Absatz 6
highlight Höhepunkt 4
hiking Wandern 3
hint Hinweis 5
home furnishings Einrichtung 7
homogenization Vereinheitlichung 6
hook something up etwas anschließen, installieren 5
hotel chain Hotelkette 4
hype hochjubeln 8

I

I'll be damned Verdammt noch mal! 6
identify identifizieren 10
idiosyncratic idiosynkratisch 6
idleness Untätigkeit, Müßiggang 3
impact Einfluss 8
impression Eindruck 7
in a snit verärgert 7
in vain umsonst 10
in your dreams! das hättest du wohl gern! 7
inconvenient lästig, ungünstig 8
increase erhöhen 9
incredible unglaublich 1
indecent exposure (Erregung öffentlichen Ärgernisses durch) unsittliches Entblößen 4
infatuation Verliebtheit 5
ingredients Zutaten 10
instead stattdessen 3
insuperable unüberwindlich 10
intercourse Geschlechtsverkehr 4

Wortschatz

interfere sich einmischen 4
intimation Andeutung 5
invulnerability Unverwundbarkeit 9
it's a trip! (etwa:) das ist ein Erlebnis! 4

K

keep an appointment einen Termin einhalten 7
keep in touch in Verbindung bleiben, Kontakt haben 4
keep up (hier:) mithalten 8
keyboard Tastatur 1
kid scherzen 1
kite Drachen 3

L

lack fehlen 5
lambaste den Kopf waschen, heftig kritisieren 8
lament beklagen 8
lend themselves to sich eignen zu 9
let alone geschweige (denn) 4
lifetime Leben, Lebenszeit 1
light fixture Beleuchtungskörper 5
lighten up sich entspannen 7
line up Schlange stehen 3
link Verbindung 10
location (hier:) Filiale 3
long for vermissen 3
longevity Langlebigkeit 9
look after sorgen für, sich kümmern um 9
look for suchen nach 10
loony Verrückte(r) 4
ludicrous absurd, lächerlich 7

M

mainly hauptsächlich 10
majority Mehrheit 10
make up erfinden 1
malevolence Bosheit 4
mate (hier:) Lebensgefährte/-in 5
material (hier:) Stoff 7
mean gemein 4
measure messen 9
meddle sich einmischen 4
melt schmelzen 10
mention someone's name den Namen einer Person erwähnen 8

merchandise Ware 6
mind-numbing (etwa:) stumpfsinnig 6
mind-popping erstaunlich 8
minority Minorität 10
mishandle schlecht behandeln 4
mix mischen 10
move in together mit jemandem zusammenziehen 5
much less schon gar nicht 5
multitasking mehrere Aufgaben gleichzeitig erledigen 8

N

national identity nationale Identität 10
nestled sich anschmiegen 6
Never mind. Vergessen Sie es. 1
nooks and crannies (etwa:) in allen Ecken 6
not necessarily nicht unbedingt 3
nourish ernähren 8
nurture hegen 9

O

objection Einwand, Bedenken 4
obsolete veraltet, überholt 8
on second thought jetzt, wo ich darüber nachdenke 3
one another einander 1
one-of-a-kind einzigartig 6
operator (Angestellte(r) bei der) Auskunft 1
or something oder so 'was 3
originally ursprünglich 1
outfit (hier:) Firma 8
oxford cloth Material aus Baumwolle 6

P

paddle Schläger 3
parking space Parklücke 3
passer-by Passant(in) 10
patience Geduld 8
patina Patina 6
pattern Muster 1
pay cash bar bezahlen 6
pen (hier:) eingezäunter Bereich 3
perform eine Vorstellung geben 3
personnel Personal 6

Wortschatz

peruse durchsehen, -lesen 6
pet food Hunde-/Katzenfutter 6
place an order eine Bestellung aufgeben 7
point out hinweisen auf 1
point to zeigen auf 10
poky Knast 4
portray darstellen 9
postpone verschieben 7
pot Topf 10
practically praktisch, fast 1
precise präzise 5
pregnant schwanger 1
pretender Bewerber(in) 5
price-wise preislich 8
pricey teuer, exklusiv 7
process an order eine Bestellung bearbeiten 7
promote fördern, werben für 9
prospective voraussichtlich 7
prove beweisen 6
provide zur Verfügung stellen 10
pull up vorfahren 4
put in a request eine Bitte äußern 8
put in (hours) (hier:) arbeiten 8
put together zusammenstellen 1

Q

quirky eigenartig 6
quote (hier:) Kostenvoranschlag 8
quote (a price) (einen) Preis nennen 8

R

race Rasse 10
raisins Rosinen 6
rarely selten 1
reach an agreement sich einigen, einen Konsens finden 3
rearrange umräumen 6
reason Grund 1
receipt Kassenzettel 6
recognize erkennen 9
recommend empfehlen 8
redeem einlösen 6
redistribution Neuverteilung 9
redo renovieren 5
reference Verweis 5

refund Rückerstattung 6
register for sich einschreiben für 1
relegate verweisen, degradieren 9
relentless unbarmherzig 8
remark Bemerkung 1
remind jemanden erinnern 7
rep = sales representative Vertreter 1
repeatedly wiederholt 10
replace ersetzen 6
represent vertreten 1
request Bitte 8
reschedule neu terminieren 7
residency Wohnort 5
resident Bewohner, Einwohner 10
respond antworten, erwidern 2
revere verehren 10
rip up entfernen, herausreißen 2
risk Risiko 9
rod Stange 7
room with someone eine Wohnung mit jemandem teilen 4
roughly grob 7
row Reihe 4
rush in sich darauf stürzen 5

S

salad bowl Salatschüssel 10
sales Verkauf 7
Same here. Gleichfalls. 1
(the) same to you ebenfalls 6
sand abschleifen 2
scold schelten 10
search for suchen nach 10
secluded abgelegen, einsam 4
see someone (hier:) mit jemandem befreundet sein 5
seem scheinen 10
segregated (nach Rassen) getrennt 10
self-employed selbstständig 1
semi- halb- 3
senior citizens Senioren/Seniorinnen 3
seriously (hier:) im Ernst 5
set up aufbauen 9
shabby heruntergekommen 6
shading Schattierung 5

Wortschatz

share teilen, zusammen benutzen 1
sheers Stores 7
shop around Preise vergleichen 8
shorten kürzen 9
sign unterschreiben 6
sign up for sich einschreiben für 1
skip überspringen 5
slash (hier:) drastisch reduzieren 8
small stuff Kleinkram 7
societal gesellschaftlich 9
soggy feucht 4
sold out ausverkauft 3
source Quelle 7
spark funkeln 10
spend time Zeit verbringen 7
spin your wheels seine Zeit vergeuden 7
splash mit Wasser bespritzen 4
split (the cost) (die Kosten) teilen 1
spread out verteilt 4
spreadsheet Tabelle 8
stand up straight sich gerade hinstellen 5
stew Eintopf 10
stock (hier:) ethnische Herkunft 10
stock boy Supermarktangestellte(r) 6
stock phrase feste Wendung, Floskel 1
store credit Gutschein 6
straighten out klären 6
straightforward einfach 5
stride Schritt 7
stroll spazieren 4
study Studie 1
stuff Zeug 3
sub (= substitute) for someone jemanden vertreten 1
subdue bezwingen 10
suffer leiden 9
supplier Lieferant 8
suppose annehmen 4
suspect verdächtig 8
sweat (hier:) sich Sorgen machen wegen 7
sweltering drückend, schwül 10

T

take advantage of something etwas ausnutzen 4
take in (hier:) anschauen 8
take responsibility for something Verantwortung für etwas tragen 9
tele-marketing Telefon-Marketing 7
tell me about it! wem sagt du das! 4
tenet Grundsatz 8
the latter das Letztere 3
tip into hineinkippen 10
toss werfen, schmeißen 8
transparent durchsichtig 7
turn out to be sich entpuppen als, sich herausstellen als 10

U

unrecognisable nicht erkennbar 10
utensils Gerätschaften, Utensilien 6

V

valance Verkleidung 7
valid gültig 9
veg out 'rumhängen 3
verbatim Wort für Wort 4
viewer Zuschauer 9
violence Gewalt 9
visibly sichtbar 10
vote of confidence Vertrauensbeweis 7

W

wait on bedienen 7
want ads Suchanzeigen 6
way Art und Weise 6
weigh wiegen 10
weight Gewicht 10
weird sonderbar 4
well-being Wohlbefinden 9
well-worn abgetragen 6
window treatment Fenstergestaltung 7
wonder sich fragen 3
work out trainieren, Fitnesstraining machen, Bodybuilding machen 3
working-class untere Mittelklasse, Arbeiterklasse 10
worth Wert 7

Y

yak quasseln 8

Quellenverzeichnis

Coverfotos:	Paar © getty images/Cultura, Landschaft © iStockphoto/Allan Robichaux
S. 7:	oben © iStockphoto/quavondo, unten © iStockphoto/Bill Grove
S. 8:	© iStockphoto/Bill Grove
S. 11:	© iStockphoto/ Klaas Lingbeek - van Kranen
S. 17:	von oben links: © iStockphoto/Richard Foreman, © iStockphoto/Vicki Reid, © iStockphoto/Gene Chutka, © iStockphoto/George Clerk
S. 19:	oben © fotolia/ Werner Stapelfeldt, unten © fotolia/dragon_fang
S. 20:	© fotolia/Werner Stapelfeldt
S. 23:	© fotolia/Doris Heinrichs
S. 24:	© iStockphoto/Dori Oconnell
S. 25:	© fotolia/detailblick
S. 28:	"Dear Anne Landers", by permission of Esther P. Lederer Trust and Creators Syndicate, Inc.
S. 33:	oben © fotolia/ Roman Hense, © fotolia/ Yuri Arcurs
S. 34:	© fotolia/Roman Hense
S. 35:	© fotolia/Monkey Business
S. 37:	von links: © iStockphoto/Nina Shannon, © iStockphoto/Pali Rao, © Colourbox
S. 38:	© iStockphoto/Blair Madigan
S. 44:	Foto © fotolia/tom anys, "Venice" from "Writing Creative Nonfiction: Fiction Techniques for Crafting Great Nonfiction" by Theodore Rees Cheney, Ten Speed Press © Random House
S. 45:	© iStockphoto/vizualbyte
S. 46:	© iStockphoto/Hal Bergman
S. 49:	oben © iStockphoto/Gregory Olsen, unten © iStockphoto/S. Greg Panosian
S. 50:	© iStockphoto/Gregory Olsen
S. 52:	© iStockphoto/Anja Hild
S. 58:	"F...!" from "Et cetera, et cetera. Notes of a word-watcher" by Lewis Thomas © Welcome Rain Publishers
S. 60:	© iStockphoto/ David Liu
S. 63:	oben © iStockphoto/Dean Turner, unten © fotolia/somenski
S. 64:	© iStockphoto/Dean Turner
S. 67:	© panthermedia/Marina B.
S. 69:	© fotolia/fotos4people
S. 72:	"Cohabitation": Reprinted with the permission of Atria Books, a Division of Simon & Schuster, Inc., from THE MIRACLE OF LANGUAGE by Richard Lederer. Copyright © 1991 by Richard Lederer
S. 74:	© iStockphoto/Jacom Stephens
S. 77:	© Colourbox (2x)
S. 78:	© Colourbox
S. 80 :	© MEV
S. 86:	Foto © iStockphoto/Don Bayley, "I'll be seeing you in all the familiar places" by Craig Wilson from USA Today, March 15, 2000
S. 89:	© iStockphoto/Heng Kong Chen
S. 90:	© iStockphoto/Floortje
S. 93:	oben © ullstein bild/Sylent Press, unten © iStockphoto/Pali Rao
S. 94:	© ullstein bild/Sylent Press
S. 96:	© panthermedia/Markus R.
S. 99:	© iStockphoto/Jacob Wackerhausen
S. 102:	Foto © iStockphoto/PeskyMonkey, "Don't worry about work" from Good Housekeeping, February 1999
S. 103:	© iStockphoto/Maciej Noskowski
S. 107:	oben © iStockphoto/H-Gall, unten © iStockphoto/Izabela Habur
S. 108:	© iStockphoto/H-Gall
S. 110:	© iStockphoto/Dino Ablakovic
S. 115:	Foto © iStockphoto/Tomml, "Just can't seem to stop" by Andy Goldberg from The Telegraph © Telegraph Media Group Limited 1999
S. 117:	© iStockphoto/narvikk
S. 121:	oben © iStockphoto/Alina555, unten © fotolia/Monkey Business
S. 123/124:	© iStockphoto/Alina555
S, 129:	"Unchanging men in changing times" from "Why Women Live Longer Than Men…and what men can learn from them" by Royda Crose, www.lifecycles.net
S. 131:	© iStockphoto/Vicki Reid
S. 133:	oben © fotolia/blende40, unten © iStockphoto/Joshua Hodge Photography
S. 135:	"The ingredients are proving slow to melt in the American pot" from "Great Third Wave on the No.7" by Patti Waldmeier, Financial Times, 18 September 1999
S. 137:	© iStockphoto/Jacob Wackerhausen
S. 140:	© panthermedia/Marion K.